Secrets of Fascinating Womanhood

To show you how to unlock all the love and tenderness in your husband.

A book you will never forget.

Inside, read how you can ...

- **Save your failing marriage.**

- **Make your good marriage better.**

- **Unlock all the love and tenderness in your man.**

- **Develop your full potential as a woman.**

- **Increase your self-confidence.**

- **Feel happier, more lovely, more feminine.**

Discover with Angela, the beautiful teachings of the world famous "Fascinating Womanhood" course that has saved thousands of marriages.

"One of the best books I have read on the subject of marriage and womanhood – I couldn't put it down."
Nancy Campbell
Editor *"Above Rubies"* magazine.

On-line edition 2009

Helen Andelin 87
Founder of
Fascinating
Womanhood.

Dedicated to Helena Andelin who has revealed the beautiful
truths of Fascinating Womanhood to so many women.

My wonderful
mother
Bonnie Coory
age 90

Dedicated also to my mother, Bonnie Coory, a
gentle, loving woman who instinctively knew most
of the Fascinating Womanhood secrets all along,
and to Marie my wife and sweetheart of 43 years, who
is fascinating in her own unique way.
David Coory

My sweetheart as
a young woman
and now my wife
of 43 years Marie
Coory

First published 1989 by Zealand Publishing House
Second edition   1990
Third edition (Revised)   1991
Fourth edition (Updated)   2007 PDF format only
Fifth edition (Updated)   2009 PDF format only

Further copies of this book can be downloaded in PDF
book form from **www.healthhouse.co.nz or www.zealandpublishing.co.nz**

Zealand Publishing House
Private Bag 12029,
Tauranga, New Zealand.

Phone   0800 140-141 (NZ only) or (07) 574-6663
Fax   0800 140-142 (NZ only) or (07) 574-5558
International: Phone   ++64 7 543-0491

Email   enquiry@zealandpublishing.co.nz
Internet   www.zealandpublishing.co.nz

Author
David Coory.

This book has been inspired by the highly successful
Fascinating Womanhood marriage course founded by
Helen B. Andelin, Pierce City, Missouri, USA. This marriage
course has saved and enhanced thousands of marriages.
The author is grateful for her kind permission to use
the true experience stories contained in this book.

The Promise of Fascinating Womanhood

When you sincerely apply and consistently live all the ten secrets revealed in this book, you will awaken deep feelings of warm and tender love in your husband. He will respect you and fiercely protect you. He will even adore you, and treat you as a queen.

The Warning of Fascinating Womanhood

When you begin to live Fascinating Womanhood,
you walk a path of no return. Your man will
never again be satisfied with the old you.

Contents

Use restraint

Apply Fascinating Womanhood with restraint at first, and with purity and sincerity, especially Secret Number Two.

Let your femininity unfold and blossom naturally, just as a fruit tree blossoms in the springtime.

If your husband should ever suspect that you are insincere, or just acting a role, he will not be able to respond fully to you. Your relationship will not bear the wonderful fruit possible with Fascinating Womanhood.

Fascinating Womanhood is an immensely powerful force for good in your marriage. However, it also gives you the knowledge to manipulate men. Please strongly resist any temptation to abuse it in this way.

Forgive yourself of past mistakes

You will almost certainly come to realise that you have made some mistakes in your marriage. But there is nothing to be gained in continuing to blame yourself. Mistakes are learning experiences and stepping stones to future success.

Real joy in life can only be experienced by first passing through sorrow.

The poet Kahil Gibran wrote: *"When you are joyous, look deep into your heart and you shall find it is only that which has given you sorrow, that is giving you joy. The deeper that sorrow carves into your being, the more joy you can contain."*
THE PROPHET

*The numerous **True Experiences** quoted in this book are extracts from hundreds of letters in the files of Helen Andelin, founder of the Fascinating Womanhood course. Only names have been changed.*

Angela's story is based upon actual events, but names and details have been changed.

Angela and her teacher are both Christians and this account reflects their Christian beliefs. However Fascinating Womanhood works for women of all beliefs and cultures. All that is required is trust in the wise plan of a loving God, and humility.

No particular religious viewpoint is intended to be expressed in this book.

CHAPTER ONE

Angela

ANGELA picked up her remote and clicked off her TV.

She rubbed her tired eyes and ran her fingers through her short brown hair. Glancing up at the lounge clock she saw that it was six minutes before midnight.

Angela sighed. She hadn't intended staying up so late. "Well at least I feel sleepy" she thought.

Sleep had not come easy this past week.

She turned off her electric heater, then leaned over and picked up the empty chocolate drink mug from the carpet. Heaving her heavy body from the couch she walked to the kitchen.

Her anger flared briefly when she saw the mess left by her two children. However she was too drowsy to clear it up now. How many times had she complained before?

She switched off the lounge lights then groped in the dark for the door to the hall, leading down to the bedrooms. Opening it, she felt for the switch and turned on the hallway light.

As she passed her son's bedroom, she heard what sounded like a sob. She stopped and listened. Yes it was sobbing. Her 12 year son David was sobbing.

Angela felt a sinking feeling inside and tensed up. Her drowsiness vanished.

David's muffled, quavering voice confirmed her worst fear.

"I want Dad to come home." Then more sobs.

"Oh no!" thought Angela. "Please God, not this."

She hurried in and crouched at her son's bedside. In the dim light she could see his straw-coloured hair on the pillow. His body was sobbing convulsively beneath the blankets. The side of his face wet with tears.

Anxiously she slipped her arms under the blankets and cradled his lanky body.

"David, it's all right. Mum will always look after you darling".

"I want Dad. Why can't Dad come home?" David seemed to be only half awake.

"Mum loves you David", said Angela, putting her face against his, her own tears mingling with her sons tears. "Oh God, what can I do?" she thought. She felt her sanity slipping.

She had depended so much on David's strength since Ted left. He had been a tall, confident boy for his age, and now this.

Yet signs had been appearing, especially during this past month. David no longer brought friends home from school. He didn't appear to have friends any more. He just lay around watching TV most of the time, even weekends.

His teacher had rung Angela last week, concerned about what she termed, "David's lack of co-operation in class."

Angela cradled her son gently for several more minutes, until he appeared to be asleep. Then she covered his shoulders with the blankets. For a little longer she softly stroked his prickly hair. Then she kissed him and went to her own bedroom.

She left the bedroom light off, so as not to awaken Tiphony, her nine year old daughter. Tiphony slept with her in the double bed.

After Ted had left, Tiphony had become frightened sleeping alone in her own bedroom. Now she slept every night with her mother. Angela was secretly grateful for the comfort.

Feeling shocked and strangely lonely after her experience with her son, Angela mechanically undressed in the dark and slipped on her nightie.

"I'll never get to sleep tonight," she thought. "If only somebody cared. If only Dad was still alive. He always cared."

Angela felt a little better thinking about her father and his cheerful, reassuring ways. She would take her problems to him as a girl and his strong arms would hold her tight as she poured out her heart.

Then he would smooth her long hair and say, "It's all right Sweetheart. Everything will turn out all right. You'll see".

And it always did. Just confiding in Dad seemed to make it better. "Why couldn't Ted be more like her father?"

She recalled again how cold and remote Ted had become these last few years. How he hardly ever spoke to her, and when he did it was mostly to criticise.

She saw no love in his eyes, only anger. She remembered again with dismay, his ugly contorted look the night he hit her. She would never forget that night.

Despair overwhelmed Angela. She went into Tiphony's empty bedroom and sat on the bed and wept bitterly.

After a while she began to felt a little better. Tiphony's bedside digital clock glowed red in the dark, 12.25 am.

Angela began to feel cold. She returned to her own bedroom and put on her dressing gown. Then she collected her cigarettes and ashtray from the living room, and returned to Tiphony's bedroom and switched on the light. She sat on the bed again and lit a cigarette and tried to calm her nerves.

Ted disliked her smoking. She had only begun again last year. It seemed to calm her temporarily and make life more manageable. She had been surprised to be told a few days ago that Ted had been seen smoking since he left. "Hypocrite", she muttered.

Angela thought back to the first week after Ted had left. Compared to the stressful months leading up to the separation, the feeling of relief was wonderful. Even David and Tiphony seemed more relaxed.

But then the pressure and stress had started building up again. Angela had returned to full time school teaching. Ted had left her the house and car, and paid child maintenance, but angrily refused to support her any further.

It seemed that she never had time for herself any more. Teaching all day at school. Working every night doing housework and lesson preparation. Working most weekends doing the lawns and garden. It wasn't how she had imagined it would be.

Other things also began going wrong. She damaged the car, and it was off the road for two weeks.

Then the lawn mower which had always been hard to start, would not start at all. The washing machine was making a funny noise. The tap in the bathroom leaked. Bills kept arriving, power, rates, water, insurance.

Then there was her mother's attitude. Ted and her mum had always got along well. He mother would say things like, "What are you doing wrong Angela? Ted's a good man."

How did she know what it's like living with someone who hardly ever talks to you. Just glares at you. Just ignores you most of the time.

She stubbed out her cigarette resentfully.

Dad would understand.

"Can you see me now Dad?" she whispered aloud. "I wonder what it's like where you are now. Oh, if only I could be with you. But my children need me."

Angela felt her warm tears well up again. They flooded her eyes and trickled down her face.

She remembered how her father would read her a Bedtime story each night when she was a child. And how afterwards he would kneel with her beside her bed, his strong arm around her shoulders and help her say her prayers.

"Always remember to say your prayers Sweetheart," he would say. "Your Heavenly Father loves you, even more than I do".

"And I haven't", thought Angela sadly as she sat alone with her tears trickling down her cheeks.

"I'm sorry Dad." she whispered, "I'll start to pray again, every night."

Then Angela got on her knees beside Tiphony's bed, and bowed her head and prayed. She whispered the words aloud, as her father had taught her.

"Dear God, my Heavenly Father, I am so unhappy. If you really love me as my Dad has said, please help me. Please find me a man who will love me and care for me. Somebody who will hold me and talk with me, and not be angry with me all the time. Please help me."

While saying these words, Angela's tears began to flow more freely and dripped down onto her hands. But she began to feel very different inside. A warm and peaceful glow was enveloping her. Her sadness and tenseness were fading.

For the first time in months, Angela began to feel serene.

She ended her prayer, but continued to kneel against the bed. The feeling inside her was wonderful and comforting.

She remembered feeling like this as a little girl when her Dad knelt alongside of her as she said her bedtime prayers.

Deep down, Angela felt that everything was somehow going to turn out all right. She resolved to pray every day from now on.

Angela's peaceful feeling gradually turned to drowsiness. She got up off her knees and went back to her own bedroom, and gently slipped into bed alongside her sleeping daughter.

In a few minutes she was sound asleep.

Life seemed a little better for a few days.

It was early spring, Angela's favourite time of the year. The Jasmine growing on the fence outside her back door was in full blossom. The sweet fragrance lifted her spirits as she left to teach school each morning.

However, despite her busyness, and the never-ending demands of raising children as a single parent, there was an emptiness pervading Angela's life.

Her friends seldom phoned or called around any more. Angela would sometimes phone an old friend, but it wasn't seem the same as before. She could detect a coolness in their response that hadn't been there prior to Ted leaving.

Angela also forgot her resolve to pray every day.

Friday evening, a man knocked on her door. Through the glass Angela recognised him as Rick, the husband of Marge, a nearby neighbour. She opened the door apprehensively.

"Angela, I seem to be having trouble with my TV reception. Could I come in and check your picture?"

"Oh Hi Rick," said Angela. She felt strangely uneasy. There

was something odd about Rick's manner.

"Well, yes, I suppose you can have a quick look."

Rick walked into the lounge and glanced at the set. "Oh, yes, there is something definitely wrong with mine. Marge has gone away for a few days. I thought I would try and fix it while she's gone. I suppose it's a bit lonely now that Ted's gone?"

"I'm managing" said Angela coolly, still standing by the door. She could smell the alcohol.

"Well, if you want any help, just ask," said Rick. He looked her up and down and gave a sly grin, then left.

Angela felt relieved when he had gone, but at the same time angry and cheapened. "Who does he think I am? I've a good mind to tell Marge when she gets back."

The burden of being a solo parent again became almost unbearable during the following week. David was becoming increasingly hard to control and disobedient at home.

Tiphony came down sick with the flu and needed to stay home from school for two days. Angela had to stay home and look after her.

Angela felt guilty when she phoned to inform the school where she taught that she was unable to come in to teach that day. The principle had answered the phone and she sensed his annoyance. When he had hired Angela he had continually stressed the need for her to be reliable.

Saturday evening the phone rang. Tiphony ran to answer it. "It's Nanna, Mum," she called out.

Angela took the phone from Tiphony. "Hello Mum. How are you?"

"I'm more concerned about you Angela. Have you heard from Ted lately?"

"No Mum, and I don't want to. It's all over. Can't you see that? I wish you wouldn't keep on about it. He doesn't care about me, and I don't love him any more. It's finished."

"Ted is still the father of your children, Angela."

"Yes Mum. I know. David went to see him yesterday. He's taking him and Tiphony out somewhere all day tomorrow. So they are still seeing him. He's picking them up at 9.30 in the morning."

"Those children need a full-time father, Angela."

"Look Mum, I'll find them a good father. Just give me some time. I prayed last week Mum, and I got a feeling that everything is going to turn out all right. It was such a lovely feeling. Oh but I miss Dad so much."

"Yes, so do I dear," said her mother. "I'm so glad you prayed Angela. Why don't you come to church with me tomorrow morning? I'll drive over and pick you up about quarter past nine. Ted will be having the children."

"No, I don't want to Mum. People will only ask me, 'How's Ted?' You know how they are. I'll be so embarrassed."

"They won't know he's gone Angela. All you have to say is,

'He's fine.' Come on. Come for your father's sake. You know it would make him happy."

"Oh Mum, . . . well, . . . well OK then. At least I won't have to face Ted when he picks up the children."

"Good girl Angela. See you tomorrow".

CHAPTER TWO

Ami

ANGELA's mother picked her up for church the next morning as arranged.

As soon as Angela and her mother walked into church, Angela saw Ami, sitting alongside her husband Bill.

Angela was surprised to see her. They had been friends since childhood, and even got married around the same time, but nine years ago Ami and her husband Bill had moved to a distant city.

Ami looked so pretty and slim that Angela felt like a frump in comparison. They were both the same age.

Angela was relieved that Ami had not seen her. So she avoided any eye contact with Ami and sat with her mother during the service.

At first Angela was self-conscious and felt that people were staring at her. But she enjoyed singing the lively hymns and by the time the service ended she felt relaxed and peaceful.

However, to avoid meeting Ami and having to answer awkward questions, Angela asked her mother for the car keys and then walked quickly out to the car park with her head down. She then sat and waited in her mother's car and soon became lost in her thoughts.

She was startled when the car door suddenly opened and there was Ami's pixie-like face beaming down at her.

"Angie! Here you are. How good to see you. I've been looking all over for you."

Angela smiled back, deeply embarrassed. She got out of the car and hugged Ami. How slim she felt. "Oh Ami, it's so good to see you too. And you look so well. What brings you back home?"

"We're living back here now. Bill's been transferred. We moved back last weekend. Oh I'm so happy. I love it here. How's Ted? Hey, we'll have to all get together again."

"Oh he's fine," said Angela, forcing a smile. "He's taken the children out all day today."

"How nice. Where to?" asked Ami.

"I'm ah, ... not sure," replied Angela, feeling uncomfortable.

"Well look Angie, I'd better not keep Bill and the children waiting any longer. I'll pop round and visit you this afternoon and we'll catch up on all the news."

"Well, . . . um, . . . I . . . well, OK then Ami. That would be nice. See you then."

When her mother dropped her off at home, Angela changed into her black slacks and put on her comfortable dark green pullover. The house was empty and quiet. Ted had obviously picked up the children OK.

While she stood in the kitchen preparing her lunch, Angela decided to tell Ami the truth about her separating from Ted. She would soon find out anyway.

Later that afternoon, Angela was sitting anxiously on the couch, smoking a cigarette and trying to read a magazine, when she heard Ami's car come up the driveway.

Her heart beat faster and her hands felt clammy. She stubbed out the cigarette.

"Come in Ami," she called, hearing her footsteps out on the patio.

Ami walked through the open door smiling. Angela thought she looked a picture of health and happiness. Her shiny black hair was flowing around her shoulders and she wore a pink dress.

Angela remained sitting on the couch, nervously rolling up the magazine. "Well here goes," she thought.

"Ami, Ted and I have separated." She said it quickly, avoiding Ami's gaze.

Ami appeared stunned for a moment. Then she sat at Angela's side and put her arm around her. "Oh Angie, no!"

Angela tried to hold back her tears, but could not. Her shoulders began to heave and she burst out in loud sobs. Ami held her tight and let her sob. She then took a tissue from her purse and gave it to Angela.

"You sit right there Angie. Let me make you a nice hot chocolate drink. Then you can tell me all about it. You seemed such a happy couple when you first got married."

"I'll come and help too," said Angela sniffing and wiping her tears as she stood up.

They both went into the kitchen, and Angela turned on the stove to heat some milk then said to Ami, "Ted has his own business now. He still fixes cars. Just him and an apprentice. He seems to have lots of work, but he works long hours. I used to do the books for him. You know how useless he is at maths. He has to do it all himself now. He's bound to muck it up."

"How long has he been gone now Angie?"

"Over two months now. It was such a relief at first. No more tension. But now . . . I don't know. I seem more tense than ever. He's changed since you knew him Ami."

"He won't do anything around the house. He hardly ever speaks to me. And when he does it's only to complain about something."

"Honestly, he criticises me all the time. I had my hair cut and permed and he said I looked awful. And it was really nice. All my friends said so."

"He just doesn't respect me any more Ami. He never discusses anything with me, just glares at me. He still does. He even beat me up."

"Oh Angie. I can't believe that. Tall, gentle Ted, beat you up? That man's as gentle as a lamb."

"Well he slapped me," said Angela.

"Did he? What led up to him doing that?"

"Nothing. I just told him that he wouldn't have a business if it wasn't for me doing his books. Which is true."

"Oh yes, and what else? I know what your tongue and temper can be like Angie."

"Well, I did tear up some of his invoice books and throw them on the floor. The way he was treating me I wasn't going to do anything more for him?"

Ami sighed, "That sounds like you Angie. But he shouldn't have hit you. Where do you keep your cups?"

"Use those two mugs over there Ami."

"And he didn't want me to go back teaching. I can't imagine why. All my friends are working. I told him he wasn't bringing in enough money. He had to borrow a lot to start his business. And on top of that he goes out and buys a new van. Anyway, I did go back to work. I was tired of being stuck at home all day."

They took their hot chocolate drinks into the living room and sat back on the couch. Angela lit another cigarette.

"I didn't think you would start smoking again Angie. Remember how we both gave up together after that horrible cancer film at school?"

"I think it helps me relax Ami. You would probably start smoking again too if you were going through the hell I'm going through."

"I don't think so", said Ami. "It's not very feminine."

"Well anyway Ami, you've heard enough about my problems. How's everything with you and Bill?"

"Oh Angie, Bill and I have never been happier. He just spoils me rotten lately. I love him so much. We've got four lovely children now. One boy and three girls. You remember Becky, the eldest, who was born here, she's twelve now."

"Yes. Her and David are the same age," said Angela.

"That's right, it was so neat when we were both pregnant together," said Ami smiling.

"Yes, it was," said Angela.

"Actually Angie, to be honest with you, last year Bill and I had a few problems too. He got laid off work, and I didn't handle it very well at the time. That's when I took the Fascinating Womanhood course."

"What do you mean, Fascinating Womanhood course?" said Angela.

"Oh, it's the best thing I've ever done Angie," said Ami, smiling widely. "I thought our marriage was pretty good, but now it's wonderful. Honest. I've never been so happy in my whole life. Bill seems happy too. And he enjoys his new job."

Angela felt a peaceful feeling come over her as Ami talked. Strangely she also seemed to sense the presence of her father in the room. She stubbed out her half smoked cigarette.

"It's a course on how to bring out the best in our husbands. You learn ten secrets about men. Oh Angie, I think you need to go through it. I really do. From what you've told me, I think you've made some big mistakes with poor Ted."

Angela's peaceful feeling suddenly vanished and she felt her temper rise. "Poor Ted? Me made mistakes?" she said. "It's him, not me. I've done nothing wrong. He won't talk to me! He won't take me out. I tried to make him go to a marriage counsellor. But would he? Oh no, not him!"

"I've done my best to change him for his own good, but all he thinks about is his stupid business. Puts it before me, and before the children. And he buys a new van. He can't afford it. The business isn't doing that well. He's just acting the big shot. And he's never home. Work! Work! Work! That's all he thinks about. I've got feelings too. And if he ever smiled at me it would crack his face."

"Oh Angie, come on now. Ted used to smile at you all the time when you were courting."

"Well he doesn't any more. I tell you Ami, he's changed. He's always grumpy, even with the children, except when he's been on the booze. Anyway its over! I don't want him any more. I told him that. I don't love him. I'm going to find somebody who really cares about us."

"Angie, you won't find anyone better than Ted. Who else will love your children like he does? He's their real father. You can't change that. Do you really think your children will accept another father? And what if you do find another man, and he has children too? You'd be their step-mother you know. Could you love them like your own? Would they love you back?"

Angela felt depressed at Ami's words. "Maybe you're right Ami. I don't know. Who would want me anyway? Look how fat I am."

"You hold the key to all this Angie. We women hold the key to happiness in our marriage. You can bring back the old Ted. The one who loved you. The Ted who married you."

"It's too late Ami. It won't work. Ted won't change. I've tried and tried and tried."

Ami smiled. "It's not too late at all Angie. Look, I'll find out if they hold a Fascinating Womanhood class here. If they do, will you take the course?"

"I don't think so Ami. I'm so busy since Ted left."

"I'll come with you if you like."

A woman can build or destroy a man.

17

"Well, . . . I might. . . . If you came too Ami."

Ami's eyes sparkled. "Good on you Angie. You'll be so glad you did. Oh I do hope they hold them here."

About an hour later, after chatting about old times, Ami said goodbye to Angela and left. She had just backed her car out onto the road when Ted drove up to the kerb in his van. David and Tiphony climbed out and ran excitedly inside to their mother Angela.

"Hi Ted" called out Ami, waving and smiling through her open window. Ted looked puzzled at first. Then he smiled broadly as he recognised her. He immediately got out of his van and walked over to her, still smiling broadly.

"Ami. Good to see you."

"Nice to see you too Ted. It's been a long time. Sorry to hear about you and Angie."

"Yeah," said Ted, suddenly looking serious and lowering his head.

"How's Bill?" he asked.

"Fine, just fine. He's been transferred back here. We moved last weekend."

"Hey, that's good news," said Ted, smiling again. "You're looking really well, Ami."

"Thank you Ted," smiled Ami. "Well I must be off."

"Bye Ami. Say hello to Bill for me."

Two weeks later, on Monday evening, Angela was serving the evening meal when the phone rang. She answered it curtly, annoyed at the interruption.

"Hi Angie, it's me Ami. Hey guess what? The Fascinating Womanhood course is taught here. They hold it in a downstairs room in the Civic Playhouse. And we've timed it just right. A new course starts soon. They're going to hold an introduction night this Wednesday at 7.30. Will you come with me? Please Angie. You did promise."

Angela couldn't help smiling at Ami's enthusiasm.

"OK Ami. I've been thinking about it. Yes, I'll come with you. And if it's half as good as you say, I'll take the course."

"Oh great! Remember it starts at 7.30. I'll meet you outside about ten minutes before, or do you want me to come and pick you up?"

"No, I'll be there Ami."

"All right. See you then. Bye Angie."

The woman holds the key to happiness in marriage.

CHAPTER THREE

Harmony

On Wednesday evening, Angela drove to the Civic Playhouse and parked her car. She looked all around for Ami but there was no sign of her. So she stood on the footpath outside the building and waited.

It was dark and there was a cold wind blowing.

While she waited, a number of women entered the building. Ten minutes went by. Angela looked at her watch. It was already 7.30. She felt cold, and very nervous.

"I think I'll go home," she thought to herself. There was housework to do and David had been teasing Tiphony a lot lately. She had reluctantly left them alone together at home.

"Is this where the Fascinating Womanhood meeting is being held?"

Angela turned, startled. A short, elderly woman in her 70's, with grey hair and a kindly face had spoken to her.

"Yes, I think so," Angela replied. "I'm just waiting for my friend. We were going to go in together."

"Well, it starts at 7.30, and it's that now," the woman said. "Why don't you come in with me? I'm Elsie," and she smiled at Angela.

"Yes, I think I will. It's so cold out here."

They walked through the main door and saw a neat handwritten notice that said FASCINATING WOMANHOOD ROOM ONE and an arrow pointing down the stairway.

They walked down the stairs and entered a red carpeted room. It was pleasantly warm, and filled with women of all ages seated in cream coloured, plastic chairs. Some of the women were chatting but most looked a little nervous.

At the front of the room, behind an oblong table sat three well groomed women. The woman in the middle looked to be in her 60's, the one on the left about Angela's age, 35, and the woman on the right in her 40's. Behind them on the wall was a white writing board.

Angela half hoped to see Ami among the women in the room, but she didn't recognise anybody.

Elsie, the elderly woman that Angela had come in with sat in one of the few remaining chairs. Angela saw only two empty chairs side by side. They were in the front row. Feeling ill at ease she walked to the front and sat down in one of the chairs. She placed her purse on the other chair to hold it for Ami if she arrived.

The warmth and cosiness of the room began to calm Angela's nervousness a little.

She studied the three women seated behind the table in front of her. Somehow they seemed different, more striking than normal.

All three were dressed in colourful feminine clothing. The serene looking, older woman in the middle and the younger woman on the left both wore their hair long.

Then the third woman, on the right, a short, solidly built, confident looking woman about 45, with shorter hair stood and motioned for quiet.

She smiled pleasantly and spoke. "Ladies, my name is Kitty. Thank you for coming along tonight to hear about Fascinating Womanhood. As you are all probably aware, we are about to start a new course, beginning next Wednesday evening. Let me explain a little more what it's all about."

"Fascinating Womanhood teaches you the art, the secrets, the laws, call them what you may, of winning a man's deepest, tenderest love. It does this by enabling you to become the kind of woman he can greatly love and respect, and even adore."

"Your man does not need to know anything about it. In fact it's far better that he doesn't. It makes you even more mysterious in his eyes, more fascinating, more delightful. Men are not permitted to attend this course." She smiled again.

"Now why is it, that a man often ceases to love and cherish his wife after he marries her? Why? It's because she stops doing the things that aroused his love when they were courting."

"So how does she re-awaken her husband's love and tenderness? Simply by obeying the unchanging feminine laws by which a man's love and tenderness are aroused and sustained. The ten Fascinating Womanhood secrets are those timeless laws."

"Yes, they are old fashioned. But they work. Truth is always old fashioned."

Angela was so engrossed in what Kitty was saying, that she did not notice Ami slip into the chair beside her.

"Sorry I'm late Angie," Ami whispered into Angela's ear, making her jump. "Bill had to work late tonight."

Angela was delighted to see her friend and whispered back. "Oh I'm so glad you're here Ami."

Angela fully relaxed now that Ami was beside her.

Kitty continued. "Now I am not saying that our husbands are never at fault, or don't make mistakes. Of course they

do. But when we women correct our own mistakes, and live the Fascinating Womanhood laws, we arouse a wonderful loving response from our men. Even harsh and cold men respond. More than you would ever dream possible."

"Yes it's true, you can experience more happiness than you've ever known before. More love, more tenderness, more caring, and you will be more respected as a woman."

"If you live these ten laws fully, I can promise you this. Your life will become richer, more fulfilling, full of surprises. I know. Mine has."

"When we live the ten laws of Fascinating Womanhood, we awaken masculine instincts in our husbands, and feminine instincts in ourselves."

"Most of us had these natural instincts when we were young girls, but we seem to lose them as we grow older. Or we have them educated out of us by modern ideas on the woman's role. But as we see all around us, these modern ideas aren't working. Everywhere we see failed marriages."

"Fascinating Womanhood teaches you ancient truths. Truths on how to live so as to become fascinating and delightful in the eyes of your man. His ideal woman. The kind of woman he dreams about. The kind of woman who arouses his deepest feelings of love. Feelings of tenderness and most important, of respect."

"You also learn how to understand men. Men are totally different from us. You will learn how to build their confidence, and their self respect. To bring out their full potential."

"You've heard the old saying, *"Behind every great man there is a great woman."* Well you learn the secret of this. How the two of you can become a powerful team. How you can bring out the very best in each other."

"You will also then know how to bring out the best in your sons, and other men you come into contact with."

"There are ten lessons in this course, one for every secret.

"Secret Number One teaches us how to minimise our husband's faults and weaknesses.

"Secret Number Two shows us how to vastly increase his self-confidence, and at the same time arouse his love and affection for us. This secret is immensely powerful and when applied brings spectacular results. But it doesn't work unless we have applied Secret Number One first."

"Secret Number Three teaches us how to comfort our man when he's discouraged. And to do it in such a way as to deepen his love for us. The kind of love that endures forever.

"This secret also shows us how to help him to be more successful in his career, and be a better provider. Many women find their husband's income increases significantly within two years of living this law of Fascinating Womanhood."

"Secret Number Four teaches us how to let go worrying about the finances. To feel secure in our husband's ability to provide for us. And to make sure he fully accepts his masculine responsibility to do so."

"Secret Number Five teaches us ways to increase our own confidence, and to develop serenity and goodness in our personality. Serenity and goodness are qualities men find highly attractive in their wife. They like to be able to put us on a pedestal, and praise us in front of other men. The more we develop these qualities, the more our men will treat us like queens."

"Secret Number Six helps us to enjoy being a mother and a homemaker. To feel fulfilled and respected for the important work we do in nurturing our children and creating a haven in our homes. This secret brings peace and harmony into our homes."

"Secret Number Seven encourages us to look after our health, and enhance our appearance. Our hair, our figure, our smile. So that we glow and look attractive to our husband."

"Secret Number Eight reveals natural secrets of feminine dress, charm and mannerisms that are fascinating, enchanting and alluring to men."

"Secret Number Nine shows us how to obtain our womanly needs and wants, and in such a way that our husbands enjoy giving them to us. And love us even more deeply afterwards. You will be surprised how simple this is."

"The final law, Secret Number Ten, teaches us how to handle anger, both our own and our husbands. And in such a way as to increase his love for us."

"Now, let me introduce our Fascinating Womanhood teacher, Harmony."

The slim, serene woman of about 65, who had been sitting between the two woman now stood. She was quite tall and her shoulder-length silver hair was partly gathered up and held with a white bow. She wore an attractive, knee-length yellow dress.

Angela was fascinated by her appearance, so unlike the matronly look of most older women.

Harmony gave a radiant smile that made her look years younger and began to speak in caring, smiling voice. Angela took an instant liking to her.

"Does your husband love you with all his heart? Does he feel a tender desire to protect you, and shelter you from all harm, from all worries, all difficulties?"

"Does he adore you, and praise you in front of other men and women? Does he want to satisfy your every need and desire?"

"Most women don't feel that men are capable of such love, but believe me, they are. Almost every man can be tender, romantic and adoring, if these passions are awakened in him by a woman."

SECRETS OF FASCINATING WOMANHOOD

"We often awaken these passions in men during courtship, but they die away after marriage. Why is this? It is because, as Kitty just said, we do not continue to arouse them."

"Fascinating Womanhood teaches you how to re-awaken those passions in your man, and fan them into a fire that will burn brightly forever."

"Are we being selfish in wanting this kind of love? No. Showing tender, romantic love for his wife is a source of great joy to a man. He feels more of a man, more masculine, more manly. You will learn in Fascinating Womanhood that feeling masculine delights a man."

"He will also have a stronger desire to succeed in his career, no matter what kind of work he does. Why? Because he has someone he deeply loves to work for. To die for if necessary. He feels fulfilled and content as a man."

"Fascinating Womanhood is about making our marriage great. We are aiming for the stars. It is a big prize. And there is a price. That price is humility."

"We need to lay aside our self-righteousness and our feminine pride. We need to realise, that many modern ideas, though they sound good in theory, just don't work in practice. Communism is one such example."

"In Fascinating Womanhood you learn ancient truths. And because they are true, they work when you apply them."

Elsie, the elderly woman who had come in with Angela hesitantly raised her hand and asked a question. "I already have a good marriage. Will this course help me?"

"Yes it will. It CERTAINLY will. Many women believe they already have a happy marriage. But after taking this course and living these ten secrets, there comes into their relationship a depth of joy and romantic love they never believed possible. I was one of those women."

"Other women, who before learning the secrets of Fascinating Womanhood, felt neglected and unloved by their husbands, are thrilled to see their relationship burst into full blossom. They see their cold, unresponsive husbands mellow, and become warm and loving."

"Even women who have been divorced and lonely for years, have reconciled with their husbands and remarried them again. They now enjoy a tender love and companionship they never knew before. I have personally taught women who have experienced this. Women who sat in the very chairs you are sitting in"

Angela could feel a tingle of excitement building inside her. Maybe it wasn't too late after all. But then a mental picture of Ted's cold eyes and unsmiling face dispelled her excitement.

"We women can build or destroy a man. Really we can. Put sand in a machine and it will wreck it. Put oil in it and it will run smoothly. Fascinating Womanhood gives us oil."

"If our husband doesn't love us, we feel empty inside. That's just the way we women are. He may buy us a beautiful house. He may give us plenty of money. But if he doesn't love us, there is nothing to make life worthwhile."

"Years of experience have proven to me beyond all doubt that the laws of Fascinating Womanhood work. They are truth. Come and discover them. Put them into practice. Then slowly but surely you will see a miracle take place in your marriage."

"But you MUST BE HUMBLE. You must set aside worldly ideas. You must set aside your feminine pride, and reawaken your natural femininity."

"These are natural laws you will learn, God's laws if you like. That's why they work. They are very different from what the world teaches. So you must be humble, and teachable. You must be willing to change old wrong ways of thinking and doing things."

"Change yourself and you can have a great marriage. I stand by that statement with my life. We women hold the key. We women have tremendous power to influence men for good."

"It's not always easy, but I testify to you IT WORKS."

As Harmony spoke these words, Angela's hopes again began to rise. The peaceful feeling that had come over her when she prayed in Tiphony's bedroom last week was returning.

"Now, sitting here on my right is Misty. She has been through a course of Fascinating Womanhood and is living the secrets. Misty has agreed to briefly share her experience with us."

"After Misty has spoken, Kitty and I will answer any questions you have, and take enrolments for our next course."

Misty (True Experience)

"I feel a woman either wants to make a marriage work or she doesn't. After ten years I still want mine to work, so I have tried hard to live Fascinating Womanhood."

"I know and believe that Fascinating Womanhood works. My husband hasn't spoken a cross word to me for months. He comes home earlier than he has in years."

"In the last six months, his earnings have increased each month. He can't seem to do enough for me. I could go on and on."

"I have never been happier, or had a happier family."

"Well, what do you think Angie?" whispered Ami, gazing intently at Angela.

"Sounds too good to be true. But I'm excited," said Angela.

"It is true Angie, and it does work," said Ami. "Like the teacher said, it's not always easy. Sometimes you've really got to bite your tongue, and sometimes you blow it. But you get there. I know you can do it Angie."

"Oh Ami, you're a real friend, really you are," said Angela

hugging her. "I'm so glad you've come back here to live. I am going to enrol. And you don't have to come along with me every week. I'll be OK. Honest."

Ami's eyes moistened and she squeezed Angela's hand.

CHAPTER FOUR

Secret Number One
Accept him

During the following week, Angela's thoughts about Fascinating Womanhood see-sawed between serious doubts and hope and excitement.

Her mother was highly encouraging when Angela told her about the Fascinating Womanhood course. She promised to come around and look after David and Tiphony every Wednesday evening while Angela attended.

On the Wednesday evening of her first lesson, Angela arrived early. The course was held in the same room in which they had met last week.

Harmony, the Fascinating Womanhood teacher looked even more striking than last week as she welcomed Angela warmly at the door. She wore a shiny turquoise blue, ankle length dress that contrasted vividly with her silver hair, swirled elegantly on top of her head and held in place with a large turquoise butterfly hair clip. But Angela was impressed most of all by her peaceful serenity.

Elsie, the elderly woman who had come in with Angela last week, had also enrolled for the course and was sitting in the room.

Angela again sat in the front row. She felt rather excited and at the same time relaxed. Her mother was not only looking after the children, but also catching up on the housework for her. She hummed softly to herself as she waited for the lesson to begin.

Angela counted eleven other women present when the teacher stood before them to begin the lesson.

Harmony smiled her radiant smile and welcomed them all again warmly. Then she said, "Let's all know each other by our first names. "My name is Harmony. As I read your names, please raise your hand."

Angela? Beth? Beverley? Cherry? Diane? Elsie? Helena? Kathy? Marina? Is Marina here? No? Sonia? All here except

Marina. Oh here she is now I think."

A plump, dark haired, brown skinned woman of about 50 entered and sat down. "Sorry I'm late teacher," she said in a soft gentle voice.

"Well that's all of us here," said the teacher looking pleased. "It's so very important that you receive all ten lessons, if Fascinating Womanhood is to bring you the happiness it promises."

"Now, if you want to ask a question at any time during a lesson, just raise your hand, and please, no criticising of men in class. I must be firm on that." She smiled. "Right, now let's briefly introduce ourselves. Joanne and Beryl are also with us, just for tonight from a previous class. We will hear from them later on."

Angela, can you stand and introduce yourself first. Then just follow on in turn."

Angela

Angela had not been expecting this. However she stood and faced the class and said, "Well as you know, my name is Angela. I have two children, a boy age 12 and a girl age 9 who live with me. I am a Primary school teacher and I'm separated from my husband, whose name is Ted. He runs a car repair garage."

Beth

Next to stand up was Beth, a slightly built woman in her late 20's. She wore a dark business suit, had straight black hair and wore oval, black rimmed glasses.

She spoke in a business-like, matter-of-fact style. "I am Beth. I am in my final year of a law degree. I am married and expecting my first child in March next year. I perhaps should be frank with you all, and let you know that it is not my idea that I take this course. My mother, who is rather old fashioned, has insisted I do so. So to keep her happy I have agreed. My husband is an accountant."

Bev

Then a large, obese woman, in her mid 40's stood. Her florid face even more red than normal with embarrassment. She had frown lines between her eyes and a wide mouth, although she appeared to Angela as though she could also be jovial. She had unstyled, frizzy, dyed gingery-orange hair and wore a floral top and blue jeans.

She spoke in a loud, rather gravelly voice. "Hi. I'm fat Bev. No good tryin' to deny it, you all have eyes. I love to eat. Yes I'm married too, although he's not much chop, and we won't be much longer if he don't shape up. I've already spoken to a lawyer. But we've been told not to criticise our other halves, so I'll keep my trap shut. Though that's hard for me."

Angela couldn't help smiling at Bev's introduction. The teacher and other class members smiled also. Angela felt a liking for Bev.

Cherry

Next was Cherry, a young woman in her late 20's. She had large blue eyes, and wavy, natural blond hair. Angela thought she looked a picture of health with her clear, glowing complexion and shapely but robust figure, which was accentuated by snug fitting, cream slacks and a colourful top. She tossed her head and gave a large smile. Her voice was confident and cheerful. Angela liked her immediately.

"Hello everybody, my name is Cherry, and I can't wait to hear these secrets. I'm married to a self-employed contractor and we have a girl aged seven."

Diane

The next woman to introduce herself was Diane, a thin, mousey looking woman, aged about 50 with slightly rounded shoulders and wearing a dark jumper and trousers. Her stressed-looking face was lined with wrinkles, especially around her eyes and mouth. Her short, permed hair was dyed a dark shade of red. Angela couldn't help thinking how much she contrasted with the outgoing Cherry.

Her timid voice was thin and expressionless. "My name is Diane. I have three grown-up children to my first husband, but we divorced. But I have married again. I enjoy handcrafts. As well as taking this course I'm also taking a night course in flower arranging."

Elsie

Next was the elderly Elsie. She was, short in stature and had white hair and a kindly face. Angela was surprised that Elsie sounded nervous when she introduced herself. She had sounded confident when speaking with her last week.

"Hello, I'm Elsie and I'll be 76 next birthday. I suppose you're all wondering what an old grand mum like me is doing in a course like this. Well there's an old saying, *"You're never too old to learn."* My husband's almost 80, and we have nine grown children. They're all married, or living with partners, which we don't approve, but we've had three divorces among our children and I don't want any more. Such terrible heartache and suffering. So that's why I'm here. My husband and I are happily married. We have eighteen grandchildren, so far and six great-grandchildren."

Helena

Next to stand was Helena, a plump, vivacious woman aged about 40. She wore a long, mid-green dress and had several rings on her fingers. Angela judged from her dark hair and olive skin that she was probably of Mediterranean descent. Helena spoke with a strong, personable voice and an air of confidence.

"Hello, it's nice to be here with you all. My name is Helena. Both my husband Spiros and I have Greek parents, so family is very important to us. I love my parents and they live with us. We have four children, two boys and two girls, all in their teens, and we want them to marry properly and be happy. And yes Elsie, I agree with you, none of this modern 'living together' nonsense. My husband Spiros runs a restaurant and I and the children, and my Mum and Dad help out. Spiros and I have a good marriage." She smiled and looked around at the class and then said. "But it could be better. I am looking forward to learning a few secrets to enhance our relationship."

Kathy

Then Kathy stood to introduce herself. She was a slim, lively, chatty woman, in her early 40's with short brunette hair and dressed in what looked like elegant, designer clothes. She had clear skin, expressive eyes and a radiant, toothy smile. She reminded Angela of Ami. Kathy seemed to lack a little confidence at first but soon relaxed. She spoke quite rapidly.

"Hello, I'm Kathy, and I have three teenagers at home and a married daughter. I'm a full time homemaker, because I believe that's where a mother should be with children at home. My husband works two jobs. Keeps him out of my hair. Oops! Naughty! Not allowed to criticise."

She smacked her own hand and grinned around at the class, then continued. "Our marriage isn't too bad. My husband is so patient. He needs to be with me. I am so impatient, and like to be the boss."

Kathy continued to chat on about her family until the teacher gently reminded her that time was limited.

If you could look through a man's eyes you would find his view of a woman is very different from your own. Men DO NOT see and think as women do.

Marina

Then Marina, the plump, brown skinned, native woman of about 50 stood to speak. Her voice was soft and gracious. She had large, gentle black eyes, natural greying hair and wore a long black dress embroidered with native designs.

"Hello darlings. I'm Marina. My family have lived around here for many generations. I have six grown-up children. Three of them are married and have their own families. I have seven grandchildren. My husband is not very well. He can't go out to work any more but he's a good gardener, and a good man. But dear me, he does have a bad temper sometimes, but it's usually my fault. Oh darlings, I shouldn't have said that, should I? Sorry teacher. I love to go to church, and I teach a Sunday School class of little children every week, and I love them. I call them my little lambs."

Sonia

The last woman to stand was Sonia, an obviously shy girl, aged in her mid 20's with long mousey, brown hair. She wore faded blue jeans and a plain white cardigan. She stood and was silent for a few moments, gathering confidence to speak. When she spoke, her voice was timid and barely

Men are impressed with sympathy, cheerfulness and childlike innocence and charm in a woman.

audible.

"My name is Sonia, and my little girl's name is Sheree. She's goes to kindy now and is three years old. My partner Andrew is an orchard worker. He doesn't earn much money, but I manage."

If you could look through a man's eyes

"Thank you class," said the teacher smiling and looking excited. "Right, let's get started."

"Have you ever been puzzled sometimes as to what a man sees in a certain woman? A woman that, to your eyes, seems to have no appeal at all? Yet the man seems totally captivated by her. It's a mystery is it not?"

"However, it would no longer be a mystery if you could look through a man's eyes. You would find that his view of her is very different from your own. Men DO NOT see and think as women do. Their needs are totally different from ours."

"The things we women admire in each other, are not the qualities that are attractive to men. In fact it's often the qualities we women condemn in each other that are the most fascinating and appealing to men."

"Now let's start solving this great mystery."

"First, what kind of woman impresses other women?"

"Yes Beth?" The slightly built, dark haired student lawyer had raised her hand.

"I believe we admire a woman who is poised and fashionably dressed. One who appears to be intelligent and talented, and holds an important position."

"Good answer Beth. Yes, I'm sure that's true of most women. Now let's look at the kind of woman that impresses a man. Lets look through a man's eyes."

The type of woman that impresses a man

"Men are impressed with sympathy, cheerfulness, childlike innocence and charm in a woman. The more tender, feminine, pure, and trusting she appears to be, the more attractive she becomes to them. Vivaciousness also enhances these qualities."

"Now let's remember, we are talking about love here. A man can easily be attracted at a sexual level to a promiscuous woman who has none of these qualities. But he could never love her. It is important that we understand this difference."

"Sexuality in a woman can stimulate lust, but it does not arouse love in a man. Love is awakened by wholesome, feminine qualities, such as sympathy, purity, cheerfulness, trust, and dependence."

"Living Fascinating Womanhood brings out these natural feminine qualities in us. Qualities that stir and soften a man's heart. We arouse in him a desire to cherish us, to hold us, and adore us. We become fascinating and delightful to him."

"And not only to our husbands, but almost all men, including our sons. I get on so well with my four sons now, since I've been living Fascinating Womanhood. Its really thrilling. They are all married, but they visit me often and they really spoil me."

"Now the face you were born with doesn't matter all that much. Your husband has already accepted that. Besides, when you make him feel wonderful, you will look beautiful to him, no matter how you look. And you'll learn how to make him feel wonderful."

"When you live all ten secrets of Fascinating Womanhood the results will be unbelievable."

Angela couldn't help smiling at the teacher's childlike enthusiasm. "It can't be that good," she thought. Still, the teacher's excitement was contagious and Angela felt excited also and was eager to learn more. Harmony was certainly an inspiring teacher.

"Now, are we all ready for the first secret? This first secret needs to be lived before you will see real results from living Secrets Two, Three and Four."

"This first secret is so important. It will probably be the most challenging of the whole ten."

She turned to the white board and picking up a felt pen she wrote:

SECRET NUMBER ONE
Accept him as he is.
Look to his good side.

Then turning back to the class she said, "This secret is your man's SECOND most important need. We learn his FIRST most important need next week."

"But his second most important need, is for you to accept him as he is, and NOT TRY TO CHANGE HIM."

"I repeat, your husband's second most important need is for you to accept him as he is, and not try to change him."

"Accepting him as he is means that you accept all his habits, his weaknesses, his dreams, or lack of them, and his beliefs. You accept him as another human being, part good, part bad, just like yourself."

"We women try and change our husbands. But they don't change. It's a very common fault with us women."

Why you must not try and change your husband

Cherry, the blonde, robust young woman raised her hand. "Yes, Cherry?"

"You say we shouldn't try and change our husbands, but I love my husband, and only try and change him for his own good, for his own happiness. That can't be wrong can it?"

"Cherry, trying to force a man to change always creates problems," said the teacher, "It just doesn't work with men. Yes, a man may give into our persistence just to keep the peace, but he hasn't really changed, not inside. And we

pay a high price for having things our way. He becomes resentful and cool, and withdraws much of his love."

"Why is this so? Because by trying to change and improve our husband, we are telling him that we are not satisfied with him as he is. His sensitive male pride is wounded."

"He knows his weaknesses. But he needs you to admire his strengths, not draw attention to his weaknesses. Your husband needs your admiration like you need his love."

"When you try and change him, he feels just as you would feel if he told you outright to your face that he didn't love you any more."

"That's why men sometimes become angry for what seems a trivial reason to you. They may go out and slam the door and not speak to you for hours. The quieter ones just clam up. As we said before, men are very different from women."

"No, trying to change a man does not work class. It lessens his love for you. It saps his self confidence and his manhood. He may even feel unworthy of you. It also breeds resentment."

Elsie, the elderly woman raised her hand and said, "Yes, that is so true. There's an old saying, *If his mother couldn't change him what makes you think you can?*"

"Yes Elsie, it just plain DOESN'T WORK. The more you pressure him, the more he resists changing. That's the way men are. We have just got to accept it."

"When we try and change our husband, he will tend to spend more time away from home. He will seek out the company of those who do accept him. Perhaps at the place he works, or with his mates. Sometimes with another woman. Or he may just close himself off from you, in front of the TV, or a computer."

"He will also tend to become critical towards you, or cold, or hardly speak to you at all."

Angela squirmed as she tried to rationalise the guilt she felt welling up inside her. She had never accepted Ted's lack of education, especially his terrible spelling and poor reading ability. Surely as a school teacher she had a duty to help him.

Sonia, the young woman with the mousey coloured hair shyly raised her hand and asked a question, "But will my partner improve if I accept him as he is?"

"Almost certainly Sonia. That's just about the only way he will ever improve. Miracles happen when a man feels fully accepted by the woman he loves. Real change only comes from within. It must be his idea. He must WANT to do it for you."

"Remember, he knows his own faults. The more a man loves you, the more he will want to please you. A man will go to unbelievable lengths to please a woman he loves."

"The famous and beautiful Taj Mahal in India, was built by an Emperor as a memorial to his favourite wife Mumtaz. He loved her dearly. She bore him fourteen children, and he

Mumtaz.

The beautiful Taj Mahal, built by a Mogul emperor as a memorial to his favourite wife Mumtaz.

Shah Jahan, husband of Mumtaz.

wept bitterly when she died."

"He also built her a magnificent, white marble palace while she was alive."

"We too can arouse these noble and gallant feelings in our men, but we must change ourselves first."

Accepting drinking and laziness

Bev, the heavily overweight, woman with the ginger-orange hair raised her hand.

"Yes, Beverley?"

"Call me Bev. Everybody does. Can we go back to this accepting thing? My husband's got this chronic drinking problem. Why should I accept that? He spends a small fortune each week on his beer, and won't lift a finger to help me round the house. He sits glued to his TV sports all weekend. Why should I accept that?"

Angela sensed desperation in Bev's gravelly voice.

"I've got a TV sports addict too," said another woman, and several others spoke.

The teacher smiled and held up her hand for silence. "Before we get too self-righteous and critical about our husbands, let's take a good look at ourselves. Are we that perfect? All right, some of us would like our husbands to give up their drinking, their TV sport and other habits. But what about our chocolate? What about our cakes and biscuits? Our tea and coffee? Our fizzy drinks? How easily could we give them up?"

"And how successful are we at keeping to our diets? And TV sports, how many of us are addicted to our soap operas?"

"And lazy husbands? What time do we get out of bed in the mornings when left to ourselves?"

"Even swearing and violence. Have we ever screamed at our children, or hit them in anger? Often the faults that annoy us most in our husbands are the same ones we have ourselves."

"One of the most useful lessons we can learn in life is to stop blaming other people for our own problems and weaknesses. We can only begin to change ourselves when we accept responsibility for our own problems."

"Yes, I know our men do lots of things that annoy us. They work late without letting us know. They get niggly. They walk mud onto the floor. They leave their clothes lying around. Their faces are prickly. They sometimes reek of BO, and often don't come to meals when we call them.

"And they leave the toilet seat up," said Cherry with a giggle. The class laughed.

"Yes Cherry, that one always comes up. Even so, we must accept our man as he is. We must forgive him and look to his good side."

What to do when a husband is unfaithful

Diane, the thin woman in dark clothes raised her hand hesitantly.

"Diane, you have a question?" said the teacher.

Diane's thin voice was emotional and wavery as she spoke. "My first husband was unfaithful to me with another woman. And my present husband was too, three years ago. I can never forgive either of them for that." Then she broke down sobbing.

The teacher moved quickly to Diane's side and put her arm tenderly around her and comforted her.

Then she said to her gently, "Diane, the secrets we learn in this course have reunited thousands of couples who have gone through this heart breaking experience."

The teacher walked back to the front of the class, paused, and then spoke in a solemn voice:

"A woman must expect two things in marriage, fidelity, and financial support."

"Let's deal first with fidelity. You cannot compromise your self-respect by living with a husband who CONTINUES to be unfaithful to you. It will lead to emotional and physical ill health."

"If it is happening, this is what I suggest you do, in all sincerity. First, be humble enough to face your part in the problem. Ask yourself, "What did I do, or fail to do, that laid the foundation for my husband becoming involved with another woman? You will more clearly understand this when you have completed the course."

"Correcting these mistakes will normally win him back, even in difficult cases. But IF HE PERSISTS, you must tell him to make a choice, or you will leave him. And BE PREPARED TO KEEP YOUR WORD. That is the ONLY thing you can do that will eventually bring him to his senses."

"The same applies to a husband who will not support you financially."

"These are the two God-given rights that every woman must expect from her husband. And provided you have faithfully done your part as a wife, God will support you in standing up for these two rights."

Angela felt thankful that Ted had never been involved with another woman. At least as far as she knew.

A tense, moody man is often in a stressful job unsuited to his talents and temperament.

Forgive him for past hurts

"Even if your husband has failed you in these two areas in the past, forgive him now in your heart, while you put Fascinating Womanhood into action."

"I can't," blurted out Diane, still sobbing. "You just don't know how much it hurts."

"Only forgiving him will ease the hurt Diane. It may be the most difficult thing you will ever do. But the Bible says, *"As you sow, so shall you reap."* This first law of Fascinating Womanhood asks that you first sow seeds of forgiveness. Then, in the years ahead, you can reap life-long love and tenderness from your husband."

"But we must accept our husbands fully, and we must forgive them fully, in our hearts for all their past mistakes.

The forgetful, thoughtless man is often a deep intelligent thinker with his mind on more important matters.

No man can love a sullen, resentful wife."

"Now please listen to me carefully. This is very, very, important. Some of you, maybe all of you, harbour resentment in your heart towards your husband because of ways he has hurt you in the past. Perhaps very severe hurt, as Diane has experienced. That resentment is crowding out your love. Let it go. Drain away the poison by forgiving him. You may need to kneel down humbly before God and ask for His help. But release the resentment. Forgive him."

"His current way of treating you may be the result of unhappy boyhood experiences when he was just a child."

"When you release your resentment, love will flow back into your heart. Only then can Fascinating Womanhood create for you the beautiful marriage of your dreams."

Look to his good side

The teacher picked up a little statue of a man and held it up. One side was painted a dark, drab grey and the other side was pure white. She slowly turned the grey side away from the class until only the white side could be seen.

The husband who seems lazy at home may be putting all of his energies into his employment outside the home, to provide for his family.

"From now on, we only look to our husband's good side. Just like this little statue. The dark grey side represents our man's faults. And this white side, his virtues, his good side."

"Some of you might be thinking, 'My husband doesn't have any virtues, or a good side.' Yes he does. Think back to your courtship days. Would you have been attracted to him if he didn't have virtues or a good side? You'll be surprised as you do your first assignment this week, just how many virtues your husband does have."

Are his faults hidden virtues?

"Often what appear to be a man's faults are really hidden virtues. The husband who seems lazy at home for instance, may be putting all of his energies into his employment outside the home, to provide for his family."

"A rude, offensive man is often of high calibre, but not valued by his boss, or his wife."

"A tense, moody man, or a heavy smoker, is often in a stressful job, unsuited to his talents and temperament."

"The forgetful, thoughtless man is often a deep, intelligent thinker with his mind on more important matters."

"Many alcoholics are sensitive men, trying to blot out guilt and shame."

"Fascinating Womanhood promises you thrilling rewards when you accept your husband as he is. His response is likely to be deeply moving. You may be lifting a terrible burden he has carried around for years."

Why you must allow him his freedom

"As women, we hold the key to unlocking the goodness in our man. Therefore, it is required of us first to forgive him. Then we must trust him and allow him complete freedom. Personal growth comes only through freedom."

"We must not restrict our husband, or cling too much to him. It makes him feel trapped. We only do it because we fear losing his love. But he will be FAR MORE ATTRACTED TO US when we maintain an air of freedom, mystery and self-confidence. Just as we did during courtship."

"However, we must never give him the impression that we do not need him. We need to be an elusive, free spirit, yet dependent on him for our support and protection. Can you understand what I mean?"

"This is natural, feminine behaviour when we have no fear of losing a man's love. After all we don't restrict or cling to our fathers do we? Why? Because we feel secure in their love."

"The relationship we have with our pets, such as a cat or dog, also illustrates this principle. Our pets are free spirits, yet they depend on us for support. And because of this freedom of spirit we love them more deeply don't we? True love can never be forced. True love requires freedom."

"If your man should ever use his freedom to mistreat you or neglect you in any way, Secret Number Ten will show you how to stand up to him and gain his respect. No man can deeply love a woman who allows him to mistreat her or use her as a door mat."

"Now let's return again to Sonia's question, 'Will a man improve if we stop trying to change him?'"

"In answer to this I say, if you live all ten laws of Fascinating Womanhood, your man's major faults will tend to disappear. He will become a finer and more noble man. I've seen it happen time and time again. But you must allow him complete freedom to live his life as he sees fit, just so long as he supports you and is faithful to you."

"You won't become a door mat. Just be patient and allow time for Fascinating Womanhood to work. Old habits take time to change."

"Our time is almost up. Now I'm going to hand you out a list of your three assignments for this lesson. I don't pretend they'll be easy, but they do produce exciting results. On the back of the page you will see a list of masculine virtues to help you with Assignment One."

Angela took her copy and began to read with interest.

ASSIGNMENTS – SECRET NUMBER ONE

ASSIGNMENT ONE. Make a list of all your husband's masculine virtues. Read them every morning and night. Continue this until you have committed them to memory.

ASSIGNMENT TWO. Forgive him in your heart for all the times he has hurt you in the past. Ask God to help you if necessary.

ASSIGNMENT THREE. Then say the following to your husband, touching him as you do so:

"I'm glad you're the kind of man you are. I haven't always appreciated you in the past, and I've made some silly mistakes. I'm sorry, and I'm glad you haven't let me push you around. I'm glad you're the way you are. From now on I'm going to try to be a wonderful wife for you."

(You can rephrase this statement with words that are more natural to you if you prefer. But do not lessen its impact.)

As Angela read the three assignments she felt her enthusiasm drain away. She could not think of any virtues that Ted had. And there was no way she could ever bring herself to say the words in Assignment Three. She would rather die first.

"Now complete these three assignments as soon as you can, preferably before this weekend," the teacher said.

"They are the foundation of Fascinating Womanhood. Do not be surprised if your husband breaks down and weeps when you've spoken the words in Assignment Three. Many men weep after hearing their wives speak these words. But please be sincere, and mean what you say."

"To close tonight's class, I've invited along Joanne and Beryl, who have already been through this course. They have very kindly agreed to share with us their experiences in applying this first secret. Joanne will you come up first, and then Beryl.

Joanne (True Experience)

"Marriage for me at age twenty was an arrangement in which I could begin to change my new husband into the man I wanted him to be, and get out of it all I could. I'd been taught that marriage is a 50/50 proposition, and I was to do all that I could to be sure that my part of the proposition was secured."

"Seven stormy years later I began to view the shambles I had created – a very unhappy, belligerent husband who had retreated into himself, and children that also reflected our home situation."

"I began to pray and ask the Lord what was wrong. At this point I heard of the Fascinating Womanhood course."

"During the course, I sought to put into practice what was being taught, and saw my husband really begin to shower attentions upon me. By the end of the course our life together was sweeter and richer than it was on our honeymoon. Whereas before, I was occupied with his faults, now these same faults, somehow, were the points I could actually admire. I found myself in the freshness of a new love for him."

"He began to tell me, for the first time in years, that he loved me. Since then our life together is continuing to improve and grow in love and friendship."

"For the first time I feel satisfied and fulfilled as a woman, and grateful for the wonderful gift of womanhood God has given to me, and all women."

Beryl (True Experience)

"My husband and I have been married twenty-one years. I had always thought we had a wonderful marriage, that is, for the first half of it. Then things began to happen. We have seven children whom we love very much, but this was not enough to hold our marriage together."

"A friend had been trying to get me interested in Fascinating Womanhood, so in desperation I thought I would try."

"My husband at the time was planning to leave me. I had told him that I thought he should, as we had nothing in common any more. He was 200 miles away looking for a new job, so I had to work fast."

"The night he came home I applied the assignment, to accept him and tell him so. I told him I would like very much a chance to prove to him that I would improve. He said nothing."

"The next night I asked him if he had thought about it and he said, 'Yes,' but he was convinced it wouldn't work. He was so discouraged, disillusioned and unhappy that he thought the only thing to do was to go away by himself."

"I cried the whole night."

"The next morning he asked me if I really meant what I said, and I said, 'Yes'. He told me that he had always loved me, that he didn't really want to leave, and that his boss had offered him a raise if he would stay. Then he held me in his arms as if he would never let go."

"I remember our first year of marriage, when he kissed my feet and called me 'His Little Angel.' I wonder how I could have been so foolish as to let him down as I did. But I feel very blessed to be given another chance."

"Thank you so much Beryl, and you too Joanne, for coming along tonight and sharing your experiences with us. My eyes fill with tears of joy when I hear such experiences."

"Good night everybody. See you again next week."

When Angela arrived home, the house was neat and tidy and the children were asleep in bed. Her mother was doing the ironing while watching TV. Angela felt her spirits lift a little.

"How did it go dear?" her mother asked.

"It was very good Mum. You would love our teacher. But I can't agree with everything she says. She teaches that we should accept our husband as he is and not try and change him. Did you ever try to change Dad, Mum? I mean, try and make him into a better man?"

"Well Angela, as you know, your father was a kind hearted man. And I did resent being left at home while he was off helping everybody else. People took advantage of him sometimes. Yes, I suppose I did try and change that side of him. But he never did change. Looking back now, I can see that I was selfish. I was the one who needed to change."

"Yes, I might have even been a bit hard on Ted at times, too. Thanks for baby-sitting Mum. It was nice to know you were here looking after things."

"After her mother had left, Angela felt too stimulated to go to bed. So she found a pad and pen and sat at the kitchen table to begin her first assignment.

She doubted that she would find any good points about Ted. She turned over the assignment sheet and began to read the virtues that were listed on the back.

Masculine Virtues

Active	Agile	Alert
Articulate	Artistic	Assertive
Athletic	Attentive	Authoritative
Bold	Boyish	Brave
Brilliant	Business acumen	Calm
Capable	Caring	Charming
Cheerful	Child loving	Clean
Comforting	Confident	Conscientious
Considerate	Contented	Co-operative
Courteous	Cultured	Curious
Decent	Dependable	Determined
Devoted	Devout	Dignified
Diligent	Disciplined	Discreet
Distinguished	Dress Sense	Dynamic
Earnest	Educated	Effective
Efficient	Elegant	Eloquent
Encouraging	Entertaining	Enthusiastic
Exuberant	Fair	Faithful
Firm	Fit	Flexible
Fluent	Forgiving	Friendly
Gallant	Gardener	Generous
Gentle	Genuine	Gifted
Good	Good driver	Good navigator
Gracious	Grateful	Handsome
Handyman	Happy	Healthy
Helpful	Humorous	Honest
Honourable	Hospitable	Humble
Impressive	Ingenious	Innovative
Inspiring	Intelligent	Interesting
Insightful	Jovial	Joyful
Keen	Kind	Knowledgeable
Leader	Likeable	Lively
Logical	Long suffering	Lovable
Loving	Loyal	Lucky
Manly	Masculine	Masterful
Mature	Moderate	Modest

Money manager	Musical	Neat
Nice smile	Noble	Non-smoker
Nostalgic	Obliging	Open
Optimistic	Orderly	Out-going
Passionate	Patient	Peaceable
Perceptive	Perfectionist	Persistent
Personable	Persuasive	Photogenic
Playful	Pleasant	Poetic
Poised	Polished	Polite
Popular	Positive	Powerful
Practical	Prayerful	Precise
Profound	Progressive	Prominent
Prosperous	Protective	Prudent
Punctual	Qualified	Reasonable
Refined	Relaxed	Reliable
Resilient	Responsive	Righteous
Robust	Romantic	Rugged
Scholarly	Secure	Selfless
Sensible	Sensitive	Sentimental
Serious	Sincere	Singer
Slim	Sober	Sociable
Solid	Spiritual	Spontaneous
Sportsman	Stable	Strong
Steady	Strict	Suave
Subtle	Successful	Superior
Supportive	Tactful	Tall
Tanned	Tender	Thoughtful
Tolerant	Trusting	Trustworthy
Truthful	Vigorous	Virile
Warm	Wealthy	Well built
Well groomed	Wholesome	Wise
Witty	Youthful	

Angela began to be astonished. As she read further she became even more astonished. Why Ted had lots of these virtues. Especially if she judged him on the way he acted towards others, rather than toward herself.

Yes, he was caring towards others, courteous, dependable, dignified, disciplined, forgiving, friendly . . .

"But why only to others, and not to me?" she said aloud.

"Was it because I tried to change him?" she thought. His terrible spelling and poor reading had always embarrassed her. She had tried to make him take night classes. She had brought him home books from the school library to try and get him to like reading.

But he had never shown interest. In fact, looking back he had seemed to resent it.

She had also pestered him to go to church with her when they first got married. That had seemed to make him resentful also.

"And I have always pestered him to come home earlier, ever since he started his business." Angela was again speaking aloud. "That didn't work either."

As Angela sat at the table she thought back on the years of her marriage.

Slowly she began to realise, that whenever she had expressed her disapproval to Ted, he seemed to become worse. Why hadn't she noticed that before?

Angela took her pen and began to write Ted's virtues. She had gone only part way through the list when she realised that her attitude toward Ted was changing profoundly. She felt she was turning a corner in her life. She said to herself, "Why, Ted has more than half these good qualities. Ami was right after all. Where would I find a better man than Ted? He has got his faults, but I could accept his faults if he really loved me." A deep sadness washed over her.

Angela eventually finished writing the long list of Ted's virtues. She wondered how she could possibly remember them all.

Then she read her second assignment, "Forgive him in your heart for all the times he has hurt you in the past. Pray for help if necessary."

It was odd. Angela didn't feel like recalling any hurts that Ted had caused her. All she could think of were the numerous virtues she had written down. But she still felt a deep sadness, that Ted did not love her any more.

She tore out the two pad pages she had filled with Ted's virtues and folded them neatly.

As she brushed her teeth before bed, Angela decided she should pray for help in forgiving Ted anyway. So she went into Tiphony's empty bedroom, closed the door, and knelt on the carpet in the dark and prayed audibly in a whispering voice.

Words flowed easily. Angela thanked God for her friend Ami, and for her good parents, and for being guided to Fascinating Womanhood. Then she added, "Please help me to see what I've done wrong in my marriage. Please help me to accept Ted as he is, and his weaknesses. And help me forgive him for all the times he has hurt me. And please help him forgive me too for all the times I've hurt him."

As Angela whispered these last words, a feeling of pure love suddenly flooded over her. It instantly dispelled her sadness and brought tears of gratitude to her eyes.

A vision of a younger Ted filled her mind. He was dancing with her, and holding her tenderly. She remembered his soft warm kisses and his loving glances. The way his strong, warm hand would often seek for hers.

For the first time in years, love for Ted welled up in Angela's heart. She sat down on the floor in the dark and sobbed for a long time, letting the warm tears run freely down her cheeks.

Although it was dark, Angela felt as if she had emerged into sunlight and blue skies, after being lost in a dark underground cave for months.

CHAPTER FIVE

Secret Number Two
Admire his masculine qualities

Angela felt that she had now reached a stage where she could fully accept and forgive Ted. However, the thought of telling him face to face terrified her.

Ami encouraged her, but Angela knew she could not do it. And even if she could muster enough courage to try, she was sure she would mess it up and make a complete fool of herself.

Because she had not completed her third assignment due to this fear, Angela did not want to face her teacher again on Wednesday night. She even considered abandoning the Fascinating Womanhood classes, but then she would have to face Ami.

So when her Mother arrived on Wednesday evening to look after the children, Angela said goodbye and drove to her class, full of anxiety.

The Fascinating Womanhood teacher Harmony, met Angela at the classroom door and smiled at her. Angela blushed, then blurted out that as she was separated from her husband, she could never bring herself to face him and say the words of acceptance in Assignment Number Three.

Harmony patted her arm gently and said. "Don't worry Angela. Most women still living with their husbands cannot bring themselves to do this until later in the course."

"And don't feel bad about your separation. A short separation can be a good thing when a marriage is in trouble. Why don't you write the assignment out in a note and hand it to him?"

Angela's spirits rose immediately. "Can I do it that way?"

"That's the best way when communication has stopped," smiled the teacher.

Angela took her seat in the front row, enormously relieved. Yes, she could hand a note to Ted.

"Good evening ladies," said the teacher cheerfully. "How lovely to see you all back again, and also our two visitors Rosalyn and Donna. We'll be hearing from them later."

"Now, before we learn Secret Number Two, let's hear how you got on with your Secret Number One assignments. How many of you completed all three?"

Only Elsie, Helena, Marina and Sonia raised their hands.

The teacher looked disappointed. "Well, who completed the first assignment?" All hands except Bev's went up. The teacher smiled again.

"Very good. Please work on the other two if you haven't yet done them, especially the last one where you tell your husband that you accept him. If you just cannot bring yourself to tell him to his face, write him a note, and hand it to him with a sweet smile."

"Now I'm sure some of you have had results already in applying Secret Number One during the week. Who would like to share an experience with us?"

Kathy quickly raised her hand. The teacher looked pleasantly surprised.

"Kathy, let's hear from you. Come out the here in the front and briefly share it with us."

Kathy's lively face shone as she spoke.

Kathy. True Experience.

"I really have a wonderful husband, but he has some habits I disapproved of, especially his smoking. I always made him go out in the garage to smoke."

"After learning the secret of acceptance, I realised how awful I had been. When he came home the next night I confessed my feelings to him and asked his forgiveness for the terrible way I had treated him, and told him I accepted him as he is."

My husband was so tenderly touched that he cried. Later that evening he told me that he loved me for the first time in two years, and he slept with his arm around me all night."

"Thank you Kathy", said the teacher, blinking back tears. "Does anybody else have an experience?"

Several hands went up.

"Cherry, let's share your experience, and then we must begin tonight's lesson."

Cherry stood up and walked quickly to the front of the class, her large eyes sparkling.

Cherry. True Experience.

"My husband has always been quite a fellow to go out

with the boys, almost every night until dawn. Each time I have been extremely angry with him. After understanding the secret of accepting him, however, I tried a different approach."

"I had our evening meal on the table and called him to come and eat, when one of his mate's came to the door wanting him to go out. He got his coat on, told me where he was going, and not to wait up for him."

"My first impulse was to hit the ceiling, but I caught myself and said instead, 'Oh I think that's a good idea, you really need to get away for a while. Have a good time and I'll have something for you to eat when you come home."

"His reaction was one of great surprise. He did go, but in 45 minutes was back home in very happy spirits, and with a box of chocolates for me."

"He spent the rest of the evening just talking with me and helping me."

"That's really lovely Cherry," said the teacher. Can you see how well these truths work class?"

"Now before we move on to tonight's secret, there's one last point I should make about Secret Number One, accepting our husband's faults."

When a man is unaware of a fault

"There may come a time when your husband is completely unaware of one of his faults. You may be the only person who cares enough to tell him."

"This happened to me once. My husband is a medical practitioner. A few years ago I learned that he was beginning to be regarded as unfriendly and abrupt by many of his patients. Yet he is a caring man at heart. It was just that he was seriously overworked at the time."

"In a situation such as this, say to your husband, 'I might be wrong, but it seems to me, etc, etc."

"Reassure him at the same time that you support and admire him. Then drop the matter completely. If he still makes the same mistakes, let him do so without comment. Accept him as he is."

"We cover the matter of giving feminine advice more fully in Secret Number Nine."

"Now, let's look at Secret Number Two. This secret satisfies your husband's greatest need."

"What is your husband's greatest need class?"

"To be loved?" said Marina.

"That's a woman's greatest need Marina, not a mans" said the teacher.

"To be fed," said Bev. The class laughed.

"This is more important to him even than food."

"It must be sex then," said Cherry. More laughter.

The teacher smiled. Then turned and wrote on the white board in big letters.

A man's sensitive pride is easily wounded.

ADMIRATION OF HIS MASCULINE QUALITIES

"THAT is your husband's greatest need."

"Yes, a woman's greatest need is to be loved, but a man is different. His greatest need is to be admired."

"He needs to be admired and praised for his masculine abilities and achievements. Deep in his heart he longs for it. He cannot get enough. Admiration and praise of his masculine qualities is your husband's greatest source of satisfaction."

"So here now is the second secret of Fascinating Womanhood." She turned and wrote on the board . . .

SECRET NUMBER TWO
Admire his masculine qualities.
Never wound his sensitive pride.

"This secret is the most powerful of all the laws of Fascinating Womanhood. Applying this secret produces spectacular results. Why? Because admiration is the food of a man's soul. He needs it daily. He yearns for it. He craves it. Men will even give their lives for it."

"On the other hand, failing to keep this law, and wounding our husband's sensitive male pride, causes him to suffer deep hurt. He becomes very unhappy. THIS IS THE MOST COMMON CAUSE OF MARRIAGE FAILURE."

Why men have sensitive pride

"Let's look first at the second part of this law. 'Never wound his sensitive pride."

"Why do men have such sensitive pride?"

"I'm going to test your humility here. Most women find it hard to accept the true answer to this question. So we are going to take it direct from the Word of God. This Bible scripture is of vital importance in understanding men."

"Angela, would you please read out this verse in Genesis that I've highlighted," said the teacher, handing her a heavy, black covered Bible. "These are the words God spoke to Eve."

"To the woman he said. "I will greatly multiply your pain in child-bearing; in pain you shall bring forth children, yet your desire shall be for your husband, and he shall rule over you."
                    Genesis chapter 3, verse 16.

"Now that last bit, *'he shall rule over you'* we women can find hard to accept. Nevertheless, whether we accept the Bible or not, that scripture is true. Fascinating Womanhood is all about truth. We women ARE born with a desire for strong and caring male leadership. While men, with their highly sensitive masculine pride, and strong muscular bodies are programmed, so to speak, to *'rule over'* women.' I myself prefer the word 'lead'."

"This strong, God-given pride is what drives men to want

to lead, and to protect, and to provide for women. God has programmed it into men so to speak."

"This strong desire in a man to protect and provide for a woman, is just like the strong mothering instinct God has programmed into we women. In the same way it drives us to protect and provide for our children."

How a man feels when you wound his sensitive pride

"A man's in-born masculine pride is so sensitive, that if challenged by a woman, the hurt cuts him deep like a knife. This often arouses instant anger and harshness. Sometimes it results in physical violence, but more often, in deep resentment."

"A man just cannot bear to have his fragile and sensitive pride belittled or ridiculed by his wife, or any other woman."

"We wives can deeply hurt our husband without realising it. Our words can cause him severe mental pain. This is why so many men erect an invisible wall around themselves. A wall of silence, to protect against this pain."

"They stop confiding in us, and only rarely have long conversations with us. They will not share with us their innermost feelings, although they long to do so."

"This can be heartbreaking for a wife. She despairs of ever breaking through his wall of silence. Yet she will sometimes hear her husband confiding to others. Sharing his thoughts and problems and dreams in a way that he never does with her. This causes her much distress and unhappiness."

Angela's heart was beating fast. The teacher was describing Ted exactly. For years now he had stopped revealing his feelings to her. She recalled how hurtful it was to overhear him sometimes, revealing his plans, thoughts and hopes to others. Ted even confided more in her mother than herself.

Her heart pounded even harder as she raised her hand.

"Yes Angela," said the teacher.

"I've got exactly that problem with my husband. We are separated now as you know. But if only I could get through to him. He really is a good man. I can accept that now, but I don't feel that he's really mine."

A murmur of agreement came from several other women. One said, "My husband's like that."

"Yes, it's more common than we think," said the teacher. "But be patient. We ARE going to learn how to overcome it. But first of all, we need to fully understand the many ways in which our husband's sensitive male pride is wounded."

"Now sometimes we deliberately hurt our husband's pride with a sharp tongue and angry tone, but more often we do it in jest."

"We laugh or mock some masculine quality about him. Or we compare him unfavourably with other men."

"When we do that, especially in front of others, we make him feel as if he's been struck with a lash. He may not say

Don't suggest he call a mechanic.

46

a word, but we have killed his affection for us, at least for a time."

"If it continues over a long period, our husband will numb his senses to minimise further hurt, sometimes with the help of alcohol, or even drugs."

"But when he does that, he also numbs himself to the finer things of life – music, sunsets, flowers, little children. He can become impotent, or sexually deviant."

"Only long term acceptance and admiration will restore him to normal."

"In less extreme cases, a man puts up a wall of silence and reserve between himself and the woman causing the hurt."

"If your husband confides more easily in others than he does in you, there IS a wall in place."

"You have hurt his sensitive pride when he has confided to you in the past. He will not want to risk being hurt again. He probably also feels resentful towards you."

As long as he is smiling warmly at you, all is well.

Angela's face flushed hotly. It was as if a blindfold had been taken off. She had always had a sarcastic tongue. As a child she had continual battles with her brothers. Even now they avoided her. And she had not spared Ted either.

Sometimes when Ted had shared ideas with her, she had scorned them as impractical, or poured cold water on them. And often, when she was angry with him, she would mock his poor reading. And more recently, she had mocked his inability to handle the book work in his business.

She could not remember the last time she had praised or admired him. She recalled the two pages of his virtues she had written last Wednesday night.

As she sat there, a feeling of love and sympathy for Ted, mixed with strong guilt, welled up inside her. There was a lump in her throat and her eyes burned with tears. "How could I have been so stupid?" she thought, shaking her head.

"Now," said the teacher, "how do we get our husbands to take down their wall of silence? Only by living the secrets of Fascinating Womanhood, especially this one, Number Two."

Wives can easily hurt their husband's sensitive pride.

Marina raised her hand. "Yes Marina," said the teacher.

Marina spoke softly, "Darling, I think I must be guilty of hurting my husband's pride, but I never mock him or laugh at him. And I try not to get angry. Are there other ways?"

"Marina there are hundreds of ways we can injure our husband's sensitive pride," said the teacher. "A common way is to show a lack of confidence in him. We have to be so careful to think before we speak. Things like suggesting he call a mechanic when he can't get the car started. Or suggesting that he doesn't earn enough money. 'We can't afford it.' Who's ever said that?"

"Admiring other men is another very common mistake. Have we ever held up our fathers as a shining example to our husband. Sometimes we forget the age difference."

"Another common one is advising him on masculine matters when he hasn't asked for our advice. We must think so carefully before speaking. Watch out for a drop in his countenance. That's a warning signal. Keep him smiling. As long as he's smiling warmly at you, all is well."

"Now I am going to hand you out a list of common ways a woman wounds a man's sensitive pride. Go through the list carefully when you get home. Mark those you are guilty of, then resolve never to do them again, not ever."

"Don't underestimate the power of these things to harm your relationship. They can temporarily kill your husband's love for you stone dead."

Angela took the handout and quickly scanned the list. Her guilt increased still further. With dismay she recognised many mistakes she had made in the past.

COMMON MISTAKES WIVES MAKE THAT INJURE THEIR HUSBANDS' SENSITIVE PRIDE

- ☐ **Criticising his weaknesses.**
- ☐ **Speaking angrily when he fails in a masculine area of responsibility.**
- ☐ **Disagreeing with him on masculine matters.**
- ☐ **Pouring cold water on his ideas.**
- ☐ **Giving him advice when he has not asked for it.**
- ☐ **Discussing his career or occupation as if you know as much about it as he does.**
- ☐ **Reminding him how you struggle on his income.**
- ☐ **Telling others how much your parents have done for you since you got married.**
- ☐ **Admiring a masculine quality in another man.**
- ☐ **Suggesting he call a repair man when he is trying to repair something.**
- ☐ **Not paying attention when he is telling you about something of which he is proud.**
- ☐ **Not praising him when he does something outstandingly well.**
- ☐ **Telling him he is losing his figure or his hair.**
- ☐ **Holding yourself up as an example for him to follow.**
- ☐ **Reminding him of your superior education.**
- ☐ **Excelling him in a male-dominated sport such as athletics, golf, swimming.**
- ☐ **Going out to work when he would prefer that you stayed at home.**
- ☐ **Telling others that you have to go out to work to make ends meet.**

The teacher continued, "All these mistakes belittle your husband. They sap his self-confidence. He feels less manly. He may feel unworthy of you."

"More often, the hurt causes him to feel angry and resentful towards you. He then shows his bad side, his ugly side. He just can't feel loving and tender towards you. No

A man needs to feel loved, but not as much as he needs to feel admired.

matter how much he knows that he should, or would like to."

"Nor can he bring himself to confide in you, although he may long to. His fear of further hurt and his resentment prevent him."

"Sometimes however, a husband will belittle himself to his wife. Why would he do that? Because he secretly hopes she will disagree with him, and praise him instead."

"Now before we move on to the positive, powerful side to this secret, there is another reason why a man may not confide in his wife, even when she is not hurting his pride. That is when she is a blabber mouth. When he cannot trust her to keep it to herself. We must learn to be discreet when our husband confides in us."

The power of admiration

"Now for the positive side of this secret. We are going to learn how to transform a man. How to draw out and develop the goodness in him."

"We are going to learn how to cause his confidence and his self esteem to soar. How to arouse his energy, and his drive."

"And most important, we are going to learn how to awaken the fullness of his love, and his tenderness for you."

"But first, a question class. Why do men try to excel in business and in their careers? Where does their motivation and drive come from? Why do they keep striving for bigger and better things, or more fame?"

Beth spoke, "For money I would imagine,"

"Yes Beth, but money is secondary. Elsie, what do you think?"

"Is it to be admired?" asked Elsie.

The teacher smiled. "Yes, Elsie is right. Admiration is their reward. The admiration of other men. And just as important, the admiration of their wife. That is a man's greatest joy."

"Remember, your husband needs your admiration more than he needs your love. Few women know this great truth. It's summed up nicely in the following couplet."

"A man needs to feel loved,
but not as much as he needs to feel admired."

"A woman needs to feel admired,
but not as much as she needs to feel loved."

"Why is your admiration so important to your husband? Because it makes him feel manly. Feeling manly is the most pleasant and enjoyable feeling a man can experience."

"Our husbands, and our sons too, often do and say things in our presence, hoping to receive admiration and praise. But most women are too busy with other things to notice."

"The woman who knows how to admire a man's masculinity is the woman who wins his heart. She is an angel in his eyes."

"Now just in passing, I would like to add that admiration

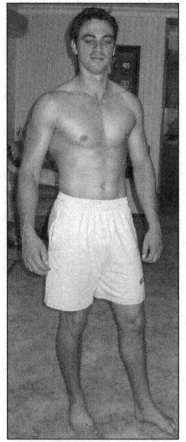
Men are very proud of their muscles.

When you praise him for manly qualities, like running, swimming, sports, work skills, you touch his heart.

is also a wonderful thing to give to our sons. It helps them grow into confident manhood. Their need is especially strong during their teenage years. You'll be thrilled at how close you can draw your sons to you by praising and admiring them. And also by resisting any urge to criticise them. In fact this applies to all our children at any age."

"We should never tease our children either. They may not mind other adults teasing them, but we parents should never tease them. It is destructive to their self-confidence."

How to help your husband become a better man

"Now, back to men. A man who is never admired becomes a lonely and bitter creature. But the man who is admired and praised, especially by his wife, grows in confidence and nobility. There is a ready smile to his face, and a spring in his step. He holds his head high."

"You can use this masculine admiration principle to help your husband become a better man. First, you need to have a trusting belief in his better side. Then, whenever he does something right, or good in his masculine responsibilities, sincerely praise him for it. Make him feel manly."

"Also remind him of good things he's done in the past that have impressed you. Do this daily in the weeks ahead, until it becomes a habit. Watch him develop and grow. You'll be so proud of him."

Elsie spoke, *"Behind every great man, there is a great woman.'*

Yes, that's so true Elsie. Now you all know that the main secret of this is praise of his masculine qualities."

"Helena, would you please read us these words from the famous German writer Goethe," said the teacher, handing Helena a card. "This goes right a long with what Elsie said."

"If you treat a man as he is, he will stay as he is, but if you treat him as if he were what he ought to be, and could be, he will become that bigger and better man." Goethe 1774

Cherry raised her hand. "When you say, 'the praise of his masculine qualities' what exactly do you mean? I mean, do I admire my husband's muscles for instance?"

"Yes, by all means," said the teacher, "men are very proud of their muscles. If your husband's muscles aren't well developed, at least admire his strength, especially when he undoes a tight lid for you, or lifts something heavy."

"We can also admire our husband's deep voice, his beard or moustache, his sex drive and ability to please you in this area. That's very important to a man."

"Or his strong build, especially if he's short. His driving skills, his gardening skills, his handyman abilities, his career skills which is another highly important area to a man."

"Admire anything he excels at of a manly nature. Just be sincere and you cannot go wrong. But don't overdo it. Don't gush. Remember, watch for his smile."

"Don't praise him for how well he does the dishes, or the vacuuming, or makes the beds. That won't stir his love for you. But when you praise him for manly qualities, like running and other sports, driving, navigation, work skills, you touch his heart."

"Even give sincere praise for small masculine accomplishments, like hammering a nail in straight, sawing a straight line, or backing a trailer."

Kathy said, "Won't he get a big head with all this praise?"

"No Kathy. Life is full of humiliations for every man. These daily embarrassments keep him from getting a swelled head. On the other hand, you become his source of inspiration, his refuge from humiliation. His source of strength. He will love you deeply for it. His confidence will soar like an eagle."

"And when combined this with the next secret, Secret Number Three, he will even worship you. I am not exaggerating."

"It's a wonderful feeling for a husband to have a wife who truly admires him. When you admire him, you make him feel like you feel when he buys you flowers unexpectedly."

"But again I must warn, BE SINCERE. This is especially important if you haven't been giving him any praise. He may be suspicious. Watch for his smile. That's the sign he has accepted your admiration. Can we accept a sincere gift of flowers from our husbands without smiling?"

"If he does not smile, he probably thinks you are insincere, or he is still harbouring resentment. That's why its so important to do Assignment three of last week's Secret Number One. Your submissive words will release his pent up resentment."

"Two other important points. First, try and touch him as you praise him, and look him in the eye and smile. It's not strictly necessary, but it adds to his pleasure."

"Second, BE SPECIFIC. Say exactly what it is that you admire about him. The more specific the better. Rather than say for example, 'What nice legs you have'. You might say, 'What strong, well-shaped thighs you have."

Cherry laughed. "If I told my husband that, he'd wear shorts all year round."

"I quite believe he would Cherry. Admiration has a powerful effect on our husbands."

How to find qualities in your husband to praise and admire

Beth spoke, "My husband is not really the masculine type. He's a good husband, and highly intelligent, but he hasn't got big muscles, and he's not a handyman."

"A good point Beth, all men have either intelligence, brawn, mental talent, or physical skills. Praise them in the area in which they most excel."

"For example, Beth might watch for chances to admire her husband's intellectual skills, especially to do with his accountancy career. A man's occupation is an important masculine function. Even after he has retired we should remind him of his past successes."

"You will get ideas for admiration from the list of your husband's virtues you made out for last week's assignment."

"But remember, only masculine things if you want to awaken his full love for you."

Pandora's Box.

"To discover even more things to admire about your husband, encourage him to talk about himself. Ask him questions that require long, thoughtful answers. Encourage him to talk about his past accomplishments. Those things of which he's proud, and his dreams for the future."

"Listen patiently. Let him see that you are interested. STRONGLY RESIST THE DESIRE TO TALK ABOUT YOURSELF."

"It doesn't matter if you don't understand all he is saying. He won't be overly concerned. It can even make him feel more manly. Just appreciate the character that is being unfolded to your view. And openly admire any noble, masculine thoughts he shares with you."

"Later on, when he regularly confides in you, you might need to show gentle, feminine dismay at any unworthy thoughts he shares, but at first, just listen uncritically."

"When your husband feels that he can trust you to respect his masculinity, he will confide to you his deepest and innermost thoughts. This is when you begin to awaken his deepest love."

"Here we have the explanation of the mystery we discussed last week. How a man can be captivated by a woman who appears to have no attractive qualities to us at all. That woman is living Fascinating Womanhood. Especially this weeks Second Secret, and next week's Third Secret of Fascinating Womanhood. Yes, we women have great power over the destiny of our man."

"But again, remember to BE SINCERE. You are dealing with your man's most sensitive area, his sense of masculinity. He may strongly resent praise that has a phoney ring to it. It can backfire on you. Watch for his smile of acceptance."

Bev grinned then said, "I don't know. I still think Kathy could be right. All this praise and admiration will give any husband a swelled head, especially mine." The class laughed.

The Fascinating Womanhood teacher smiled. "Maybe it will Bev, but he will return you so much love and kindness that you won't mind one little bit."

"But remember again, that even though your husband is lifted by sincere admiration from you, his wife, he is still coming into contact with other people in his life. People who discourage him, mock him, reprimand him, and humble him. This is enough to keep his head the proper size."

"So to sum all this up, *'A man's greatest pleasure is when his masculinity is admired by a woman. His greatest pain is when his masculinity is belittled by a woman."*

The 'Pandora's Box' reaction'

"Now before we close tonight, I need to forewarn you about a surprising reaction that can occur in your husband when you live the first two secrets of Fascinating Womanhood."

"It is especially likely when he has built a wall of silence around himself. It's called the 'Pandora's Box' reaction."

"This is an unexpected outburst of angry feelings toward you. Angry feelings that he has bottled up for years."

"Don't be shocked. Be glad if this happens. Even encourage it to happen. Why? Because it means that he now feels safe to release his resentment. It means he does not need to keep it bottled up any more. It's the beginning of him confiding in you."

"Above all, DO NOT ARGUE BACK. Just sit down and take it. Even agree with him. For when 'Pandora's Box' is empty, he will have a wonderful feeling of relief. The resentment locked up in his heart is now gone. His heart can now fill with so much love and tenderness for you that you will scarcely believe it possible. His wall of silence will vanish at the same time."

"Provided you continue to live the principles of Fascinating Womanhood, he will continue feeling safe in confiding in you. This will be the foundation of a beautiful, trusting relationship."

"Now, it has been a longer than normal lesson tonight, but a very, very important one. I'll hand you out this week's assignments and then we'll hear from our two guests."

ASSIGNMENTS – SECRET NUMBER TWO

ASSIGNMENT ONE. Praise one of your husband's masculine qualities before he goes to sleep tonight. Watch for his smile.

ASSIGNMENT TWO. By asking questions that require long, thoughtful answers, and giving admiration, try and have your husband talk to you about a past achievement, or a future dream, for at least five minutes. (Be openly attentive and DO NOT INTERRUPT HIM WITH YOUR OWN THOUGHTS as he speaks.)

ASSIGNMENT THREE. Every second day, sincerely tell your husband how much you admire him for one of his virtues that you listed as part of last week's assignment. Touch him and smile as you do so. Continue doing this until you have praised him sincerely for all the virtues you have listed.

"Angela, as you are not living with your husband we can excuse you from this week's assignments, at least for a little while, but all of you who have not yet completed last week's assignments, please do them as soon as you can. They are the foundation of Fascinating Womanhood."

"Don't tell your husband what your assignments are, just do them. They are far more effective that way."

"Now, Rosalyn, would you come up and speak to us first, and then Donna will share her experience with us."

Rosalyn. True Experience

"I first became acquainted with Fascinating Womanhood about four years ago, through my sister. I was sceptical at first, but finally I was able to set aside my overgrown pride and ask the Lord to help me in a last desperate attempt to save a failing marriage."

"It wasn't easy at first. I wondered how I could have been guilty of so many wrong attitudes, and that female pride kept sneaking back."

"I put the teachings into practice. I was so frightened. All I could do was to pray for the courage that I seemed to lack."

"He was about three hours late coming home, but I didn't, as usual, question him or complain. I simply said, 'I know you must have put in a hard day Honey. You deserve some time away from everything. I kept your meal warm so I'll bring it right to you.' Suddenly an expression of confused pleasure came over his tired face."

"After he finished eating I curled up by his feet on the floor and began. 'Honey, I want you to know that I appreciate you for the strong man that you are. And I realise that you must say no to me once in a while for the good of both of us, and I really respect you for it.' (I had been begging, pleading and crying for a new outfit I'd seen, but couldn't have). 'I couldn't feel safe or secure with someone who let me push him around. I just want you to know I love you as you are, and wouldn't change a single thing about you."

"Well, I can't even begin to describe the expression that came over his face. I only know it was one with deep warmth and love for me. Then he pulled me close to him and held me for a long time. He actually wept, and I wept with him out of happiness for the moment and of real hope for the future."

"The next day he came in acting rather strange and with a big box. And do you know what he had done? He had gone shopping and bought a complete outfit for me and both of the children. It was all there, from shoes to hats. I just couldn't believe it. Now it was my turn for tears. I knew that I was on my way to being a Fascinating Woman."

"That was four years ago. He still surprises me with flowers, or some little token of his love, and I still shed a tear or two."

"He says it makes him feel great to know he can make me happy. Our marriage is indestructible. Fascinating

Write in your Love Book all the tender romantic things your husband says to you as you live Fascinating Womanhood.

Womanhood is absolutely beautiful, and never stops snowballing into something bigger and better everyday."

Donna. True Experience

"My husband and I had been married thirteen years, most of them unhappy. We had separated three times, and I had decided to leave him for the last time. I had given up on him."

"About this time a friend of mine told me about Fascinating Womanhood and encouraged me to take the class. I told her that nothing could be done for that stubborn husband of mine, and I might as well give up, but she begged me to take it. By then we had already separated."

"I was worse than miserable. A numbness went through me. After the first class, I prayed as I had never prayed before. I prayed that my husband would want to see me and talk to me. He did."

"I decided to take him back, but I was afraid. How was I to know it was going to work."

"At the next class the teacher told us to compliment our husband on his manliness, muscles, etc. I didn't think I could bring myself to say something like that."

"Finally, just before the next class, I knew I had to do something, because the teacher would ask us about it. So I waited until we were in bed and the lights were out. I thought I would faint. Finally I told him what beautiful muscles he had."

"As soon as I said it, he took me in his arms and kissed me over and over. This is when our new marriage began."

"I was told not to expect material rewards, but a happy marriage. I received both. Some of the things my husband has bought me without asking are; a beautiful nightie, a typewriter, a trip to Hawaii, a new stove, table and chairs, bedroom carpeting, perfume and flowers."

The teacher wiped tears from her eyes as she thanked Donna, and Rosalyn for coming along tonight. "These are not isolated experiences class. All of you can have similar, beautiful experiences. Remember, admiration is your husband's life blood. Just as tender, romantic experiences are a woman's lifeblood."

"Before we say good night, can I suggest that you start a Love Book. A Love Book is a little pink or red notebook in which you write all the tender, romantic things your husband says to you as you live Fascinating Womanhood. I have one. I've kept it for years. It's the most priceless treasure I own."

Angela felt excited as she drove home. It was all starting to come clear to her now. Ted had been starved of admiration for years.

She now felt real hope. Deep down inside she felt that everything could turn out fine.

Before going to bed that night, Angela wrote Ted a note of acceptance to complete her assignment for last week.

Dear Ted,
I have had a lot of time to think since you have been gone. I have not appreciated you in the past, and I have made some silly mistakes. I am sorry, and I am glad you have not let me push you around. I am glad you are the kind of man you are. If you give me another chance, I promise I will be a wonderful wife to you.
Love Angela.

It was difficult and humbling for Angela to write these words. She had felt her heart beating fast as she wrote. She wondered if she had used the right words, and whether she could live up to them. However after several rewrites she finally felt satisfied with what she had written.

She put the note in an envelope and took it outside and put it in her car so she would not forget it tomorrow.

Then she went to bed. But she was so stimulated by tonight's lesson, and the writing of her note to Ted that it was a long time before sleep came.

Angela awoke the next morning after a vivid dream that Ted was alongside her in the bed. She was brought back to reality when she opened her eyes and saw Tiphony's long blond hair on the pillow alongside her.

Today Angela did not feel at all confident about taking the note to Ted. However, as she had firmly decided last night that she would take it to him after school this afternoon, she would see it through.

Angela was so anxious all morning as she taught her class that she developed a tension headache. At lunch time, she did not feel hungry, so decided to take the note to Ted during her lunch break and get it over with.

She drove to his workshop and saw his van parked outside. She had been half hoping he wouldn't be there.

Her heart pounded as she walked into the work bay. The area was full of cars, but there was no sign of anybody.

"His apprentice is probably out to lunch," she thought, "But Ted should be here."

Then she heard voices coming from Ted's small office. She glanced through the open door. Yes, Ted was in there, standing talking with a customer wearing a business suit.

Ted saw Angela, but ignored her. He looked flustered and closed the office door.

Angela was undecided what to do next, so she waited. It soon became obvious from the tone of the customer's voice that he was highly displeased with Ted.

Angela overheard snatches of his words . . . *"paid for that last month"* . . . *"sloppy account system"* . . . *"sort this mess out"* . . . *"not paying until"* . . . Then the door opened and the customer strode out of the workshop. Ted came out also, looking grim and cold eyed.

"What do YOU want?" he said harshly to Angela.

Angela felt shattered. It was hard to breathe. Tears welled up. She couldn't trust herself to speak and just held out the envelope.

Ted took it. "What's this?" he said, glaring at her.

"Please read it later," she said, her voice breaking. Then she hurried back out to her car. Her hands shook as she fumbled with the seat belt and drove off. She did not dare look back.

The tears came again that evening when Ami phoned and Angela told her what happened. "It's no good Ami," she said. "He's worse than ever. He'll never change. And now he'll think I'm stupid, writing him a note like that."

Ami was comforting. "It was just bad timing Angie. Can't you see how terribly his pride was hurt. You saw and heard him being humiliated by that customer. You could not have arrived at a worse time."

"I tell you what Angie, our car is nearly due for a warrant of fitness. Bill would want Ted to do it. I'll go and book it in tomorrow and see how he is."

The next morning Ami put on an attractive white dress with feminine frills on that she had made herself, and drove her car to Ted's workshop.

"Where can I find Ted?" she asked the apprentice who was lying underneath one of the cars.

"He's in the office over there," he said, indicating with his head.

Ami saw Ted sitting in front of a small laptop computer, on a desk covered with papers. He had a worried look on his face.

"Hi Ted," she said airily.

Ted looked up with a start. "Oh, hello Ami," he said. "I didn't expect to see you here. What do you think? I've just bought this new computer to do my accounts."

"Wow!" said Ami smiling. "Can you work one of those things? I'm always messing up Bill's one. You men have such good minds for computers."

"Oh there's nothing to it," said Ted brightening. "Just a matter of following the instructions."

"Hey, this is a nice place you've got here Ted. Clean, painted floors, and look at all the cars you've got to work on. You must be doing a good job."

Ted's worried face broke into a broad smile. "Well, yes, we always try and do a good job. *'Do it once, do it right'* that's my motto."

"Bill would like you to give our car a warrant of fitness check Ted. Can I book it in?"

"Well, I am booked up until the end of next week, but for an attractive customer like you Ami, I can do it right now while you wait if you like."

"Oh thank you Ted," said Ami giving him a big smile. "That's kind of you."

Ted blushed. Ami remembered how he often blushed as a young man. She also noticed that he whistled as he checked her car. This was the same Ted she had always known. His reddish brown hair had receded a little and was starting to grey around the temples, but he was still the same Ted inside.

Ami spoke to the apprentice while she waited, "What's it like working for Ted?" she asked.

"He's a good mechanic. Knows his stuff. So you know him?"

"Yes, I went to school with him. How do you find him?"

"He's a good boss. Though he's not the same since he broke up with his missus. Bit moody most of the time. Seems happy enough now though, you must have cheered him up. Haven't heard him whistle for months."

"Perhaps you could remind him from time to time what a good mechanic he is," said Ami.

Ted was still whistling as Ami drove away twenty minutes later.

CHAPTER SIX

Secret Number Three
Make him Number One

DAVID'S behaviour was worsening.

His teacher phoned Angela again on Friday to say that David had been caught fighting at school, and that his school work had deteriorated further.

David was also becoming cruel and hurtful at home towards his sister Tiphony. This, along with his increasing insolence and disobedience toward her, was causing distress to Angela.

On Monday evening, David said to her in a sullen voice, "It's your fault Dad won't come home. I want to go and live with him."

David's words stung Angela. Her relationship with her son had now, in many ways become as strained as her relationship with Ted. She was finding it difficult to love David as she once did.

When her mother phoned late that evening, Angela poured out her frustration to her about David's behaviour.

"Why don't you practice Fascinating Womanhood on David," said her mother. "Isn't it supposed to work on all males?"

Angela thought it was an excellent idea. She wondered why she hadn't thought of it herself. She recalled how Harmony the Fascinating Womanhood teacher had told the class several times how effective Fascinating Womanhood could also be with their sons, and how close it had brought her to her own sons.

When she hung up the phone, Angela reflected on the ways she spoke to David. She soon realised she was making the same mistakes with David, that she had made with Ted. Trying to change him. Criticising his weaknesses. Nagging about his reluctance to help with the housework.

When was the last time she had admired him? She could not remember.

She recalled how earlier, this very evening, she had mocked him in anger about not having any friends. He had stormed off to his bedroom and slammed the door behind him.

The more Angela cast her mind back, the more guilty she felt. Then an idea came into her head.

She went and found the list of masculine virtues from her first Fascinating Womanhood class. Then she sat down at the table with her pen and pad and began listing David's virtues.

After a few minutes she was again astounded. Just as she had been when listing Ted's virtues. David seemed to possess even more virtues than Ted. Her heart softened greatly toward David.

Angela remembered the little grey and white statue of a man that the Fascinating Womanhood teacher had held up in class.

Angela firmly decided, there and then, that from now on she would only look on David's good side. She would accept him, and not try and change him, and tell him so.

She felt excited and wanted to start immediately. "I wonder if I could do something right now," she thought.

She arose and went to David's bedroom. His door was still closed. She opened it and said softly, "Are you still awake David?"

"Yeah. Whadda yer want?" David's voice was surly and muffled, and resentful.

Angela felt her anger rise again at David's response. But she held her tongue and composed herself.

"David," she said quietly, entering the room and standing next to his bed, "I want to tell you that I'm glad you're the kind of boy you are. I haven't always appreciated you, and I've said some things that aren't true about you. I'm sorry David. I'm glad you're the way you are, and I'm proud of you. From now on, I'm going to try to be a wonderful mother. And I'm going to do everything I can to make Daddy want to come home."

David remained silent. Angela bent down and kissed him on the forehead. As she did so she saw his closed eyes flood with tears. Angela felt a lump come to her throat. Her own tears came as she left the room. She continued to weep freely as she sat at the dining room table, and finished writing the long list of David's virtues.

The next morning David awoke in high spirits. He did not tease Tiphony once.

Before he left for school, Angela hugged him from behind as he was making his lunch in the kitchen. Then she rubbed his shoulders and said, "Such a tall, strong boy." David seemed embarrassed, but grinned broadly.

"Bye Mum. Bye Tiphony," he called out cheerfully as he rode off early on his bike, I'm going to Damian's house before school.

"David seems happy today Mum," said Tiphony. '

"Yes dear. He is happy today," replied Angela smiling.

Angela also noticed that David had made his bed. The first time in weeks without her having to nag him about it.

Angela felt at peace all day.

She was delighted when she got home to see that David had brought his friend Damian home with him from school that afternoon.

That evening Angela called her two children together. She gave them each a pen and paper and suggested they both write a letter to their father. They eagerly agreed to do so.

Angela wrote Ted a short letter also.

Dear Ted

I really mean what I said in the note I handed you last week. I know now that you have been a good husband to me, and a good father to David and Tiphony. I am sorry I never fully appreciated you in the past.

You are also an excellent mechanic, and I am proud that you run your own business.

Love Angela.

Angela also made a firm decision that evening, to definitely give up smoking, and also, to lose weight. She would try and become more like her friend Ami.

The next morning Angela arose early to go for a run to the Post Office, just over a km away and post the letters they had all written to Ted last night.

She squeezed into her old running shorts and sports bra, pulled on the running shoes she had bought several years ago, but had hardly used and set off.

But she rapidly became exhausted and breathless and had to walk most of the way, there and back. However she enjoyed a tingling glow when she arrived home.

The days were now becoming longer as summer drew near. It was a beautiful, sunlit spring evening when Angela drove to her third class. The flowers and trees of the suburban homes she passed looked fresh and bright. Angela felt a sense of well-being.

Tonight the Fascinating Womanhood teacher wore a flowing, long white dress, with her hair french-plaited down her back. Angela thought she looked like a mother angel.

She welcomed the class, then smiled at Kathy who was sitting in the front row.

"Kathy, have you managed to accept and admire your husband yet, as we have discussed in our first two secrets?"

Kathy, who was elegantly dressed as usual said, "Well, yes I have. Would you like to hear what happened?"

"We would love to Kathy?"

Kathy stood and turned to face the class. She seemed a little embarrassed at first, but spoke very clearly.

Kathy. True experience

"Trying to tell my husband that I accepted him and that I admired him was a very hard thing for me to

come out with. First of all, I'm not the kind of person to say something like this, and secondly, I thought I would start to giggle."

"I tried three or four times to do my little speech, but always ended up turning and walking out of the room."

"Finally I was going to do it, no matter what kind of mess it turned into. So I walked into the room and started."

"Well, the look in his eyes was just unbelievable. Never can I remember such a look. He had so much pride in his eyes, and it was not for himself, it was for me."

"Later in the week he took me out to dinner and made two comments. One hurt and the other felt great. He said, 'For the first time he felt I really cared.' He had never thought I cared what happened to him. Secondly, that he 'never loved me more than he did then."

"What more can a woman ask for? Isn't this what we really want, and makes it all worth it."

Make him Number One in your life.

"Yes Kathy," said the teacher, "it is so worth the effort we make. It may not always be easy, but it's so very worthwhile. Anybody else? Has anybody had a 'Pandora's Box' reaction yet?"

Marina raised her hand. "Yes, darling, I have."

"Marina, how exciting. Come and tell us about it."

Marina. True experience

"Well, I've been applying what I've learned, and my husband seemed happier. Then last week tension began to build a little, not bad. Then two nights ago, wham! A Pandora's Box' reaction. It seems as if all the pent up feelings he had came out, and at the same time his walls of silence came tumbling down. Pretty dramatic. And pretty wonderful!"

"Now he tells me he has never been so happy in all his life, and I feel the same way."

"Last night my husband spent three hours just talking to me, telling me more about himself, his past and dreams than I have learned in the years I have known him."

"Oh, I just love hearing your experiences," said the teacher, looking radiant. "They just thrill me."

"Now for our third secret. But first, there's a little saying that's been around for years. We should teach it to our daughters. You'll like this Elsie. Let me quote it to you before I introduce this powerful secret."

> *A good woman inspires a man.*
> *A brilliant woman interests him.*
> *A beautiful woman fascinates him.*
> *But a sympathetic woman gets him.'*

"Now here is Secret Number Three." It's a two part secret. She turned and wrote on the board.

SECRET NUMBER THREE
Make him Number One in your life. Comfort him tenderly when he is tired or discouraged.

"The first part of this secret tells us to make our husband our king, our hero, Number One in our life."

"The second part is the powerful effect a woman's sympathy can have on a man."

"Let's look at the first part, why your husband should be Number One?"

"Now be honest, all of you, who or what do you really make Number One in your life? Is it your husband? Is it your home? Is it your children, your parents, your career?"

Elsie spoke, "I think many of us women put our homes before our husband, and sometimes even before our children too."

"Yes Elsie, some of us do. But isn't the king more important than the castle? Fascinating Womanhood teaches that, first our husband, and then our children, should come before our home. Our husband should be Number One and our children Number Two."

Elsie spoke again, "Yes, I strongly agree with that. And another reason to make our husband Number One, is that our children grow up and leave home. As you know I've raised a large family, nine children. All of them have now left home. My youngest son left over ten years ago now. They all still visit of course, but there's just my husband and myself most of the time."

"That's true Elsie. Yes our husband and wife relationship continues long after our children have left home. Long after our parents pass away. Does it ever end?"

"This Third Secret is a lovely law of Fascinating Womanhood. When we make our husband Number One, our children feel secure and happy, and the love between us and our husband increases dramatically. It's so rewarding."

"You make him King, and you become his Queen."

Why some husbands resist having more children

"Most women begin marriage this way. They make their husband Number One, until the first baby is born. You know what I mean, or soon will. We have all brought adorable babies into the world, or like Beth, are about to."

"However it is so vitally important that our husbands still remain Number One at this critical time. No matter how adorable our babies might be."

"When a husband is restored to Number One again, often his resistance to having more children vanishes."

"Like Elsie, I've also raised a large family, seven children, not as many as Elsie, but what a source of joy they are to me now. They're just wonderful. Mind you that wasn't always the case when they were younger. Toddlers can be a real handful and teenagers test us to the absolute limit. But life is rich in our mature years after raising a large family, especially when they all turn out well."

Elsie said, "I couldn't agree more. There's a lovely saying, *"Your hands full now, your heart full later.'* Our children and our in-laws just spoil my husband and I. And oh, how I love my twenty-one precious grandchildren. I spoil them too when they come and stay with us, or we visit them. Sometimes they write me the sweetest notes and draw me pictures. I save them all."

"Yes class, Elsie is right. We should not follow the world and limit our families. I believe *'the larger your family, the richer your life,'* and it becomes even richer as life goes on."

At these words from the teacher, Angela couldn't resist turning her head to see what Beth, the young career woman's reaction would be. She saw Beth roll her eyes at Cherry in disbelief.

Angela was surprised however to see Bev smiling and nodding her head. Helena was beaming.

Angela tried imagining what it could be like to have a large family. The idea was attractive in many ways, especially if it had still been the norm nowadays to have a large family, as it was in her grandmother's day.

Ted came from a large family and was willing to have more children.

Angela was impressed with the genuine joy that Elsie and the teacher were obviously receiving from their large families. However, she wondered if she could cope with sarcastic remarks of some women who firmly believed that two children nowadays were more than enough.

The power of sympathy

"Now," said the teacher, "lets move on to the powerful, sympathy part of this secret."

"You remember last week, how we learned about the sensitive pride of men? And how painful it is for them when we women wound it. And also how easy it is for us to do so? Well, we wives can learn not to hurt our husband's pride, but we can't stop other people hurting it. And they will hurt it."

"Many times your husband will come home to you, tired and discouraged. Not because of over work, as you might think, but because somebody has wounded his pride."

"Perhaps he was not shown appreciation for something good he had done. Or he may have been criticised or reprimanded by a superior. Maybe a customer, or a work colleague made a hurtful remark. He may have made a foolish mistake that embarrassed him in front of his co-workers. That's very common."

"Most men are too ashamed to reveal the real reason for their discouragement, so resist the urge to pry. He'll tell you if he feels like doing so."

Try and appreciate the heavy responsibility your husband carries throughout his life, especially his working life..

"However, this is the time he needs you most. THIS IS THE MOST IMPORTANT TIME OF THE DAY FOR THE FASCINATING WOMAN. This is the time to heal his wounds."

"Ignore any grumpy remarks. Make allowances. Don't react. Remember he is your Number One."

"The children can wait. The meal can wait. Make him comfortable. Listen to him talk if he wants to."

"Give him at least thirty minutes of peace and quiet. That's not too much to ask is it? His better side will soon surface, especially after he has eaten."

The teacher held up the little grey and white statue again and turned the white side to the class."

Bev held up her hand. "Yes Bev," said the teacher.

"Hey what about me? I've been slaving away at home all day. Four noisy boys. I would love thirty minutes of peace and quiet."

Several other women made similar remarks.

The teacher held up her hand and smiled. "Yes, many women object to this vital part of Fascinating Womanhood. But this is very, very important."

"Going home to an unsympathetic wife is the main reason a husband leaves his wife for another woman. And always, for a woman who is more sympathetic to his needs. A woman who soothes his hurt pride. A woman who gives him some admiration."

Bev reddened and said no more. She recalled her painful experience of several years back. What had her husband seen in that cheap, repulsive woman? She cringed at the memory.

The great responsibility men carry

The teacher continued. "Please try and appreciate the heavy responsibility our husbands carry throughout their lives, especially their working lives."

"When a man marries, he takes on his shoulders the burden of providing for a family. He cannot lay this burden down with a clear conscience as long as he lives. He knows his family's success and welfare rely heavily on his efforts."

"The burden is with a man twenty-four hours a day. Most men take this responsibility very seriously."

"A feeling that he is failing in this masculine role can hurt his pride so much that he can turn to drink, or drugs, to dull the pain and disgrace he feels."

"Also, your husband's work world is competitive. His job is never 100% secure. There's often constant pressure on him to exceed last year's efforts. Pressure to keep up with competitors, and his peers. And as he ages, energetic younger men sometimes surpass him and are placed in positions over him."

"Why some women want to choose a life career in that masculine, high pressure environment I do not understand. It's not the glamorous world we daydream it to be."

"I don't agree with that," said Beth. "I find it exciting."

"Well, yes it can be Beth, for a few years, but the pressure is relentless, and eventually it takes its toll on a woman's femininity. We look at this a little deeper in Secret Number Six."

Why you should comfort him lovingly when he arrives home

"So when your husband arrives home, even if he's in a good mood, don't greet him with your problems. Don't let the children go to him with their problems. Don't quiz him about his day."

"Rather, just give him smiles, comforting words, and a sympathetic ear. A man cannot help but deeply love a woman who treats him lovingly, and comforts him when he is tired and discouraged after a long day."

"Take the time to look your best for him. Wear feminine clothing, of the kind you know he likes to see you wear."

"Organise the children and the evening meal to give him his thirty minutes peace and quiet to recover. Then wait until he has eaten before raising problems that need his attention."

"Turn a blind eye to his less than best behaviour as he collapses and unwinds. He has come home to you to recover. He is tired of being his best all day."

"Mother him a little. He will quickly bounce back, and treat you like a Queen."

Why he comes home late

"Bev you have a question."

"Yes, now what about when my husband comes home late for his meal. I find that very annoying."

"Most women do Bev. Just be forgiving. It's not that serious. He's more important than a cold meal. When you live Fascinating Womanhood, your husband won't be late without a good cause. A man's job is important to him. And customers and bosses sometimes make extra demands on his time. Remember he's out there working to provide for his family, for you."

"Yeah, well, maybe you're right," said Bev. "I never quite looked at it like that."

Cherry spoke, "My husband nearly always comes home late too. He runs his own business and always seems to be working. I feel he neglects our little girl sometimes, and I can't get him to do any work around the house. He's a good man, but how can I get him to think of me and his daughter a bit more, and do more around the house?"

"Who's he working for Cherry? He's working for you, and his daughter. Some men show their love by working hard, but we wives don't always see it that way. Appreciate what he's doing."

"Sometimes a man has to work long hours to build up a business, or get out of debt. He may put all his energy into

his work and neglect the house maintenance for a time. But we learn how to handle this problem in Secret Number Nine."

"Class, if you have a hard working husband, be proud of him. And don't encourage him to take retirement early, if at all. That's not good for a man. Edison the inventor was a hard working man. He worked right up to his death at age 84. His hard work gave us the blessing of electric lights, recorded music, motion pictures, and other inventions."

"However, I can promise you all, that when you live Fascinating Womanhood fully, your husband won't spend any longer time at his work than he really needs to. The same applies to other activities that take him away from you."

"We must attract our husband home, not try and force him home. It just does not work."

"So to sum up, your husband needs you to comfort him when he's discouraged. He needs you to heal the wounds that others have inflicted on his pride."

"When you do this, you become indispensable to him, and he will love you tenderly in return."

"Many women also report that their husbands become more successful in their work when they apply this Secret Number Two in their marriage. I firmly believe it."

Why husbands seldom offer to take their wives out to dinner

"Now this is a good time to explain a common problem. Many wives wonder why their husbands never offer to take them out to dinner."

"To understand this, we need to look at our homes through a man's eyes. You see, home to a man, is like a restaurant is to us women, a place away from the never ending demands upon our time."

"So a night out to dinner is nowhere near as attractive to him, as it is to us, particularly when he also has to pay the bill. And this can be half the week's housekeeping food money."

"However, a man willingly makes sacrifices for the woman he loves. And he enjoys doing so."

"When you live all ten secrets of Fascinating Womanhood, your husband will delight in fulfilling your innermost needs."

Your husband is far more likely to come through a crisis successfully when you are fully behind him, believing in him, trusting him.

How to comfort your husband during a severe crisis in his life

"Now, let's look how we can apply this secret to a man who has suffered a severe blow to his pride. A man who is going through a crisis. Cherry, you have a question?"

"Yes. Are you sure this comforting and sympathy works for all men? My husband's business is in trouble. It even looks as if it might fail. When he told me about it this week, I was sympathetic. But do you know what happened? He got angry at me. He told me to shut up!"

It was apparent to Angela that Cherry was not her normal cheerful self tonight.

The teacher looked concerned. "What exactly did you say to him Cherry?"

"I said to him. 'Don't worry John. If you fail in your business it doesn't matter. I'll be happy if you just have an ordinary job.' And I get told to shut up."

The teacher smiled. "This is a good case to illustrate what I was about to talk about. Cherry, you broke an important law of Fascinating Womanhood. Can anybody tell Cherry why her husband got angry with her?"

"Yes I think I can," said Angela. "She hurt his pride when she belittled his ability to save his business."

"Correct Angela. Well spoken. Yes, I think we can be certain that Cherry's husband wants her to have confidence in him. To believe that he can be successful in his time of crisis. Our husbands are far more likely to come through a crisis successfully when we are fully behind them. Believing in them. Trusting in them."

"Cherry's case reminds me of another crisis situation that came up in class some years ago. This woman's husband had just become redundant. She rightly said to him, 'Henry, this may be the door to opportunity, a stepping stone to greater success'."

"Her husband was so relieved he almost wept. And she was right. Her husband went on to become a very successful manager of another company."

"So when your husband suffers a severe blow to his pride, sympathise with him. But also let him know that you still believe in him. That's what he needs most, your trust in him. Remain calm and optimistic. Don't tell him to count his blessings. Don't offer advice to solve his problems, unless he asks you. Just sympathise with him, support him, trust him."

"When he feels better, again express your confidence in him. Let him know you trust his ability to overcome the crisis."

"Don't minimise his problems, or make it sound too easy. You'll rob him of his potential heroism. Let him feel that no matter how great the struggle, you are confident he will be successful.

"And whatever you do, don't take over the reins. Let him remain in control."

"Hold him as you sit with him. Look into his eyes as you speak to him. Remind him of his strengths. Truly trust him. He won't let you down. Love is the greatest power in the universe."

Angela saw that Cherry was now smiling and looking her old cheerful self again. She obviously understood what the teacher was saying. Angela liked Cherry.

When your husband confides an ambitious plan to you

"Another critical time for your husband's pride is when he first reveals to you an ambitious plan. Or a noble idea that he has been secretly considering."

"We must not let our feminine fears, our need for security, dampen his enthusiasm, or hold him back."

"Never pour cold water on his ideas. It's a common female trait to do this. Doing so often causes a man to erect a 'wall of silence'."

"Rather, let your husband know that you believe he can achieve it. If it's impractical, others will point it out to him in due course. But he will be comforted to know that his wife believed in him."

"If he goes ahead with his plan, support him all the way. He'll probably make mistakes, but mistakes are stepping stones to success."

When your husband does something dishonest

"Now, what do you do if your husband does something really wrong, and you get to hear about it. Not unfaithfulness, we'll deal with that shortly, but something dishonest or shameful? Here's what Fascinating Womanhood teaches."

"First, don't ignore it, or pretend you don't know. But do show a reluctance to believe he did it. Let him clearly know that you did not believe he would do such a thing. That it must have been a temporary lapse. Let him feel your disappointment. But reassure him of your unwavering belief in his better side. Then say no more about it, ever."

"NEVER LOWER YOUR STANDARDS TO HIS. For a man to love you deeply, he must always feel that you are a better and more noble person than him."

The alcohol or drug addicted husband

Bev spoke. "Good grief. My husband's always doing wrong. He's an alcoholic. What can I do about that? God knows I suffered enough with my own father. He was an alcoholic too. Now I'm married to one."

"Well Bev, I don't mean to be unkind, but a daughter of an alcoholic often marries a man with an addiction. She thinks he will change if she gives him enough love, but it doesn't often happen."

"The main problem with most addicts is a poor self-image. Addictions such as alcohol, drugs, including prescribed tranquillisers and sleeping pills, tobacco, pornography and gambling are a major problem today. But they can all be overcome with God's help."

"Let's look at why a man becomes an addict. An addict is usually a sensitive man, with a poor self-image, who often suffers emotional pain. This emotional pain usually comes from criticism by others, or perhaps, to put it another way, the lack of admiration of others."

"Or the emotional pain can come from his conscience,

from the guilt of past wrongdoing. Or even from the every-day pressure of just earning a living in the modern world."

"An addict often only enjoys a feeling of normal well-being when he has deadened his higher mind with alcohol or drugs. The so called 'high' he feels, is just the way a normal person feels most of the time. But to the addicted man, by comparison to his usual depressed or anxious self, it is a wonderful feeling. He is at last temporarily freed from his emotional pain."

"These personality disorders can often be traced back to childhood influences, especially growing up without parental discipline. Many addicts were spoiled as boys by parents who never taught them to cope with the responsibilities of life."

"And even more often, they have grown up with lack admiration from their parents. We learnt last week in Secret Number Two how important admiration is for both boys and men."

Elsie spoke. "Yes Harmony, your point earlier about mothers spoiling their boys is very real. The youngest son in a large family is especially at risk. Sometimes we mothers won't let our last child grow up. I was guilty of that. I was still calling my youngest son 'my baby' when he was 20. He didn't seem to mind, but my husband firmly insisted that I not spoil him. Anyway, he's turned out fine. A very confident boy. Sorry, I'm still doing it, a very confident man. He's 30 years old."

"Thank you Elsie. Yes that's a very good point. Motherhood is so wonderful, but what an important responsibility. We look at motherhood in Secret Number Six."

"Now just a final point about overcoming serious addictions. Usually the only effective way is with the help of another person who has overcome a similar addiction."

"Groups such as Alcoholics Anonymous are most effective. The cure starts with a simple phone call. But it needs to be by the addict himself, and to the organisation best able to help him. They are listed in the phone book. If an addict is unsure which organisation is best to use, he can phone Alcoholics Anonymous for advice."

"Of course there are numerous other common addictions, for both men and women, like TV, especially soaps and sports, sweet, fatty foods like chocolate, fast foods, over eating in general, gambling, shopping, spending, love stories, over-cleaning and hypochondria."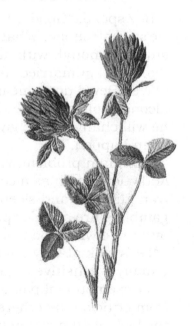

"When we're addicted to something, we feel a strong craving when we're denied our addiction for several days. We will go to great lengths to obtain it."

"We learn how to overcome these lesser addictions in Secret Number Five, but serious addictions nearly always need outside help and prayer."

When you don't love your husband any more

Bev spoke again. "I don't know if its worth the trouble. I

don't love him any more. I can put up with his drinking. It's not that bad lately."

"Bev, it's not uncommon for us to avoid change," said the teacher. "We become comfortable with a situation, even when it is painful. But you wouldn't be taking this course if you didn't hope for something better."

"I challenge you to fulfil your secret dream of what your marriage could become. I care about you Bev. I believe you can do it. You hold the key."

Bev blushed and bowed her head.

"Have you done the three assignments for Secret Number One yet?" asked the teacher.

Bev shook her head.

"Please do the first one tonight Bev. Make a list of your husband's virtues. Will you do it?"

"Well, if you think there's hope, yes, I'll do it," said Bev, her voice breaking. She blinked back her tears. It was the first time in her entire life she could remember anybody saying to her *"I care about you Bev."*

The teacher continued, "Many women married to alcoholics, addicts and men with personality problems have lost all love for their husbands. What should they do? Well here are four thoughts to any woman who is in this situation."

"First. Remember that your husband was once an innocent little boy. His addictions and bad habits have all been learned. So they can all be unlearned, if he has the will, and your support, and the right help."

"We need to look closely at ourselves. Is our behaviour providing the climate for him to really want to change? DO YOU REALLY WANT HIM TO CHANGE? Or are you making it easy for him to continue with his problem, by shielding him from the consequences of his behaviour? We've all heard many times how most people need to hit rock bottom before they will seek help."

"Second. In the beginning, you were both attracted to each other as people. You chose each other. You vowed to stay together for better or worse."

"Third. If he has fathered your children, he can never be replaced in their eyes. Your children are an eternal link between you both. Nothing can change that – ever."

"Fourth. That same man, if you give him acceptance, admiration and sympathy, make him Number One in your life, and allow him to take his proper place at the head of the family, will, with the right help, which he must seek out for himself, eventually mature and become a wonderful husband."

"I've seen it happen time and time again. These men often become highly considerate husbands. It seems they want to make up for the years they have disappointed their wives."

Make your first marriage work

The teacher's face became serious. She said, "You know class, I cannot emphasise enough that we should try our utmost to make our first marriage work. We have God on our side. For in the Bible, in Malachi 2:15-16, God says these words to men; *"Let no man be unfaithful to the wife of his youth. I hate divorce."*

"So if we ask for help, God will help us, for He hates divorce. But His help will come, not in changing our husbands, but in changing ourselves. Then we will arouse a desire in our husband to want to change also."

Angela couldn't help nodding her head in agreement. She recalled her prayer to God for help, the night she heard her son David sobbing.

"I've been teaching these classes long enough now, to know beyond any doubt, that our first marriage has the greatest potential for happiness. But we must put in continual effort. It's like looking after a garden. If we neglect our garden, it quickly becomes a terrible mess."

"Falling in love is an illusion, a temporary state. It's not true love. True love only takes root and grows as a husband and wife satisfy each others emotional needs. As we mature together, and sacrifice together."

"I know what true love is. Elsie knows what true love is, don't you Elsie?" Elsie smiled in agreement. "I know that we can all experience the thrill and security of true love, by living these wonderful Fascinating Womanhood principles. That's why we're here."

When your husband has been unfaithful to you

"Now what can a woman do when she is faced with the shattering truth that her husband has become involved with another woman?"

"Many women deny the obvious for as long as possible. But if your husband is suddenly away from home for long periods at night, or overnight, for various vague reasons. If he is paying more attention to his appearance, you have every reason to be suspicious. Confront him with his behaviour. You have a God-given right to fidelity in marriage."

"If it is true, first honestly face your part in the problem. What did you do, or fail to do, that laid the foundation for this to happen? What need is this other woman meeting in your husband, that you failed to meet?"

"Correcting these mistakes, forgiving him, and living the laws of Fascinating Womanhood will nearly always win him back. But you must never raise the matter again. And although it may be very difficult, you must trust him 100%."

"Never quiz him as to where he's been. Trust is so vital in rebuilding the relationship. If it was an isolated occurrence in middle age, it is unlikely to be repeated. And many men, in trying to atone for their severe guilt, become highly considerate husbands afterward."

"If he is not prepared to give her up, tell him firmly, and plainly, that he must choose between her and yourself, and be prepared to keep your word."

"It is mentally destructive for you to continue in such a situation. It can quickly lead to emotional disorders, and a serious breakdown in your health."

Tell him plainly what you would like him to do. Then ask him to tell you what he wants.

Chastity, your most precious gift to your husband

"Now I'm sure you all understand how important your own chastity is to your husband. It can be the height of emotional agony for him to imagine another man being intimate with you. It is the ultimate blow and insult to his sensitive male pride."

"We must constantly teach our daughters this fact also. That the most precious gift they can give to their future husbands is their chastity."

"Class, never become involved in an affair. Never even think about it. Not for an instant. It might seem exciting to imagine, but adultery is a serious wrong in the eyes of God. It shatters entire families. We will never, never find happiness that way, only misery. If any of us have ever been guilty of this, we should humbly ask God for forgiveness, and never do it again."

How to overcome sexual difficulties in your marriage

"Now we're going to discuss a little about the sexual side of marriage. We don't talk a lot about sex in Fascinating Womanhood. That's because sexual difficulties are mostly due to only three things, resentment, fear of pregnancy, and lack of communication."

Therefore sexual difficulties nearly always resolve themselves when we live Fascinating Womanhood."

"However, as part of this Secret Number Three, Fascinating Womanhood offers you three guidelines for sexual contentment in your marriage."

"Firstly. For most men, their sexuality is a central part of their masculinity and self esteem. Therefore it's an area where just ONE WRONG REMARK can deeply hurt them for years. However, on the other hand, it is also an area where a little admiration can boost them a long way for a long time."

Cherry gave a loud giggle and said, "So we should tell them their 'you know what' is super big."

"Oh Cherry!" said Elsie. The class laughed.

The teacher smiled, "Well yes we could Cherry, but I won't comment any further on that."

"Secondly. It is important for most men, not all the time, but most of the time, to lead or pursue in sexual intimacy. He likes to seduce you. That's why some husbands can lose interest when their wives offer themselves too freely, or seem too eager."

"Thirdly. It is also important to your husband that you enjoy his attentions. And that you appear to be satisfied with his performance. So give sex joyfully, even if you occasionally act a little more enthusiastic than you feel. It means so much to your husband. He wants you to enjoy his attention."

"Any remaining sexual problems after you live Fascinating Womanhood usually yield to better communication. Tell him plainly what you would like him to do. Then ask him to tell you what he wants."

"Now a warning about communication in this area. Never, never talk about any sexual experience you may have shared with another man. Even if your husband questions you about it. Assure him that he is by far the better lover, then say no more."

"Any questions?"

Sonia shyly raised her hand.

"Sonia you have a question?"

"Yes teacher. But it's a bit embarrassing . . . I mean. . . I think my partner might be oversexed. I mean, how often is normal?"

"Don't be embarrassed Sonia. That's a very valid question. Some men use sex as an emotional outlet for tension, discouragement and often boredom. They can make excessive demands on their wives."

"Living Fascinating Womanhood can help overcome this problem. A wife can meet her husband's emotional needs in better ways."

"There is an opposite situation to this also. When a man is deeply involved in a stimulating project, one into which he is putting a lot of energy, his sex desire can drop temporarily. His energy is being channelled elsewhere."

"Also, contrary to what most people believe, abstaining from sex can decrease the need for frequency. It's rather like our appetite for food. If we eat often, we get peckish often, but if we eat only one or two meals a day, our appetite adjusts accordingly."

"Now in answer to your question Sonia, reliable research points toward an average of about nine times during a woman's monthly cycle as being normal for most younger married couples."

"During and after menopause, frequency can drop considerably, or cease entirely. There is often a difficult adjustment period. This varies from woman to woman. Our husbands do need to be extra caring during this sometimes troublesome time."

"Looking back, I must have been very difficult during those three or four years of menopause. But my husband loved me, and was very tolerant, bless him. Most men are extremely tolerant if we treat them right. More so than we women."

"Helena, did you have a question too?"

"Yes, I probably speak for most of us here. I feel like being cuddled and spoken to after sex, but my husband just goes off to sleep." The class laughed in agreement.

"I wish I could solve that one Helena," said the teacher. But that's just seems to be the way most men are. I guess we've got to accept it. Tell him how you feel anyway. He'll probably try and make an honest effort."

"Any last question, our time is nearly up. Yes Marina."

"Should we ever refuse our husbands?" Marina's voice was even softer than normal.

"Do we give our children cookies every time they ask for them?" said the teacher. "No, we would spoil them. Most men don't appreciate sex which can be had too readily. Remember, they like to seduce you. If you definitely don't feel in the mood, you can say gently, 'Some other time,' or 'Tomorrow'. But don't leave him uncertain. And say it before he becomes strongly aroused."

"Allowing our husbands to become strongly aroused and then refusing them, is unkind. It can result in silent resentment, sometimes for days."

Don't leave him deprived of sex for long

"And when you deprive your husband of sexual release for long periods, other women, even plain women, will appear sexually attractive to him, on a physical level. A hungry man thinks often of food. It's just not worth the risk. Too many otherwise good marriages have been destroyed by sexual deprivation alone. Just do what's necessary. It doesn't take much to satisfy a man. It doesn't require full intercourse."

"Here again, communication is the best long term answer. Talk with him. Ask him what you can do to help him when you don't feel in the mood."

"Also help your man understand how a woman varies in her responsiveness during her monthly cycle. Decide on some basic guidelines as to when, and where, and how, and try and stick to them."

Sow the seeds of Fascinating Womanhood first

"Thank you teacher," said Marina. "Can I ask one final question, not about sex? You are telling us to make our husbands Number One, but aren't these secrets supposed to make us Number One, to him?"

"Oh yes Marina. Very much so. It will happen. But we need to sow the seeds first. When we live all these secrets we become the most wonderful person in the world to our husbands. Just like Mumtaz was to the Emperor. Remember the Taj Mahal last week. We become his Number One, his Queen, and he is our King."

"Now here are your assignments for the coming week.

Please do your assignments. Every one of them. Don't put them off until the perfect moment. It seldom comes. Do them as soon as you can."

"But only do Assignment Three when you really mean it. Assignment Three is an immensely powerful statement for a man to hear from his wife. There can be no turning back after you have said that."

ASSIGNMENTS – SECRET NUMBER THREE

ASSIGNMENT ONE. At least twice during the week, greet your husband when he comes home, with a smile and looking your feminine best. Have your home quiet and organised. Make him comfortable. Listen to him if he wants to talk. Don't speak about your day or your concerns until after he has eaten.

ASSIGNMENT TWO. In your own words say to him, *"I'm beginning to realise the great responsibility you have, to provide for me (and the children). I do appreciate it. It must be a big load to carry."*

ASSIGNMENT THREE. Say to your husband, *"I want you to know that you're the most important person in my life, and always will be."*
(You must really mean this and never give him a reason to doubt it in the future.)

As Angela read the assignments, she decided to write Ted another note during the week to fulfil Assignments Two and Three.

Angela felt saddened that she had so miserably failed in comforting Ted during the years they lived together. Almost every time he had come home from work she had unloaded all her problems and frustrations on him. The very moment he walked in the door. No wonder he worked late so often. Yes, she could make him Number One from now on, if only he would come home and live with her.

"Judy and Blossom are our two visitors tonight. Come and share your experiences ladies," said the teacher and sat down.

Judy. True Experience.

"Our sex life was good, the only good part of our marriage it seemed. I told my husband so. But the trouble was, that was the only thing I complimented him for, or admired him for."

"I certainly didn't accept him, or praise him. He was never treated as Number One."

"Because of this he turned to other women, who made him feel Number One and admired his manly attributes."

"He turned to women who would listen to his stories and give him the time and attention every man needs."

"I hated him for having other women. I couldn't

understand why he wasn't satisfied with the sex
I gave him."

"After Fascinating Womanhood, I could see that it
wasn't sex he needed from these other women, but
acceptance, admiration, and being Number One. By
withholding these things from him, I had driven him to
unfaithfulness."

"But I have no fears that he will have another
escapade, because I know what kind of woman a man
wants."

Blossom. True Experience.

"My husband and I have been married six years. We
have two children. When I became pregnant with my
last child, my husband became very cold and indifferent.
He said he didn't love me. He began having an affair
with another woman."

"After being separated for three months we went back
together on six months trial. We were both miserable,
separated."

"During this trial period our marriage was shaky, and
wasn't what I wanted and needed so desperately."

"I didn't feel loved like I wanted to be. I felt helpless
and worried constantly that my husband would find
another woman to have an affair with."

"At this time I heard about Fascinating Womanhood
and attended the classes."

"The first time I practised it, I saw my husband's face
light up and felt a tenderness, though small, towards
me."

"We had very little communication, but when I
started admiring him, and giving him the sympathy
that we've heard about tonight, he became a changed
man."

"His wall of reserve has disappeared, and he tells me
all his problems and treats me with a lovely, tender
feeling. It is a marvellous experience. One I have always
dreamed of, but never had. The more I admire him, the
more love I feel from him."

"I now have a wonderful peace within. I receive the
love I so desperately need."

"Thank you so much Blossom, and you too Judy for
coming along tonight. Yes, sympathy has a powerful effect
on our husbands. So does acceptance and admiration."

"These three qualities in a woman stir a husband's deepest
emotions. They arouse a magnificent response in his heart."

CHAPTER NUMBER SEVEN

Secret Number Four
Allow him to lead

THURSDAY evening, after David and Tiphony had gone to bed, Angela took her writing pad and sat at the dining room table to write Ted another note. This was to fulfil Assignments Two and Three from the previous night's lesson on making your husband Number One.

She planned to tell Ted how much she appreciated his past support of her and the children. And also to tell him how important he was to her, and that he was now Number One in her life.

As she sat wondering how best to start, the phone rang. Angela reached over and answered it.

"Hello?"

"Ted here Angie."

Angela felt her heart beat faster.

"Hi Ted." Her voice was high and nervous.

"Are the children still up?"

"No I sent them off to bed early. But they're probably still awake. Do you want to speak to them? I'll go and get them."

"No, no, no. It's all right. I . . . I ah . . . I read your letter."

"He's been drinking," thought Angela. "I can tell by his voice." Despite her nervousness, she felt her familiar anger begin to rise. Then she remembered the first secret of Fascinating Womanhood, *Accept him as he is."*

So she breathed deeply and said, "I really meant what I wrote Ted. I am just about to write you another one." Angela tried to gather enough courage to tell Ted that she planned to write about making him Number One in her life, but she couldn't do it.

"I'll look forward to that," said Ted. Then silence. Angela sensed that Ted wanted to say more, but couldn't trust himself.

"Well . . tell David and Tiph I rang. Ask them if they want to come to the Stock Cars Saturday night. Tell David to come and see me at work on his way home from school tomorrow.

He can let me know then." Another silence. "Well, I'd better go."

"OK then. Good night Ted."

Angela's palms were clammy when she hung up the phone. Why did she get so nervous when speaking to Ted? He seemed to be just as nervous as her too.

"A couple of nut cases," she said aloud, picking up her pen again.

Angela felt much better when she had finished writing the note. She read it through.

Dear Ted

It was nice of you to ring tonight.

I would have liked to have told you this on the phone, but I have decided to put it in writing.

Ted, I now realise the great responsibility you have carried over the years in supporting me and our children, and in providing us a home. I do appreciate it. It must be a big load to carry.

I want you to know that even though we are apart for now, you are the most important person in my life, and always will be.

Love,

Angela.

Angela smiled and felt a glow of satisfaction inside as she sealed the envelope. She walked outside to put the envelope in her car, so that she would be sure to remember to post tomorrow.

However, it was a clear, mild night and Angela suddenly felt full of energy. She decided to go for another run to the Post Office and post Ted's note tonight.

She went back inside and put on her running clothes and shoes, tucked the envelope inside her bra and set off.

Angela was surprised at her energy. This time she was able to run nearly all the distance to the suburban Post Office. She only slowed to a walk twice to get her breath. However she was puffing furiously when she arrived.

She posted Ted's note, and then enjoyed a peaceful walk back home through the tree lined streets of her quiet suburb. The fragrance of spring blossoms scented the night air. Despite her problems, Angela felt glad to be alive.

As she prepared for bed she felt relaxed and warm. She remembered to kneel and say her prayers. She forgot to do so most nights. She prayed that Ted would accept her note and that everything would turn out well. She got into bed and fell asleep in just a few minutes. The next thing she heard was Tiphony snoring softly on the other side of the bed and it was morning. Angela again felt alive and full of energy.

Early Saturday evening, David and Tiphony excitedly left to walk round to Ted's flat, to go to the Stock Cars with him.

Later that night, Angela waited up for them to come

home. Just before 11 pm she heard Ted's van come up the driveway. Apprehensively she went out to meet him.

The outside security light came on and Angela immediately noticed the deep shine on the van's paint work and some new stripes that Ted had added. She walked up to his window. Ted lowered the window with an uncertain look on his face.

"Hey, you've got your van looking really snazzy Ted" she said. "I like your new stripes," she added, remembering to be specific in her admiration.

Ted's face broke into a shy grin. Seeing this, Angela relaxed and smiled back at Ted. She felt a warmth in her heart. That was the first time she had been able to smile at Ted in over two years.

"We had a neat time Mum," yelled David as he climbed out of the van. "And Dad bought us a hot dog."

"Did he now?" said Angela. "Well come on you two, off to bed. It's late."

She felt prompted to invite Ted in for a warm drink, but didn't feel she could handle it yet.

"Good night Ted," she said smiling at him again.

Ted again looked at her uncertainly, then gave another shy grin.

"Good night Angie" he said, then reversed out of the driveway.

Angela walked slowly back inside and slid the ranch slider door closed behind her. Tiphony was in the kitchen.

"Did Dad say anything tonight?" asked Angela.

"Not much," said Tiphony tossing her blond hair as she poured a glass of milk. "I told him you were giving up smoking. He seemed happy. And he doesn't smoke Mum. You told me he smoked now."

"Well I'm pleased to hear that Tiphony. Did he tell you he doesn't smoke?"

"Yes, I asked him," said Tiphony.

Angela felt good inside. "Well, off to bed Tiphony."

"OK. Good night Mum."

"Good night Tiphony."

"I think I'll sleep in my own bed tonight Mum."

"If you like dear."

It was soon Wednesday evening again.

"Good evening class," smiled the Fascinating Womanhood teacher Harmony. "You seem in fine spirits tonight. I'm guessing you have all done your assignments."

There was a murmur of agreement. Except for Bev. She made the excuse that her husband had been a pain this week and she hadn't felt like doing them.

The smile vanished from the teacher's face and she said, "Oh Bev. I'm disappointed. Please try and do them this week. I really do care about you. Ignore his bad behaviour and just do them. Especially the listing of your husband's good points."

SECRETS OF FASCINATING WOMANHOOD SECRET 4 – ALLOW HIM TO LEAD

Angela heard Bev mutter, "What good points?" But the teacher did not appear to hear.

"Right, let's begin as usual by hearing two experiences from during the week. Who would like to go first?"

Diane raised her hand. "Diane. Good, lets hear from you first. Come out to the front here."

Angela noticed that Diane looked more attractive now than she had in the first class. At that time she had appeared depressed and had broken down in tears. She also seemed to have gained some weight, stood more erect, and was much happier. Tonight for the first time she wore attractive, feminine clothes and her voice was more confident. It had lost its thin monotone and now had expression and personality.

Diane. True Experience.

"I had been extremely happy all day, but when my husband came home he cast a shadow of gloom and was grumpy."

"I was determined not to let his gloom rub off on me. So as we learned last week, I made him comfortable and invited him to talk over the day."

"He just wanted to relax, so I continued to prepare our evening meal."

"When I went to call him to dinner, his head was bowed and there were wet tears on his cheeks."

"Tenderly, I softly said, 'Dear, share it with me."

"All of a sudden he burst into deep sobs, and he opened the lid of 'Pandora's Box'. He had lost all faith in womanhood through the tragic experience of a previous marriage. Out stormed all of his resentments, hatred towards women, and fears of the future. He had opened his shell."

"Since that evening last week, our love has had the freedom to grow, even to the height of him telling me with a big hug that I am everything a man could want in a wife."

The teacher stood and hugged Diane a long time when she had finished talking. Diane looked even happier as she took her seat.

Angela felt happy for her also. She could barely believe a woman could change so much in a few weeks. There was a hunger in her heart for a similar experience with Ted.

Cherry now had her hand up and was waving it around. "Cherry, do you have another experience?" said the teacher. "Come on up and share it with us."

Cherry. True Experience.

"I had a perfect opportunity to use the secret of sympathy on the day after last weeks class."

"When my husband came home from an unusually bad day at work, he was in a terrible mood, ready to pick a fight over the least little thing."

81

"Instead of being on the defensive and arguing with him as I usually do, I simply told him how glad I was to have him home. Then, since he didn't seem to want to talk about anything to me, I just left him alone."

"Instead of asking him to watch our little girl while I fixed dinner, as is the usual routine, I made some comment about his working so hard and needing to rest and I took care of her. I did my best at being cheerful, though it was very difficult."

"However, I won out in the end. For that evening after dinner, for the first time since we've been married, my husband didn't leave the table immediately, but sat and talked to me for a good hour."

"It was a wonderful feeling. I felt as if we had really communicated with each other."

"That's wonderful Cherry," said the teacher, looking excited. Her face was glowing and Angela thought she looked twenty years younger.

"Remember, the time when your husband comes home is the most important time of the whole day." she said. "Prepare for it. Make it special for him. You'll hardly believe the difference it will make."

"Now, for the Fourth Secret of Fascinating Womanhood we turn to the Bible again." She picked up the heavy, open Bible off the table and handed it to Helena.

"Helena, would you please read for us the lines I've highlighted here in Genesis. The first part is the verse we read in Lesson Two, on explaining a man's sensitive pride. Remember, this is God speaking to Eve."

Helena read, *". . . your desire shall be for your husband, and he shall rule over you."*

"OK now Helena, read further down what God says to her husband Adam."

"By the sweat of your face you shall obtain your food, until you return to the ground from which you were taken."

"Thank you Helena," said the teacher, taking back the book. "Now these two decrees of God are the foundation of Secret Number Four."

She turned and wrote on the board.

SECRET NUMBER FOUR
Your husband's God-given role is to lead you and provide for you. Allow him to do it.

Beth, the slim, young, career woman said. "Oh come on teacher. That's a bit old-fashioned? Nowadays marriage is a partnership. I know mine is. Like most husbands and wives we both work to provide. You can't survive on one income today?"

"Thank you for being frank with us Beth," said the teacher. "Yes class, what Beth has said does seem to be the view of much of the world today."

Elsie spoke, "But there's a saying Harmony, *"When you are in step with the world, you are out of step with God."*

"Thank you Elsie. Yes I believe Elsie is right. In Fascinating Womanhood we return to correct principles. Principles that are true and are known to work. True and proven laws that God has given us in the scriptures."

"Allowing our husband to lead us and provide for us BY HIS OWN EFFORTS ALONE, greatly enhances his feeling of masculinity. Remember, that's the most pleasant feeling a man can have."

"The more we woman take over a man's role, the less masculine he feels. And the more masculine we become."

A man is suited to his God-given role of provider.

"That's not to say that we shouldn't be capable of handling his role in an emergency. But unless it is forced on us by our husband's absence, we should keep out of it."

"Yes Beth, it can be a struggle on just one income in our early married years. We may not be able to buy luxuries that others can on two incomes. But deep down, a man still prefers to provide for his wife alone."

"He likes to feel that we depend on him. The more dependent on our husband we appear to him to be, the more tender and caring he tends to feel toward us."

"Now I'm not saying this is always possible. Buying a first home is very expensive, but parents can often help out here, but it is the lovely ideal to aim for."

"When our husband provides for us alone, he becomes more confident and more masculine. We in turn become more feminine and delightful to him."

"Luxuries never bring the lasting happiness we think they will. Only living God's laws bring us lasting happiness."

Beth spoke again. Angela detected an edge to her voice, "Well then, what do you say IS the woman's role?"

The teacher smiled. "This is our role" she said, and turned and wrote on the board:

A WOMAN'S GOD-GIVEN ROLE
    Companion
    Mother
    Homemaker

A MAN'S GOD-GIVEN ROLE
    Leader
    Provider
    Protector

"They fit together like a horse and carriage Beth. Both are equally important, but clearly different. And yes, it's true that the roles are blurred in today's western society. This blurring of roles causes much strain and unhappiness. It's the root cause of an enormous number of unhappy and failed marriages."

Different characteristics of men and women

"To find contentment and satisfaction in our lives, we need to live our God-given roles. God has suited us to these roles."

"Most men are, by their masculine nature, born leaders. They tend to be decisive, and have logical, able minds. They are also competitive, muscular, and have a strong desire to excel. Nor are they afraid of spiders, or the dark, or strange noises at night."

"But we women are different. We tend to be intuitive, and nurturing, and need security. We often hesitate, and change our minds when it comes to decision-making. Also we have a strong need to be loved and protected."

"And men like us this way. It makes them feel protective. Men love to protect a woman. When we make our man feel protective, it arouses his tender feelings. Just as tender feelings are aroused in us, when we feel protective towards a small child."

"And when we feel protected by a man, it awakes in us gentleness and femininity."

"Beth is right about marriage being a partnership, but it is a complementary partnership. Husband and wife have different roles. The husband leads, provides and protects his wife and children."

"His wife helps him, gives him cheerful companionship, consoles him and admires him. She is mother to his children, and ensures that his home is a peaceful haven for him to come home to and recover."

"When we fulfil our role well, our husband will love us and cherish us. He just can't help doing so. That's the way God made him."

"We and our husbands are two different halves of one complete whole. Put us together, add love, and we become a beautiful, complete, well rounded personality, much stronger than our two separate halves."

"Here's a little poem adapted from Longfellow that says it nicely:"

The string is to the bow,
As the woman is to the man.
Though she bends him, she obeys him.
Though she draws him, yet she follows.

A family needs a leader

"All organisations need a leader. A ship needs a captain. There needs to be a single person to make final decisions in important matters. A ship cannot have two captains."

"The family is no exception. As we read earlier, God has placed upon the husband, this right to finalise important family decisions. But only after consulting first with his wife, and if need be, with his children."

"The man is the head, or the ship's captain of the family

so to speak. We women are his first mate and the heart of the family."

When you disagree with his decision

"Kathy spoke, "But what happens when we disagree with a decision he makes?"

"Well Kathy, we must support our husband, even when he makes a final decision we don't agree with. However, if you strongly disagree with a decision he has made, you should tell him so, but IN A GENTLE, LOVING VOICE. You must also tell him, at the same time, that if he goes ahead with his decision, YOU WILL STILL SUPPORT HIM."

"It is very, very important that we honour our husband as leader in our home. For God has not only made him the leader, but also the shepherd of our family."

The key to our husband's tenderness and love

"Now class, I'm going to write a very emotional word on the board. This is a word many women reject angrily. Yet it is probably the most magical quality a woman can possess, if she wants to awaken all the tenderness and love in her husband." She turned and wrote:

SUBMISSIVENESS

Both Bev and Beth reacted indignantly. Angela felt mixed emotions.

The teacher held up her hand for silence. Then she smiled and said gently, "When we follow the leadership of our husband, and are submissive to his wishes, there comes into our homes a sweet spirit of peace and harmony."

"Our husband's heart is softened by our yielding spirit. It awakens his tenderness, his sense of protection, and most of all, his deep love."

Bev scoffed and said in a hostile voice. "You're saying I should be obedient to the old drunk?"

"We never criticise our husbands in Fascinating Woman-hood. But yes Bev, submissiveness is an important part of Fascinating Womanhood."

"That's asking too much!" snapped Bev. "What if he makes a wrong decision? And boy, he's made plenty. I don't trust him. I'm a better leader than he is."

Angela was shocked at the vehemence in Bev's voice.

The teacher's response was calm, "All men make mistakes Bev. Some just hide them better than others. We women make mistakes too. That's how we all learn."

"We just need to be humble, and willing to trust our husbands' decisions. We must be prepared to risk our security, our comfort, and our money if need be. We have to give him the reins and trust him to learn. In the long run it will be for the best. Remember, God has placed him at the head."

"Let me read what a Christian writer, Orson Pratt wrote about this, back in 1840."

Children feel secure when their father leads the family.

"The wife should never follow her judgement in preference to that of her husband, for if her husband desires to do right, but errs in judgement, the Lord will bless her in endeavouring to carry out his counsels; for God has placed him at the head, and though he may err in judgement, yet God will not justify the wife in disregarding his instructions and counsels, for greater is the sin of rebellion than the errors which arise from want of judgement; therefore she would be condemned for suffering her will to arise against his."

"Be obedient and God will cause all things to work for good, and he will correct the errors of the husband in due time. A wife will lose the Spirit of God in refusing to obey the counsel of her husband."

"Those are lovely words teacher," said Elsie. "I firmly believe them to be true."

"Thank you Elsie," said the teacher. "Yes I also testify that those words are true. Fascinating Womanhood teaches us true principles. Yes, these principles conflict with modern ideas, but they are still true. And because they are true, they work."

"Of course, most husbands will largely delegate decision making to us when it comes to running our household. After all that's our own domain. But even so, he still has the right to the final say in all matters."

How your children benefit when your husband leads

"Our children also feel secure, when male and female roles are clear. When their father is respected as head of the family, and both father and mother present a united front."

"This can also protect our children against the risk of homosexuality. A warm loving father who leads and encourages his family, and a gentle, feminine mother who remains at home while they are growing up, almost guarantee that our children will mature into well adjusted adults. Nearly all child psychologists agree on this."

When a wife wants her own way

"Of course, most of the time we are happy to let our husbands lead us. But there are times when want things our own way, especially when it comes to where to live. Women use all kinds of pressure on their husbands to influence them in this area. We may not want to leave our parents, or our friends, or our familiar surroundings."

"But remember Secret Number One, 'Accept him.' We must accept his judgement, even if it means postponing our dreams."

"Even when we feel he is wrong, we must give him the ball and let him run with it."

"Happiness and true love are found in warm, affectionate relationships, not in houses or localities."

When your husband is about to make a serious mistake.

Elsie spoke. "I agree with all you are saying Harmony. I probably wouldn't have thirty years ago. But I now know what you are teaching is true."

"Thank you Elsie," said the teacher.

"However, there is one point I really would like guidance on, and probably the others would too. What if our husband is about to make a really serious mistake. A decision that we know for certain is not the right one?"

"Good question Elsie. And there is an answer. Now let's assume that we've already given our husband our views in a feminine manner, but he's still determined to go ahead with a disastrous decision. This does happen. It has happened to me a few times, and I'm going to share a little secret with you that has worked every time for me."

"This is what I do. I don't say another word to him. I remain quiet. I just offer a silent prayer in my heart to God, that everything will turn out for good. Not to change my husband, but just that everything will turn out for the best."

"And do you know what happens? Every time this has happened. My husband changes his mind. Dramatically. Just like that. Every time has been a miracle. I never needed to argue or oppose his decision."

"I testify to you class, prayer has great power when we are trying our best to live right, and we have done all that we can ourselves."

When a father is hard on the children

"Helena, you have a question."

"Yes. My husband is very much the leader in our family, but I think sometimes he's too hard on our children. I tell him so. They're good teenage kids. Am I right in doing that?"

"Well Helena, unless our husband actually injures our children, we should let him have a free hand. We should not undermine his authority."

"We women tend to be more gentle in disciplining our children, but children respect a firm father. It won't do them any harm, as long as they feel he loves them."

"More harm is done by lax discipline in the home. Ask any policeman. He'll agree on that."

"In a sad situation, where a father does physically abuse his children, living the first four secrets of Fascinating Womanhood will nearly always solve the problem."

"Sexual abuse of children by a father is a totally different matter. Do not ignore it. If it is happening you must immediately separate your children and yourself from him. Sexual abuse by a father can do enormous damage to children."

When your husband won't lead

Sonia shyly raised her hand. "Yes Sonia?"

"I would love my partner to lead me. But he won't. I often

have to take over, especially in money matters.”

"We're just coming to the problem of a husband who won't lead his family, Sonia. Thank you for raising it.”

"Now when a husband won't lead, the reason is usually ingrained lack of responsibility, or low confidence in himself. Perhaps he was spoiled as a child, or never admired by his parents.”

"Irresponsibility in a man is a very difficult problem. As parents we must be careful not to shelter our children too much from the harsh lessons of life. We are not doing our children any favours, long term.”

"However, when we live the first four secrets of Fascinating Womanhood:”

1. Accepting him.
2. Admiring him.
3. Making him Number One.
4. Allowing him to Lead.

"We cannot help but raise a man's confidence, and hopefully his sense of responsibility. Fortunately a man's sense of responsibility usually improves as he ages and has children of his own.”

"However, he may still cling to past bad habits. You will probably need to encourage him to overcome them. So here's what to do.”

"First, remind him that it's his God-given role to lead you, and that he is therefore qualified to do so.”

"Even though he might not believe in the Bible, read him at least one Bible scripture about his leadership role. Bible scriptures have a power all their own. You could well be surprised at the powerful, long term effect on your husband of a Bible verse on his masculine role, even though he might scoff at first. Truth is powerful and has a certain ring to it that is hard to deny.”

"I'll list three good ones on the board. Make a note of them. The first is the one we read earlier.”

Genesis	Chapter 3, verse 16.
Ephesians	Chapter 5, verses 22-25.
1st Peter	Chapter 3, verse 1.

"Second, tell him that you need him and WANT him to lead, and that you trust him. Then hand over the reins and let him go. DON'T TAKE THEM BACK AGAIN, NO MATTER WHAT HAPPENS. Support him 100%. Allow for his mistakes. Praise his successes. He will nearly always grow into his role, and you will blossom in yours.”

The sensitive area of finances

"Now, we're going to enter the war-zone of finances. This is a very sensitive area in marriage, because it's tied so closely to your husband's sensitive pride.”

"It is also tied closely to our womanly need for security.”

"Before we look at who should handle the finances, let's listen to this tape of a typical husband–wife discussion.”

"Listen to how easily a husband's pride can be hurt, and how misunderstandings easily arise in financial discussions. I'll comment as we go along."

"We hear the husband speaking first. He's just arrived home from work and is looking at a bill that came in the mail that day."

HUSBAND. "It sure takes a lot of money to raise a family nowadays." (TEACHER. *"He's hoping for some admiration from his wife on his ability to provide."*)

WIFE. "Well it's not my fault. I scrimp and scrape to make ends meet. Other women buy more expensive clothes than I do for me and the children." (*"She's wrongly taken his remark as a criticism of her spending habits."*)

HUSBAND. (Defensively). "I earn more than most men, and you don't have to go out to work like other women." (*"He's still desperately hoping for some appreciation and admiration. His sensitive male pride has been deeply hurt, consequently his anger is rising."*)

Put the worry of the finances on your husband's shoulders, where it belongs.

WIFE. (Irritably). "Yes, well as soon as Mike starts school I'm going out to get a job and earn some money. Then maybe we can afford some new carpet for this house. It looks awful." (*"She's just broken the first four secrets of Fascinating Womanhood. Her husband feels angry and resentful. He also feels a failure. His self-confidence and esteem have plummeted."*)

"Now let's hear how a woman who lives the principles of Fascinating Womanhood handles the same situation. Of course ideally, she would wait until after she has pampered him a little and he has eaten, before letting him see the bill, preferably unopened."

HUSBAND. "It sure takes a lot of money to raise a family nowadays."

WIFE. "It sure does. And you're managing so well darling. It must be a big responsibility for a man." (*"She has intuitively sensed the importance of this moment and has stopped what she was doing and come over and squeezed his hand and is looking him in the eye as she speaks."*)

HUSBAND. "Well, I don't mind the load, but yes it can be tough at times." (*"His confidence and self-esteem have doubled. He's feeling manly inside. His love for his wife soars."*)

WIFE. "I'm lucky to have you for a husband to care for me." (*"He's just put his arm around her shoulders and kissed her cheek lovingly."*)

The teacher switched off the tape. "That's Fascinating Womanhood in action," she said smiling. "And yes, she might have laid it on a little thick, but men don't mind. Even a lazy, irresponsible husband will change when he's inspired like that.”

"I get letters from women who have gone through this course. They often tell me that their husband's income has increased greatly since they've been living Fascinating Womanhood.”

Why your husband should manage and worry about the finances

"Now, who should manage the finances? Who did God make responsible to provide for the family? Remember what God said, *'By the sweat of your face you shall obtain your food.'* Adam, right? Or in other words, our husband.”

"Our role is to support him and spend his money wisely. But his responsibility is to provide and manage the income.”

"Another question. Whose role is it then to WORRY about the finances?”

"Well, ours I suppose,” said Diane.

"Both of us,” said Angela.

"It's my husband's role,” said Helena. "I don't want to worry about the bills.”

"Yes, Helena is right,” said the teacher. "We women should NOT have to worry about money. That's our husband's role. We women worry too easily about money. A man is much better equipped to worry about such things. Most men would rather work harder than worry about money. That's the way God made them.”

"We women are different. Worry dulls our feminine charm and sparkle. We become depressing to our husbands. We can't function properly in our role.”

"So put the worry on your husband's shoulders. Put it where it belongs. Let him provide and manage the money. Then boost his manly confidence and watch him take care of the problems.”

Know enough about the finances to cope alone if necessary

"I must add however, that although our husband should carry the burden of the finances, we still need to know enough about what's going on to cope, if our husband were to be taken from us, or become very ill. Let's be realistic about this. We women do live longer than men.”

"But while you're both healthy, put the worry fair and square on his shoulders, where it belongs.”

How to organise the finances

"You're not saying that our husbands should do all the shopping are you?” asked Elsie.

"No, we do the regular shopping Elsie. Besides most men hate it.”

"Let me suggest a simple plan that works with most couples. Some of you are probably doing it already.”

"Sit down with your husband once a year, and UNDER HIS LEADERSHIP work out how much money you as the homemaker of the family, need each week to cover the housekeeping expenses and your personal needs. These are the expenses that are normally paid for at the point of sale – groceries, clothing, toiletries, petrol if you have your own car, and such like. But not the electricity, rates or mortgage. Those bills are his concerns."

"This amount becomes your household allowance, or budget, and is provided for you each week or month by your husband, and perhaps also partly by a government child subsidy for some women. This allowance is yours to spend as you see fit. No questions asked. Any money you save from your allowance by being thrifty, belongs to you to spend as you wish."

"All other expenditure, including all bills that come to the home, are paid for by your husband, without you having to worry in the slightest."

"Sounds neat," said Sonia, giving a rare smile.

"What about investments?" said Diane.

"Yes, also investments. Don't worry about them. Let it all go. Trust him. Don't concern yourself. Providing for the family is his area. Let him worry about it. You will help him much more by being a delightful, feminine wife."

"Even if he should lose everything, with your support and the knowledge he will learn from his mistakes, he will soon bounce back. Most millionaires have gone broke several times in their life before they've learnt enough to be highly successful with money."

Helena spoke, "My husband Spiros and I handle the finances the way you recommend. It works well."

"Yes Helena, it does," said the teacher. "My husband and I do it that way too. I haven't had to worry about bills for years. So many problems are avoided by using this method."

"Sounds like heaven," said Sonia.

Why you should ask your husband for your financial needs

Beth raised her hand. "Yes Beth," said the teacher.

"It certainly doesn't sound like heaven to me. That means if I'm not working and want to buy something for myself, and I can't save it out of housekeeping, I have to go and beg my husband for the money. I would hate to do that."

"Beth, that's a common attitude with many women. But really its only pride at the bottom of it. We have to lay aside that female pride. It causes no end of trouble in our marriages."

"You see, men love to buy things for women they deeply love, when they can afford to do so, and even when they can't afford to do so. It makes them feel manly. It thrills them."

"However an important part of awakening that deep love in men, is that we women ask, not beg, for our needs. We learn more about this in Secret Number Nine."

"A woman who supports herself, or continually sacrifices

and does without, will not be loved as deeply as a woman who asks her husband for her needs."

"It's better that our husband spoil us a little. Really it is."

When you are better at managing the finances

"Angela, you have something to say?"

"Yes. I'm just trying to take all this in. It's so different from what I've always believed. In fact it sounds too good to be true. Yet it sounds so right. But I have a question, 'What if a woman is better than her husband at managing the finances? I know I am, and so I've always managed them."

"Yes Angela, most wives ARE better than their husbands at balancing and paying accounts. There can also be a heady and somewhat masculine feeling of power and satisfaction in doing so, especially when there's enough money to go around. However that feeling of power and satisfaction rightly belongs to our husband. Our old enemy, female pride is coming in here again."

"But sooner or later, the time comes when there isn't enough money to go around. Then YOU have the worry, and not your husband. He is insulated from the worry and does not experience the natural male urge in such circumstances, to work harder and earn more money. It puts you in a very unfeminine position."

"Another common problem when you manage the finances, is that it often puts your husband in the position where he must ask you for money. This can be painful to his sensitive masculine pride. He is belittled in his own eyes. It can arouse much resentment in his heart and trigger many arguments."

"And if he buys you an expensive gift, you might think how the money might have been better spent."

"You will almost certainly think this if he buys one for himself."

"Fascinating Womanhood says, give the finances to your husband. If he doesn't know how to manage them, let him learn."

What to do when your husband
continually gets into debt

"Cherry. You want to say something?"

"Well yes, I agree with you that our husbands should manage the finances, and my husband wants to. But whenever I've let him, he's always got us into debt. I become a nervous wreck. I've always had to take them back over again. What can I do?"

"This is a common problem Cherry. Ideally this is the way to handle it, and it's tough. When a woman hands back the finances to her husband, she must let go completely. SHE MUST TURN HER BACK ON IT, COME WHAT MAY. No checking up. No questions."

"If he makes a mess of it, let HIM suffer the consequences. Refer all debt collectors to him. Don't shield him in any way.

He must suffer. That is the ONLY way he will learn."

"With experience and time he will learn to cope. Be prepared mentally to lose all your possessions if necessary. It seldom comes to that however."

"Always remember, especially as you watch him suffer, that you are building a man. A man whom the Bible tells us will live forever. This is the man who is your life-long companion. Your Number One."

"He will be twice the man when he finally masters his weakness. Not only will he be a more successful provider, he will have far greater self-confidence."

"To use the common vernacular, your husband has to feel like a 'real man' before he can love you deeply. He can't feel like a 'real man' when he has to come and ask you for money. He can't feel like a 'real man' when he sees you sick with worry over not being able to pay a bill."

"Now its very, very important, when your husband is going through a financial crisis, that you live all the secrets of Fascinating Womanhood. Otherwise he may become too depressed to cope. He must be sincerely praised and admired for every little success along the way."

A compromise plan for chronic over-spenders

Elsie spoke, "I believe what you say will work in most cases, but I think there will still be a few men who will never learn to discipline their spending. I have a son like that. Money has burnt a hole in his pocket ever since he was a little boy. Without his wife to control his spending, I dread to think what would happen."

"Well yes Elsie. This can be a real problem with some men, and women too. There is an answer however. If we have handed the finances over to our husband completely, and let him suffer the full consequences of his irresponsibility, and after a year or two, he still shows no sign of curbing his chronic over-spending, then we can fall back on this compromise plan. But only as a last resort."

"In this compromise plan, your husband deliberately delegates all large purchases and bill paying to you. He needs to do this willingly mind you, and he must still feel that he's in overall control. One way to do this is for you both to sit down, and under his direction, work out a yearly budget together."

"As part of this budget, he allocates himself an allowance for his personal expenses. This is the opposite of what we discussed earlier, where you the wife are given an allowance. His allowance really needs to be paid into a personal bank account so that his masculine pride is not belittled by his wife handing him cash each week."

"However he must never be insulated from the true financial position. He needs to have input into all major purchases and should authorise all the larger payments. He also needs to see the remaining bank balance every month."

"This plan is rather like the boss of a small company,

who delegates the bill paying and purchasing to an office clerk. The boss is still responsible, and authorises all the large purchase orders and sees all the large bills before authorising payment. Yet his clerk organises the purchases and payments within the budget set by the boss."

"Thank you Harmony," said Elsie, "That sounds like a very good solution for a spendthrift husband."

How your husband feels deep down when you go out to work

Angela raised her hand. "Yes Angela," said the teacher.

"I like what I'm hearing, but I am still puzzled about something. I went back to work last year as a Primary school teacher. My husband had just started his own car repair business, so I mainly went back to work to help with the expenses. I used nearly all my take home pay for the household budget. I thought he would be grateful to me for this. But instead he begins criticising me worse than ever. It really hurt. Why didn't he appreciate what I was doing?"

A look of concern came over the teacher's face. Then she said, "Angela, if you think about it, I'm sure you will understand why. Did your husband ask you to go out to work?"

"Well, no. He was against it at first. But we needed the money, and I was able to earn more than him at the time."

"Were you showing confidence in your husband's business ability, by going out to work?"

Angela felt her face begin to burn. Her thoughts raced. Could that have been the problem? Surely not. But he did change so quickly. But she was only trying to help him.

The teacher continued. "A man needs to feel that his wife depends on him, and trusts him. He needs to feel important. He needs to feel that he is excelling in his masculine role of provider."

"Almost always, a woman's decision to go out to work worsens a marriage difficulty."

"Yes what you say is true," said Kathy. "My husband doesn't want me to go out to work. I did once for a few months, but boy, was he a grouch? Luckily I didn't earn more than him. I don't know what might have happened to our marriage if I had."

Diane raised her hand. "Yes Diane."

"Are you saying a woman shouldn't go out to work?"

"No Diane. But Fascinating Womanhood says that she does pay a price. A husband will always feel more of a man when he fully provides for his wife by his own efforts."

"A man likes to feel that you really need him. That you are dependent on him. That he is important. He will love you more tenderly and deeply when you are dependent on him. It's a big part of his masculine feeling of fulfilment."

"Even when it's his idea that you go out to work, and it often is. A newer car, or a bigger TV can be very tempting. But he will still love you more deeply if he can provide these things for his family by his own efforts."

"We too of course need to play our part. We must try and live within the income of our husband. Typically the amount he can earn working a normal forty or forty five hour week. We should not expect him to work long hours, or all weekend, away from the company of his family, or unhealthy night shifts."

"Nor should we expect luxuries he cannot afford at the present time. Luxuries will come later as his career develops more fully and his income increases. And this nearly always happens when we boost our man's self confidence by living the principles of Fascinating Womanhood."

The most common reason married women go out to work

"Why DO women go out to work? Let's be honest now. What are the real reasons? Angela told us that she went out to work to help her husband financially."

"Not many husbands appreciate that. Not deep down. Though they gladly accept the extra money. But something dies within them. They feel less manly. It nearly always results in a lessening of their tenderness and love."

"What other reasons are there why women go out to work?"

"Boredom," said Diane. "I work because I get bored sitting at home."

"Yes, boredom is a common reason," said the teacher. "But does a woman have to be bored at home? We learn how to be happier at home in Secret Number Six."

"Any other reasons? Yes Beth?"

"Fulfilment. Women go out to work to find fulfilment. That's why I have a career. I'm pregnant now. But I still plan to carry on my career after my baby is born."

"Fulfilment?" said the teacher. "Yes, many women believe they will find fulfilment in a man's world. You may find our next two secrets thought provoking Beth."

"Let me suggest the real reason why most married women work. Whether we admit it or not, isn't it to buy luxuries? Come on, lets be honest. I know we can always come up with more noble reasons. But what if we asked ourselves. 'If I was not allowed to spend the money I earned, myself, would I still want to go out to work, or would I rather stay at home?' We are touching on female pride here again."

"Now I'm not against luxuries, but we often pay a high cost for them in the loss of our husband's love. Even when he himself encourages us to go out to work, he gives up some of his masculinity. Very often he is the one who most wants the luxuries. But he will still not able to feel as tender towards you as he did before."

"There are no luxuries worth the loss of human love. Ask any lonely millionaire, male or female."

Working wives and other men

"There is another aspect of going out to work that can

Children need the secure feeling of knowing that 'Mum's at home' and 'all is normal'.

seriously lessen love in our marriage. Work often brings a wife into the unnatural situation of taking directions from another man, and working in close contact with him."

"She sees this man daily at his dynamic best, and then returns home to her husband at his weary worst. This can easily breed dissatisfaction toward a husband, in any woman."

How children feel when their mothers work

The teacher continued, "Now I don't want to embarrass Beth, but I believe it's clearly not right for a woman to work when she has pre-school children at home. Nor for a woman to be still out working when her children come home after school."

"Even our conscience plainly tells us that this is not right. Only in a severe financial emergency should a mother deprive her children of her presence by going out to work."

"We can rationalise about quality time, but what our children really need is the secure feeling of knowing that 'Mum's at home' and 'all is normal'. We just need to BE THERE."

"An empty house breeds insecurity in a child. A school psychologist once said that a common complaint he hears from emotionally disturbed teenagers is that *'there's nothing worse than coming home to an empty house and waiting for Mum to come home."*

"Oh our children are so very, very important. We mothers have incredible power to influence our children for good, and to build their self confidence. They need to know that we are there, at home. They need to feel that we care about them."

First four secrets the most powerful

"Well that's our lesson for tonight class. These first four secrets of Fascinating Womanhood are by far the most powerful. They are to do with meeting our man's deepest emotional needs. When we meet these emotional needs in our husband, he is stirred within to respond to us, and to treat us tenderly and lovingly. By living the Fascinating Womanhood truths we cause our husband to become deeply in love with us."

"In fact we can cause almost any man to fall deeply in love with us. So we must use this knowledge responsibly. To entice another woman's husband is a serious sin in the eyes of God. We will never find happiness that way."

"The next six secrets help us to become more contented and fascinating as women. More lovable to our husband, so that he will not only love us, he will worship us."

"I promise you all, that when you live Fascinating Womanhood fully, the happiest days of your marriage lie ahead of you."

"Now there are two assignments to do this week. The first one might seem a little childish to us as women, but it will have a deep, symbolic effect on our husbands."

"Bev, you won't let me down this week will you?"

"I'll do my best." Said Bev, going redder than normal.

ASSIGNMENTS. SECRET NUMBER FOUR

ASSIGNMENT ONE. Draw up a 'Certificate of Leadership' made from cardboard, or make some other symbol of leadership that will last a life time, and present it (as an entire family if possible) to your husband. Tell him (and really mean it) that from now on, you will all follow his leadership 100%.

ASSIGNMENT TWO. If you are managing the finances, or any other masculine role, say to your husband, in your own words, "I don't want this responsibility any longer. It's a burden for me. You're a man. It's much easier for you."

"Our two visitors tonight are Rosemary and Karen. I'm so grateful to you both for coming along tonight. Can we hear from you first Rosemary, and then from you Karen."

Rosemary. True Experience.

"The turning point in my marriage came dramatically when I learned through Fascinating Womanhood of the separate responsibilities of husband and wife."

"During the six years we have been married, my husband has handed all but a small amount of his salary over to me, to spend and pay bills as I wanted."

"After that class, the one we had tonight, I drove home with my mind made up that I didn't want control of the money."

"I approached my husband by saying that I could no longer carry the burden of handling the finances, that he could do it much better, and that all the worry was getting me down, and that I was not doing a very good job."

"Well he just exploded. He said. 'So, you don't want to worry! Tough! You are going to, because I don't want it! If you haven't done a good job, it's your fault, and you're going to learn to do a good job, and you are going to continue!"

"He walked around, saying that he never had a say in the money, or what I did."

"I promised him I would change. He just laughed, as though he did not believe me. I was crying. He was so angry he threw all the books and bills on his footstool."

"I then asked him to read from my Fascinating Womanhood book where it talks about man's God-given role of being a leader, provider and protector."

"He was quiet for a little while, and then a very small smile came across his face, and he said to please bring all the bills, bank books and cheque books. He worked

from 10.30 pm until midnight."

"The next week he gave me $25 saying he had that much extra and to buy some things I had been wanting."

"My husband has complete control of the money now, and I am very happy. I now ask my husband for what I need. I know he will give it to me if he can afford it."

Karen. True Experience.

"My biggest problem was love. I had not been taught what love was like. Accepting my husband was the key for me."

"Wow, how I love that man now. No more picking. He's too perfect. He has his faults, but not many. He's the boss! How wonderful it is to have a man to lean on. He makes the decisions. Since it's been this way, he always makes them in my favour and consults me frequently."

"I turned the budget over to him. It was a mess. I told him how it affected me to worry about it. I just get sick thinking about finances."

"I asked him the other day how we were making out. He said. 'Don't worry about it. I've got it all figured out.' He has too, right to the cent."

"I feel great. I could go on forever. The happiness we share is the most beautiful and precious possession I have. I no longer look longingly at those few successful and happily married couples. You know, the ones that glow, because now we are one of them."

"Aren't they delightful experiences class? Thank you both so much Rosemary and Karen."

"Well that closes tonight's lesson. Remember the experience Rosemary has just shared with us. She was relieved of the burden of finances within hours of her lesson."

"By the way, how are your 'Love Books' coming along?"

Elsie reached into her purse and held up a little red notebook.

"Very good Elsie," said the teacher beaming. "See you all next week. Good night."

CHAPTER EIGHT

Secret Number Five
Inner serenity

On Friday evening at 8:30 pm, Angela ordered her children David and Tiphony off to bed and then drove around to her mother's house and borrowed her lawn mower.

As she was driving back home, unknown to her, Ted phoned her at her house. Tiphony took the call and chatted to her father until her mother came home.

Angela arrived home a few minutes later and parked her car in the driveway. As she struggled to lift the heavy mower out of the car boot, she had great difficulty and lost her temper with it.

When she finally walked into the house, she saw David still lying on the floor watching TV.

Angela exploded.

David!" She yelled, "I told you to turn that thing off and go to bed! Why can't you do as you're told? Turn it off now!"

"Tiphony was watching too," said David sullenly, getting up to switch it off."

Angela saw Tiphony sitting at the dining room table hanging up the telephone.

"And who do you think you're ringing this time of the night girl?" she demanded.

"That was Dad," said Tiphony. "He's just bought himself a cell phone and was waiting to speak to you, but he heard you screaming at David and said goodbye and hung up.

Angela was horrified. Ted had often complained about her bad temper and harsh voice.

"Did he say anything else?"

"Yes, he said, 'Oh no! She hasn't changed a bit."

"Well if you kids would only do as you're told I wouldn't have to lose my temper! Your father complains about me screaming at you, and its all your fault! Now get off to bed

both of you!"

Angela felt utterly miserable as she prepared for bed. She wanted to phone Ted and explain, but did not have his new cell phone number. She would have to wait until Monday and phone him at work.

She felt depressed all weekend. Perhaps all her efforts so far had been undone in those few angry seconds.

She shared her feelings with Ami at church on Sunday.

"You can't blame the children Angie", said Ami. "It's your bad temper that's the problem, not them. Men don't mind if we quietly lose our temper for a good reason, but they can't stand hearing us use an angry voice, or yelling. It's just not feminine. It's too masculine."

"Men want us to be much better than them. They want us to be refined, and cheerful, and gentle and feminine."

"Now whatever you do, don't make excuses to Ted. Don't blame the children. Just apologise humbly."

On Monday morning, before leaving for work, Angela sent Tiphony out to wait in the car. David had already left for school on his bike. She then phoned Ted, hoping he was already at work.

"Good morning, Jarden's Auto Services." It was Ted's voice.

"Mrs Jarden here," said Angela brightly, trying not to sound nervous.

"Oh Hi Angie," said Ted. He sounded cheerful.

"I rang to say I'm sorry Ted, for yelling the other night when you rang. I know I've got a bad temper, and I'm going to learn to keep it under control."

"That's all right Angie. I'm glad you're trying . . . I've been reading your two letters to me Angie . . . They make me feel . . . well, sort of . . . "

Angela couldn't be certain, but it sounded as if Ted was fighting back tears. His voice became emotional.

"When I rang you Friday night, I really felt my old love for you Angie, and I wanted to tell you. But when I heard those angry words, well . . . my love just seemed to shrivel up again."

Ted's voice broke. Angela could hear him sniffing. "He is weeping" she thought.

"Oh Ted, I love you. I'm sorry. I really am. I promised you I would be a wonderful wife and I will if you'll let me."

"Angie, it's got to be different if I come back. There's been too many hurts." Ted's voice sounded more composed now.

"Tell me what you want Ted. Tell me what upsets you. I won't be offended, honest I won't. Please tell me."

"Well . . . it's mostly your grouchy mouth. You really want me to be honest? OK, I will. So many things you say hurt Angie. You don't seem to realise how much they hurt. And when I hear you yelling angry words, well my love just shrivels up inside."

"What else Ted? Please tell me."

"Well, . . . there's your smoking. I don't know why you

100

have to smoke. It pongs the house out. It's not a good example for David and Tiph. And those black trousers you wear all the time. . . I mean, when Ami came in last week she looked great."

Angela was hurting, but was determined to keep going. This was the first time Ted had opened up to her since her courting days.

"I agree Ted. Please let me know everything."

"Well, there's your hair. I love it long and shiny, and now its short and frizzy like a man's. You know I like it long. And you've let yourself get a bit flabby. You know, fat rolls don't look very sexy."

"Is there anything else?" Asked Angela, desperately hoping there wouldn't be. "I've given up smoking, and started my running again."

"No . . . , there's nothing else that really bothers me. I mean I'm not perfect, I know that. It's just your mouth mostly. The way you criticise everybody, and shout, and moan about things. I hate coming home from work when you're in one of your grouchy moods."

"And you could show a bit of appreciation for me now and again. I've worked hard for you and the kids over the years, and now I've got my own business. I felt good the other night when you said you liked my van. That's the first time in years I can remember you saying something nice about me."

"And your letters are nice Angie. They even brought tears to my eyes. I don't mind admitting that. Look, I've got a customer coming, I'd better go."

"OK Ted. Goodbye."

Angela walked out of the house, stunned, hurt, and somehow elated all at once. Knowing the problem is half the solution she thought. Well now she knew the problem, or rather, the problems. And her notes had made Ted cry. She hadn't known Ted to cry in years.

She suddenly felt an exuberant thrill of excitement run up her spine.

Angela left early on Wednesday evening to drive to her Fascinating Womanhood class. She parked and was walking toward the building when an expensive looking car pulled up at the curb. The driver, a slender, well dressed, silver haired man of about 65 got out, walked around, and opened the passenger door. The Fascinating Womanhood teacher stepped out.

"Bye Sweetheart," she heard the man say to the teacher as he put his arm around her shoulder and kissed her on the cheek.

Angela felt warm inside, "How beautiful," she thought. Her eyes met those of her teacher.

"Hello Angela," said her teacher smiling. Meet my husband Milton. Milton this is one of my students, Angela."

"Nice to meet you Angela," said Milton. He shook her hand

and smiled warmly at her. Angela felt herself blush.

The class started on time as usual. All the women appeared to Angela to be in good spirits tonight, Bev especially so.

When the teacher asked who wanted to share an experience, half the class raised their hands.

"Helena, you look especially happy tonight." said the teacher. "Let's hear your experience."

Helena. True Experience.

"Sunday, after church, my husband and I read the scriptures about the man's role together, and talked about what they meant. This was the first time we had read the Bible together."

"Then that evening, after dinner, the children and I presented him with a 'Rod of Authority' which we had all made most enthusiastically. We told him just what it meant for each of us."

"He was overwhelmed and overjoyed, and said, 'I will try to be a good leader."

"All evening he sat there with it in his hand. Several times he said what a wonderful thing we had done."

"Very good Helena." Said the teacher. "What an excellent idea. A 'Rod of Authority'. I like it."

This prompted Angela with an idea. She would suggest to David that he make a king's sceptre in his school woodwork class. Then they could all present it to Ted and tell him he is their king.

"Kathy, you look especially happy tonight too. Come and share your experience."

Kathy. True Experience.

"This week was my husband's birthday, so I fixed up a 'Letter of Leadership'. He was very pleased with it. He has shown everyone, even his boss."

"His boss asked his wife why she didn't do things like I did, so she called me and asked me to stop by, as she was getting into trouble with her husband."

"My husband really likes the certificate and still brags about it. It has made him feel more like a man."

"And I feel more like a woman who is loved. And I feel more feminine."

Queen Victoria of England 1819-1901 with her husband Prince Albert. After her husband died when she was aged 42, she so inspired the men around her that the British Empire reached it's largest expansion and rose to its greatest height under her reign.

"Thank you Kathy. Yes, most women don't realise how powerful these Fascinating Womanhood secrets are, until they put them into practice. Men are so different from us women."

"Now, the first four secrets we've learned so far, teach us how to meet our husband's masculine needs. Neglecting just one of these four important secrets can cause our marriage to fail."

"Millions and millions of marriages all over the world fail, because women don't know these laws. Nearly all these broken marriages could be saved and made happy again. Even after years of divorce. It happens. I've seen it happen. Please live these four secrets class. Even if you don't live the other six, please at least, live these first four. And let other women know about them."

"It might seem as though we do a lot of giving in Fascinating Womanhood, but the rewards are rich. We are rewarded many, many times over. It's like planting a seed. We can plant just one tiny apple seed, and are soon rewarded with bucketfuls and bucketfuls of apples, year after year after year. That's what Fascinating Womanhood is like."

"The next six secrets teach us how to become more lovable and highly fascinating to men. Tonight we learn Secret Number Five.

Secret Number Five is like Secret Number One, it lays the foundation for all the secrets that follow. It is the most important of the six remaining secrets."

"This secret teaches us how to create within ourselves, two spiritual qualities. Qualities that men deeply admire in women. All great women who have inspired men to noble deeds over the centuries have had these two qualities. Mumtaz, whom you remember we spoke about in Secret Number One, had these qualities."

Men find fascinating the mysterious inner serenity of the woman in the Mona Lisa painting.

Queen Victoria of England, also had these qualities. Her husband Prince Albert died when she was only 42, leaving her with nine children. However, because of these two qualities in her character, this warm hearted and lively woman rose above this setback, and so inspired the good men around her, that the British Empire reached it's largest expansion and greatest height of power under her reign."

"When you possess these two qualities, and live all the other laws of Fascinating Womanhood, the love and devotion of your husband will know no bounds. He will even worship you."

"Without these two qualities, we severely limit the depth of love our husband is able to give us. Even if we keep all the other secrets of Fascinating Womanhood."

"Here is the secret." The teacher turned and wrote on the board . . .

SECRET NUMBER FIVE
Men deeply admire inner serenity and goodness in their wives.

"You must be joking," laughed Bev. "Me be serene and good? Do you know what my husband calls me? 'The Grouch!'"

Most of the class laughed. Angela didn't laugh. Ted had sometimes called her a grouch also.

"We do tend to live up to our labels," said the teacher. "Sometimes these labels are attached to us from childhood. But we can peel them off and change ourselves using this

Secret Number Five, if we want to strongly enough."

Why men want us to be better than they are

"Now the two qualities we have been speaking about, that we must develop if we want our husband to love us deeply, are 'Inner Serenity' and 'Goodness'."

"Men joke about their wives being their 'better half'. This is based on the truth that men sincerely want us to be just that."

"Men expect us to be better than them. To be more cheerful. To be kinder, more forgiving, more caring, more spiritual."

"They also like us to have a mysterious serenity about us. They find it fascinating. That's why the Mona Lisa painting stirs so many men's hearts. But not many women's hearts."

"No man can deeply love a sullen, resentful woman. Nor a promiscuous one. Nor a noisy argumentative one who is always yelling at the kids. No man can be happy with such a woman."

Angela felt uncomfortable.

"But a cheerful, serene wife, one who is good and noble in her personality, is highly attractive to a man. She meets a deep need for virtue and wholesomeness in his life."

"He needs such a wife to create the peaceful and feminine home atmosphere so necessary to renew his spirit."

"He wants such a woman as this, to be the mother of his children. And children need a mother like this, if they are to develop into warm, caring adults."

"We can be so disappointing to our husband when we lower our standards. Sometimes our husband will even test us, just to reassure himself that we're as good as we seem. Men like to put us on a pedestal."

"Men like to put us on a pedestal."

Serenity an end result of goodness

The teacher turned and underlined the word <u>serenity</u> on the board.

"How do we become serene?" she asked.

Elsie raised her hand. "Yes Elsie?"

"It comes from within us," said Elsie.

"Yes. Elsie is right," said the teacher. "Serenity does come from within us. It is the end result of goodness. Serenity and goodness go hand in hand. We cannot have serenity unless we have a clear conscience."

How serenity in a woman affects a man

"We are going to learn tonight how to create a serene spirit within us. We are going to learn how to become more pure, more sweet natured. The kind of woman that inspires and uplifts a man. A woman he can respect, and cherish, and even adore."

"You mean you're going to perform a miracle," said Bev.

"Fascinating Womanhood is full of miracles," smiled the teacher.

How we lose our serenity

"First let's understand what causes us to lose our serenity. Most of us had serenity as little children growing up. That's what made us so delightful to our fathers. Why then do we tend to lose this as we get older? Anybody?"

Elsie spoke, "I think as we grow up, we lose our child-like humility. When we stop listening to our conscience and start doing wrong things."

Bev added, "We lose respect for ourselves by not being able to control our weaknesses, like overeating."

Angela said, "We give in to anger and yell at our parents as teenagers. At least I did to my Mum."

"Yes, all good answers class. So we lose our serenity by doing things that our conscience tells us are wrong, especially during our teenage years. We tell lies. We steal. We criticise. We gossip. Or we become jealous, or tell tales and so on. All these things destroy our goodness and of course, our serenity."

The importance of unconditional love

"We are breaking the laws of God when we do such things," said Marina softly.

"Yes, very true Marina," said the teacher. "The laws of God are based on love. On unconditional love. When we can love all people unconditionally, even at the expense of our own comfort, we are on the path to inner serenity."

"I believe that unconditional love for other people is the main lesson we are here to earth to learn. A religious lawyer once asked Jesus, 'What is the greatest commandment?' Jesus gave him a clear answer. Can you remember what that answer was Marina?"

Marina smiled. "Yes I think I can teacher. Jesus said, *'You shall love the Lord your God with all your soul and with all your mind. This is the great and first commandment.'*

"And the second is like unto it; You shall love your neighbour as yourself. On these two commandments depend all the Law."

The teacher beamed. "Very well done Marina. You have an excellent memory. Tell us what happened next?"

"OK darling." said Marina. "Then the lawyer asked Jesus, *'And who is my neighbour?'* To answer this, Jesus told the parable of the Good Samaritan. This is the story about how a Samaritan man, when out travelling in the countryside, came across a stranger lying injured on the road. He had been badly beaten and left for dead by robbers. So he stopped and treated the man's wounds. Then he put the man on his own donkey and took him to an inn and looked after him all that night. And the next day he gave the innkeeper two days wages to look after the man. And promised the innkeeper more money if needed, when he returned."

"Marina, thank you. You explained that so well. Yes

When a woman is serene and cheerful her husband's love knows no bounds.

the parable of the Good Samaritan illustrates the kind of unconditional love that God wants us to have for each other, and especially for our husbands."

"Unconditional love is the only way we find real joy in this life, and in the next life too, I believe. That's why I run these Fascinating Womanhood courses. They give me real joy."

How to make good choices

Marina raised her hand. "Yes Marina?"

"If I'm ever unsure that something I want to do is right, or wrong, I just ask myself, 'What would Jesus do? And instantly I know. It always works for me."

"Thank you Marina," said the teacher, looking pleased. "Yes, that works well for me too."

Beth spoke, "I ask myself, 'What would my parents expect me to do?'"

"Yes Beth, another good idea."

"So we've learned so far, that to be serene we must love people unconditionally, and always do the right thing, no matter how hard it might be. And to know what's right, we can do at least three things. Let's write them on the board."

1. Listen to our conscience.

2. Ask ourselves, "What would Jesus do?"

3. Ask ourselves, "What would my parents expect me to do?"

The power of negative emotions

"So we can see, it's not too hard for us to KNOW the right thing to do. Why then is it so hard for us to always DO the right thing?"

Bev raised her hand. "Yes Bev?"

"I know why. Because our emotions are stronger than our will power. That's why I eat too much sweet food. That's why I watch too much TV. I know I shouldn't, but I just can't stop myself."

"A very good answer Bev. You are exactly right."

Angela saw Bev smile. She looked years younger. If only she would do something about that frizzy, orange hair.

"Now class, we are getting a little closer to knowing how to obtain our goal of serenity. We know that to have serenity we need to always do the right thing. And we've learned how to know the right thing to do, but our emotions often get the better of us. Agreed?"

The class generally agreed with the teacher.

Angela spoke, "Yes, what we're talking about is very true. It's coming much clearer to me now. But it does seem to me to be more our actions, than our thoughts, that cause us to lose serenity. I mean, negative thoughts come to me lots of times, but I still feel OK, until I put my negative thoughts into words. The moment I speak them, I feel depressed."

"Yes, a very good point Angela. What we actually speak, or do, has a far greater effect on our serenity than our thoughts alone. But emotions give rise to our thoughts, and our thoughts prompt our actions. So if our emotions are good, and our thoughts are pure, our actions should be good too. That makes sense doesn't it?"

"Our goal is to be serene and cheerful, if not all the time, at least most of the time. We can only achieve that by being full of goodness and practising unconditional love."

"But as Bev pointed out, our emotions are powerful. So if we can control our emotions, so that they are nearly always good and loving, then it follows that our thoughts and actions will always be good and loving also. That makes sense doesn't it?"

The class murmured in agreement.

So we need to find a way to put strong, negative emotions right out of our lives, right? Fascinating Womanhood teaches us a way to do this.

We are going to learn a way to get rid of the strong negative emotions that keep getting the better of us."

"And when we've learned how to get rid of our negative emotions, we are going to learn how to replace them with good healthy emotions."

How to permanently rid ourselves of strong, negative emotions

"Now the strong negative emotions that control us so much of the time, mostly arise from our sub-conscious or spiritual mind. They are often triggered, or made far worse, by nutritional imbalances, especially fluctuating blood sugar levels. But we learn about good nutrition in Secret Number Seven. However the core thoughts are generated mostly as a result of unhappy memories of people that have angered and hurt us throughout our lives. Hurtful actions toward us that we have never forgiven."

"And also, guilty feelings for our own hurtful actions, where we have deliberately hurt other people."

"When we completely purify our mind of these hurtful memories, both those done to us, and those we have done to others, a miracle begins to occur. We find serenity and peace of mind. We rid our lives of so much misery."

"We become a woman with no uncontrollable emotions, no desire to smoke, or to constantly overeat, or lose our temper. No more nervousness. No more tranquillisers. No more addiction to TV, or spending binges. Just a sweet tranquil spirit and a loving desire to reach out and help others."

"Men find such a woman fascinating, even mysterious, and highly appealing."

"Sounds too good to be true," said Diane.

"Believe me it is true. It works. You've started down this path already Diane. I've seen big changes in you since this course began."

"Our spiritual or sub-conscious mind is very powerful, for good, or bad. We're going to learn to use it for good. We do it in three stages."

In Stage One, we permanently purify our mind of hurt. Hurts that other persons have caused us."

"In Stage Two, we permanently purify our mind of guilt. Guilt for the hurts we have caused others."

"In Stage Three, we reprogram our mind with positive and uplifting goals and messages. Good seeds, so to speak. To replace the weeds. Seeds that will bear good fruit and bring us serenity, all the days of our life."

We must stop blaming other people or circumstances for our problems

"Now before we start these stages, it is so important that we stop blaming other people, or circumstances for our problems. That's only an excuse that will hold us back. We must now accept full responsibility for our life. We are now going to take control of our life. So here is Stage One:"

STAGE ONE: How to permanently rid your mind of hurts other people have caused you

"First find a pad, or some sheets of paper and a pen, then go to a quiet place where you are not likely to be disturbed. Late at night can be good, or even in bed. Settle into a position where you are comfortable and could easily sleep."

"If you believe in the power of prayer like I do, you should first pray for God's help. He loves to help you do this sort of thing."

"Then relax and calm your mind, so that your memory for past events is clear. If other thoughts keep crowding in, try counting slowly backwards from ten, one count for every two breaths."

"If you still find relaxing your mind difficult, do some deep, slow breathing. Your tummy should go up and down when you're breathing properly. Relax your whole body during each slow outward breath, especially your tummy area. Let your breath just flow out through this relaxing of your tummy. Don't force it, just let it flow."

"Now when your mind is fully relaxed, take a sheet of paper and draw a line down the middle, from top to bottom, so you have two columns. In the left column, at the top, write your name, or just the word 'Me'. In the right column, at the top, write your father's first and last name."

"Now go back to the left column, under your own name and write, 'I now forgive (write your father's first and last name) for this hurt:'"

"In the right hand column opposite, write the first negative thought, or unhappy memory that comes into your mind."

"Go back again to the left column and write again, exactly the same, 'I now forgive (write your father's first and last name) for this hurt:' Then opposite again, write the next unhappy thought or memory that arises."

"Keep writing like this, backward and forward, until no more negative thoughts or sad memories arise. Let your mind search way back, as far as you can remember. Don't hold back anything."

"If you write something you can't bring yourself to forgive your father for, keep writing the same thing over and over, until you can write the forgiving words and REALLY MEAN THEM. You should be able to smile as you write them, and feel unconditional love in your heart for your father."

"If you just cannot bring yourself to forgive, kneel down and pray earnestly to God for help. Remember God loves you, just like a kindly parent and is waiting for you to ask for help. Even if you've never prayed to God before in your life before, do it now. Prayer is the only thing that will work in difficult cases. This is so important. You will never find inner serenity without first forgiving your father any wrong he has done. You must leave judgement for those wrongs in the hands of a just God."

Marina spoke softly, "You are right Teacher. One of God's Ten Commandments is to honour our father and our mother."

"Yes, exactly Marina. It's not our place to judge our parents. God will do that in his own good time."

"Now, when you pray, just talk to God your Father, in your own words, as if he was standing in the room with you. Keep praying until all the anger and resentment is gone."

"Unforgiven anger and resentment toward other people, especially our parents, is the main reason for negative, hard to control emotions arising when we are not feeling our best."

"Helena, you have a question?"

"Yes. I love my father very much. I don't think I could remember any bad things about him at all."

"Me too," said Angela.

"That's just fine," said the teacher. "If nothing comes up when you write the first forgiving statement, and you can smile and feel good inside, just move on to the next person. There's a whole list to work through. We start with our father because he normally has the most profound effect on our personality."

"Now the next name you write in the right hand column is that of your mother. The forgiving statement you write in the left hand column is, *'I now forgive* (write your mother's name) *for this hurt.'*

"Same process as before. Keep writing, backwards and forwards, until you can read all the hurts and still smile and feel unconditional love inside for your mother."

"After that, carry on the same way. Next come your brothers, and your sisters, one by one."

"Following them come your school teachers. And then you move on to your husband, and then any other man who may have hurt you."

"If you have been sexually abused by a man, you will probably find it extremely difficult to forgive him. But YOU

MUST FORGIVE HIM. This is so necessary. You will never find serenity until you do. It might help to realise that most men who sexually abuse women, have themselves been abused in some way as innocent children. An emotionally healthy man generally has no desire to sexually abuse a woman."

"Don't get this wrong. You are not letting him off free by forgiving him. You are leaving him in God's hands for justice, either in this life or the next. God is fair and just. He loves you. He will take care of it. Justice will be done. You can be sure of that. God will not let you down. He knows exactly how you feel. God promises us in the Bible that he will eventually make up for all wrongs done to us, and wipe away all our tears."

"But his Son Jesus taught us, that only when we have enough love in our hearts to forgive those who have hurt us, and are able to pray for them, is God our Father able to forgive us of our wrongs. The Lord's Prayer talks of this."

"Now finally, we forgive any other woman who has hurt us. Here again it is hard for a wife to forgive a woman who has had an affair with her husband. But without forgiveness, we will never find serenity. We can trust God to right the wrong in his own time."

"Some of us might feel the need to forgive ourselves, for past misdeeds that we have done, but that is covered in the next stage, Stage Two.

We might also feel the need to include God in our forgiving statements. Perhaps we blamed God for the death of a loved one. So you can do that too."

"Bit I want to tell you class, that I firmly believe God loves every one of us, and knows what's best for us. Just like we love our own children. If we trust him, everything will work out for the best in the end. You will see."

"Now, is Stage One clear to everybody?"

"How long should this take?" asked Beth.

"Well that depends on how many negative thoughts and memories we need to write out and discard from our minds. We clear out years of accumulated poison by this process. The more poison to be cleared, the longer it will take us."

"You might do it all in a few hours, or you may need to lay it aside and do some more the next day, or the next few days. Sincere prayer can speed up the process."

An effective way to pray

"Let's talk a little about. Prayer is an important part of attaining serenity and goodness. I don't want to interfere with your personal beliefs, but I have found the most effective way for me to pray is be alone, and to speak aloud, so that I can hear the words I pray. I also use my own words, as if I'm talking to somebody I love, here on earth."

"And I address my prayers to God, my Heavenly Father through the name of Jesus Christ. That's the way Jesus

God answers our sincere prayers when we purify ourselves from anger, resentment and lack of forgiveness.

taught us to pray."

"God loves us greatly, and is always able to answer our sincere prayers, once we have cleared out all our guilt and anger and resentment and lack of forgiveness in our hearts."

"We still need to do all we can for ourselves, but he will bridge the gap between what's humanly possible for us and what requires his help."

"We can liken this to teaching our own children to feed themselves. Once they learn, we don't expect to have to do it for them any more. But when they ask us to teach them a new skill, like cooking a new food, we are happy to show them how. I believe that's how our Heavenly Father works with us."

STAGE TWO: How to permanently rid your mind of guilt for hurts you have caused others

"Now, when we have rid ourselves of all our hurts and anger and resentment, we are now ready to rid our minds from guilt. Guilt is just as painful as past emotional hurts, and has a similar effect on our minds."

"Just what is guilt exactly? Anybody? Marina?"

"Yes darling, guilt is that awful feeling we have when we've hurt somebody, by doing something wrong."

"Yes Marina, or by NOT doing something right."

"Guilt destroys our serenity more quickly than anything else. Some of you probably feel guilty about some of the mistakes you made interacting with your husband in the past. But guilt can be a good thing if we learn from the pain, and make changes in our lives."

"So again we take some paper and a pen, and find somewhere peaceful and quiet, and totally relax. If you can't find a quiet spot in your home, you can perhaps drive off in your car somewhere, or go to a park."

"It's important that you not be under the influence of any alcohol, tobacco, or tranquillisers. These dull our conscience. It's important that our conscience be bright and active."

"Take a sheet of paper and write across the top, 'I (write your own name) *have hurt the following persons during my lifetime.'* Then below your name draw a line down the middle of the page as before."

"Now begin listing in the left hand column, the names of everybody, living or dead, including yourself, and God if necessary, whom you believe you have hurt by doing something wrong, or failing to do something right."

"As you list each name, write alongside that name, in the right hand column, the nature of the hurt, or hurts that you feel guilt for doing."

"Go right back to childhood and work forward. You might write alongside your mother's name, *'I stole $15 from Mum's purse.'*

"Or maybe you remember taking, or deliberately destroying, something belonging to your brother, or your sister. You might remember some blatant lies you told your parents, or school teachers, or some hurtful gossip to your friends about somebody."

"You will probably remember times you said hurtful things to your parents, your brother or sister, your friends, your husband, your children. This Stage Two can take a long time. One guilty memory can bring up a string of others."

"If you feel guilty when you recall them, they are harmful to you. Get all the poison out. Get it all out on to paper."

"Remember too the things you failed to do, like not standing up for somebody who was being bullied at school, or going along with the crowd and doing things you knew were wrong."

"When you can let your conscience roam free as a bird, right back to childhood and not come up with any more names, write the following at the bottom of the page."

"*I* (write your name) *am deeply sorry and repent of all the hurt I have caused these persons. From now on I will be especially kind to these persons, inasmuch as I am able, and I will follow my conscience in the way I act towards everybody.*"

"If you can't feel real sorrow for some of the hurtful things you have written down, pray for help and then rewrite the last statement again. Keep doing this until you can feel sorrow for all the wrong actions you have written, and wish that you had never done them."

"What if I can't remember a persons name?" asked Bev.

"Good point Bev. If you can't recall the persons name, just make up a title, like *'lady in blue house'*, or *'old man who collapsed on the footpath'*. Quite often we can't remember or don't know the names of people we hurt. But be sure to include everybody in your list. Even if you have to use pages and pages."

Bev raised her hand again. Angela noticed that she was smiling again.

"Yes Bev?" said the teacher smiling back.

"What we are doing is repenting aren't we? I remember repenting years ago before I got married. It was a lovely clean feeling. I was going to Mass every Sunday at that time. I felt so happy and pure. But it didn't last long. My old habits got the better of me." The frown lines came back into Bev's face and her appearance aged instantly.

"Yes, Bev is right. We are repenting," said the teacher. "It's a wonderful, serene feeling to be at peace with God and with all other people."

"We can feel that way for the rest of our lives once we clean our minds of unforgiven hurts and repent of all our wrongs."

"I also find it helps when I read two pages from my Bible every morning. It makes me feel close to God. Sort of peaceful and care free. Like a little child. It's that lovely clean feeling that Bev spoke about."

"Bev, you can feel that way again. All of us can. Stage Three teaches us how to stop our bad habits returning."

STAGE THREE: How to re-program your mind

"What we have done so far is to rid, or clean out of our mind of all bad emotions, all hurts, all anger, all resentment and guilt. It's like clearing a computer of viruses."

"Now we need to re-program our mind with good, emotional messages to change the old habits and create new good ones. We have to prevent any more negative emotions taking root."

"We do this by using a Goal List. A Goal List is just what it says, a list of goals for us to achieve in our life. It's a very powerful tool for changing our life."

"You can screw up and throw away the lists you made during Stages One and Two, but keep a record of what you write during this last Third stage."

"We need to read our Goal List every morning and every night. This should be done as long as we live. Most men are good at this sort of thing. Men are goal orientated. We women are not so goal orientated, but it works just as well for both men and women. When you see the results you'll find it exciting."

"Again find a quiet, peaceful placc. Take another sheet of paper, a smaller, brightly coloured one this time. Bright yellow is good, because you want something you won't easily lose."

"Head it up 'Goal List'. Or you can call it another name if you like, perhaps 'My Goals.' The name's not important. One woman in a class I taught called it her 'To Do List.'"

"Now we are going to write ourselves five, positive, emotional goals. These five goals must be so positive that they give us a mental uplift. If any of them don't uplift you or excite you when you read them, re-phrase them until they do."

"For the first one, we take our greatest weakness and turn it around into one or more positive goals. For example, suppose we have been addicted to junk food and are now 20 kg overweight. Let's say we presently weigh 80 kg. So we might write, *'I enjoy plain, healthy food like whole grain bread, fresh fruits, nuts and vegetables.'*"

"And a second goal to go along with it. *'I now enjoy running 2 km every morning, four days a week. I feel fit and energetic and weigh 60 kg.'*"

Some of the class laughed.

"It's as simple as that," smiled the teacher. "Write each message as though you have already achieved it. And when you read it, each morning and night, picture yourself doing what you write. See yourself enjoying wholesome food. See yourself running effortlessly and being trim and fit."

"It's important to be clear in your goals. Put specific detail in them so you can picture them easily. For a running goal like the one I just mentioned, picture your running shoes, and your favourite running route."

"That's all there is to it," said the teacher cheerfully.

"Suppose yelling at the children is a problem. You could write, *'I am gentle, peaceful and serene at all times.'* And a second one. *'I always speak kindly and gently to my children,'* and a third, *'I always encourage and praise my children."*

"Are you getting the picture? You can do as many as you like, but I've found about five or six at a time is best. And review them once a week."

"I have been doing this for years. I review my goals and rewrite them every Sunday evening, after my husband has gone to bed. Usually I change a few words as I rewrite them, and when a goal has been fully achieved, I'll add a new one. It's so exciting. I look forward to it every Sunday night."

"I also plan my coming week at the same time, but we'll cover that next week in Secret Number Six."

"In your goals, try to bring out your natural feminine qualities of humility and kindness and love."

"They don't all have to be goals either, they can be truths that we need to be reminded of. One of the first I used was, *'God loves me as much as I love my own children."*

"You might also like to add this classic, positive thought to your list, *'Every day in every way, I am getting better and better and better."*

"Now remember, you must read them every morning and every night. Read them out loud if nobody's listening. And it's so important that as you read them, you picture yourself having already achieved what you have written."

"Leave the list next to your bed at night, or somewhere you will notice it every morning and evening."

"Don't share these personal goals with anybody else, not even your husband. Just you and God. Keep them locked up in your mind. Somehow they lose their energy if they are shared with others."

"Group goals are different. They should be shared with all members of the group. They are a powerful way of achieving great projects. But tonight we're talking about our personal, life changing goals."

"This sounds exciting to me," said Bev. "Would you believe I used to weigh 60 kg before I got married? I'm double that now."

"It is exciting Bev," said the teacher. "It works. I'm not entirely sure why, but it does. I've used a Goal List for years. I was quite big back then too. That was my first goal on the list. To be honest class, my life became a mess when I went through menopause about ten or twelve years ago. But now I can truly say I've never felt happier or more content. And my health seems very good. We learn secrets of good health in Secret Number Seven."

Angela was becoming stimulated by this. She remembered finding notes that Ted had written for himself about his goal

We must beware of pride and self-righteousness. Remember that for all his vast power, Jesus was humble enough to wash the feet of his twelve disciples.

to start his own car repair business. She also remembered how a series of small miracles had occurred to make it possible. She asked the teacher, "How long do we keep the same message in our goal list?"

"Well," said the teacher, "as I mentioned earlier, I rewrite my Goal List every Sunday night, so that the goals sink a bit deeper into my mind. And I also try and enhance the wording a little as I rewrite them. But as soon as I feel a goal has been achieved, or an inspiring message has been anchored in my mind and is producing the right thought pattern, I remove it and write a new one. Sometimes I feel the need to again include an old inspiring message, especially if I find myself slipping back into an old bad habit."

"Now our time has run out. But when we follow the steps we've talked about tonight, we just can't help but grow in goodness, and in love for others. Also in self-respect and in contentment. And then, we will have the beautiful quality of serenity."

"Goodness and serenity is so necessary for our husbands to love us deeply, to cherish us. The kind of love where our husband will want to honour us in front of other men, and women, and fiercely protect us."

"But we must beware of pride and self-righteousness. Remember that for all his vast power, Jesus was humble enough to wash the feet of his twelve disciples."

"Now your assignment for this week is to put all of this into practice."

ASSIGNMENTS. SECRET NUMBER FIVE

ASSIGNMENT ONE: (Stage One, Forgiveness, see pages 107-110 for more details.)

Become totally relaxed. Divide a sheets of paper into two columns. At the top of the left column write your own name. At the top of the right column write the name of the first person listed below (ie, your father).

Then under your name, in the left column write, *"I now forgive* (father's name) *for this hurt:"*

In the right-hand column opposite, write the first negative thought or memory that arises. Keep writing out the forgiveness message, and opposite any other negative thoughts or memories, until no more arise and you can smile and feel love inside you for the person concerned. Pray for help if forgiveness is difficult.

Start with your father, then your mother, then your immediate family members, and then any of the other persons listed below who may have hurt you in any way.

Father	**Husband**
Mother	**Other men**
Brothers	**Other women**
Sisters	**Yourself**
School teachers	**God**

ASSIGNMENT TWO: (Stage Two, Repentance, see pages 110-111 for more details.)

Become totally relaxed. Write across the top of a sheet of paper, *"I (your name) have hurt the following people during my lifetime."*

Divide the rest of the sheet into two columns and then list in the left hand column the names of all the persons, living or dead, you have ever hurt. And in the right hand column, opposite each name, briefly write the nature of the hurt. Keep adding names and using more sheets of paper as necessary, until your conscience is totally clear.

Then, below your list of names write, *"I, (write your name) am deeply sorry and repent of all the hurt I have caused these persons. From now on I will be especially kind to these persons, inasmuch as I am able, and I will follow my conscience in the way I act towards everybody."*

Finally, in the days ahead, do all in your power to make amends to the people you have hurt. For those whom you cannot make amends, ask God to bless them.

ASSIGNMENT THREE: (Stage Three, Re-programming your mind, see page 112 for more details.)

Begin a Goal List of five positive, emotional goals. Re-state your weaknesses as clear, positive, detailed goals you want to achieve. Leave you list by your bed and read them every morning and evening. As you do so, picture yourself having achieved and enjoying the goal. Also include at least one inspiring message on your list.

Examples: *'I now enjoy running 2 km, every morning, four days a week.'*

'I feel fit and energetic, and weigh 60 kg."

'Every day in every way, I am getting better and better and better."

Rewrite your goal list once a week, perhaps on a Sunday evening, rewording and replacing your goals and inspiring messages as they are achieved or mastered.

"Now class, let me introduce our visitors for tonight. We are happy to have Jocelyn and Teresa to share their experiences of Fascinating Womanhood. Jocelyn would you be kind enough to speak first, and then we'll hear from you Teresa."

Jocelyn. True Experience.

"I had been on the battlefield of marriage for twelve years. I fought daily for what I wanted out of marriage, and it had taken its toll. I had nervous tension and I was bitter and resentful."

"No victory had been gained, not even a small one. I was losing ground. Our innocent children were suffering.

116

My husband was sleeping on the couch."

"I felt I just couldn't continue any longer. It was then I was invited to attend a Fascinating Womanhood class."

"Now I've given up my war for peace. The tension and weariness is gone. I'm happy and secure. I meet my domestic responsibilities with joy in my heart because I have handed back those that belonged to my husband."

"Fascinating Womanhood gave me more victories in four months than I had ever seen in twelve years, and I didn't fight for one of them. They were given to me without even asking."

"I feel loved and cherished and it is beautiful. Even my appearance has changed. My face has a new light, my eye a new twinkle, and real joy radiates from my inner being. Friends compliment me on how pretty I look."

"My husband is now drawing up plans to remodel our house, including a new bedroom for us."

Teresa. True Experience.

"I had always read extensively on the subject of marriage, because I wanted my marriage to be a happy one. From each book I read I gleaned something helpful, and our marriage seemed to be successful. But I always knew that it wasn't what I had always dreamed a marriage should be."

"We went through some extremely trying times. We have wonderful children and worked harder and harder at keeping our marriage together. But the harder we tried to make it work, the more frustrated and discouraged we became. Nothing we tried seemed to work."

"I blamed our difficulties on my husband's background. He served in Vietnam and developed a drinking problem which he has now overcome. He also suffered from war trauma."

"I truly believed that I was a good wife. After all, I had stayed with him during those impossible years. I often thought how different our lives could have been if only he were different, and if only he didn't have so many problems."

"Then during one particular trying time, I was taught the secrets of Fascinating Womanhood. I began to see that I had been making serious mistakes. I came to realise that all of our problems were NOT his fault. In fact most of them were mine. I was devastated at first to discover how wrong I had been."

"I had been trying to be a good wife, but going about it all wrong. In books I had read, much of the information was wrong."

"Fascinating Womanhood taught me how to be the wife my husband needed. Something inside of me seemed to jump up and down. I just knew it was right.

It was truth, and I saw that it was possible to change. For the first time for a long time I saw hope for our marriage."

"We women usually do all we know to make our marriage work, but once we've 'tried everything' and still aren't loved and cherished as we dreamed we would be, we lose hope."

"I began to see how my attitudes about marriage and my role as a woman had been influenced by the feminist movement, television advertising, and books full of ideas contrary to God's principles. It is only when we function in our God-given role that we can be truly happy and fulfilled."

"And the best part is that along the way our husbands are happier, and we find ourselves being treated like Queens. And we are no longer a hindrance to our men becoming what God intended them to be."

"These Fascinating Womanhood principles have been a real key to happiness in my own marriage. Good things happened. We overcame discouragement and found joy in being together."

"I have the most wonderful husband in the world and I am truly grateful to Fascinating Womanhood for finally showing me how to be the wife he needs me to be."

"Don't you get a thrill when you hear such beautiful experiences. Real life fairy tales, with happy endings. Thank you so much for coming along to share your experiences Teresa, and you too Jocelyn."

"Now let's see how serene and content we can become for our husbands this week. Remember, it is the gentle, sympathetic woman that moves a man's spirit. A woman who is serene and cheerful, even in times of hardship."

"May we all be such women, by always doing right."

"Bev, how are you getting on with your assignments?"

Bev smiled and her 'years younger' look appeared again. "I did the list of virtues," she said. "And you know what, he's not such a bad old stick after all. In fact he's a better person than me. But boy, have you got me fired up tonight to change teacher."

"I think she's got us all fired up," said Kathy, smiling broadly as she stood to leave.

"Well good night everybody," said the teacher, looking pleased.

Later that night, after her mother had gone home and the house was quiet, Angela relaxed on the couch in the living room. She began to calm her mind, preparing to do Stage One of her first assignment, on forgiveness.

But first of all, she did as the teacher had suggested and closed her eyes and prayed for divine help. Then taking a pen, she divided a sheet of paper into two columns and wrote her name at the top of the left column and her father's name in the right column. Then she wrote the words of forgiveness.

Angela had not expected any bad memories to arise concerning her Dad. She had loved him deeply when he was alive. She was therefore surprised to recall the angry thoughts she felt after her father's fatal heart attack.

In her deep loss at that time, the angry thought had kept occurring to her, *"If Dad had looked after his health better, this heart attack wouldn't have happened, and Mum and I wouldn't be suffering this terrible loss."*

Instead of repressing the thought as she had always done in the past, this time Angela accepted it. She felt prompted to write the angry thought on the sheet of paper in the right hand column, and did so.

Then she wrote in the left hand column, *"I now forgive my father for all the hurt he has caused me."*

As she wrote these forgiving words, Angela felt a flood of warmth and affection for her father, more so than ever before. The unpleasant thought she had written, suddenly seemed to lose all power to affect her.

Tears of love filled her eyes, and she sung quietly to herself the song she loved so much 'Oh My Papa'.

"Oh my Papa, to me he was so wonderful."
"Oh my Papa, to me he was so good."
"No one could be, so gentle and so loveable."
"Oh my Papa, he always understood."

No more negative thoughts arose concerning her father, so Angela moved on to her mother.

It took Angela nearly two pages to write down all the negative thoughts and memories that arose to do with her mother. She was amazed how they kept coming and coming. Mostly to do with her mother's bossiness and the angry, unfair accusations her mother had made against her during Angela's rebellious teenage years.

Finally Angela was able to write the forgiving words and really mean them. As she finished writing, Angela felt a new intimate closeness and warmth toward her mother. She saw for the first time how much like her mother she was herself. Especially the way her mother had been in earlier years.

When Angela came to forgive her brothers, she was dismayed at how much resentment she still felt toward her older brother Robert.

Robert had often teased and been cruel to Angela when they were young. Angela had always excelled Robert in school work and to get her own back at him for teasing her, she would constantly remind him how dumb he was. He was a large boy and so she had nicknamed him Dumb-Ox. His teasing had turned to cruelty when she did this.

But for Angela to forgive him for all his cruelty seemed unfair to her. Robert should be asking her for forgiveness.

She recalled bitterly the years of teasing, and hitting, and playing mean tricks on her. Whenever Robert found a spider, he would try and put it down her back. She shuddered at the memories. He had even got drunk at her wedding and deeply embarrassed her.

The hurts kept welling up in Angela's memory. She wrote them down continually. When she had finished writing down all the hurts she could remember, it was well after mid-night. But Angela still could not feel to forgive Robert.

She got ready for bed, then knelt at her bedside to pray. Angela had set a goal to do this every night now, and planned to put it on her Goal List when she made one up. At the end of her prayer she added, "And please Heavenly Father, help me to forgive my brother Robert for all the hurt he has caused me."

Almost instantly, a transformation occurred in Angela's mind. Instead of seeing Robert as a cruel and hurtful big brother, for the first time she saw him as a man. Full of sensitive masculine pride, with a need to excel women in masculine things. The first two laws of Fascinating Womanhood ran through Angela's mind, 'Accept him as he is and look to his good side' and 'Admire his masculine qualities'.

She could see now how terribly she must have provoked and hurt Robert's sensitive masculine pride over the years with her tongue.

She also remembered some kindnesses that Robert had done for her in later years. She had forgotten all about those.

A feeling of sorrow, and then love for Robert, swept over Angela. Her bitter resentment vanished. She even decided to make a list of Robert's good points when she had finished her three Assignments for the week.

The following evening, Thursday, Angela finished Stage One of her assignment with no more difficulty. She was surprised that Ted's name did not bring up any new hurtful memories. She was able to write her forgiving words with love.

Friday evening, Angela did Stage Two, on repenting of the hurts she had caused others.

There was much guilt that arose in her mind, especially to do with her mother, her brother Robert, and Ted. She was struck by the similarities in her wrong doing towards both Robert and Ted and wondered if there was a connection.

Later that evening, as Angela wrote out her final statement, expressing her sorrow and repentance, she felt very peaceful, and close to tears. She felt as if she could unconditionally love every person in the entire world. She could never recall feeling as serene, peaceful, and clear minded as this, ever before in her life.

When Angela took her empty hot chocolate mug to the kitchen, before going to bed, she was confronted by another mess, left by her children.

No anger arose, instead the thought occurred to her of deducting a small amount from their allowance each time she had to clean up after them, and also offering them each a weekly bonus, every time they went a whole week keeping the house tidy.

Still feeling serene and peaceful, Angela retired for the night. Tiphony was now sleeping back in her own bed.

The next morning, Saturday, Angela awoke very early. She did not have the slightest craving for a cigarette. Every morning since she had given up smoking, she had awoken with some craving.

Feeling refreshed from her sleep and full of energy, she decided to go for another run. She set off just after the sun had risen. The low, early morning sunlight appeared to cast a magical glow on the trees and flowers and lawns. Angela's body appeared to have boundless energy and she ran for a full two kms at a steady pace without stopping. Then she walked briskly home.

It was still early morning. So Angela took her pad and the Fascinating Womanhood checklist of masculine virtues and sat in a shady area out on the patio to cool down, and to make a list of her brother Robert's virtues.

After doing so, she then wrote a letter to Robert, expressing her acceptance of him, and her admiration for his sporting accomplishments and his business drive, both of which featured strongly in his list of virtues.

Her son David came out of the house as she was finishing the letter. He saw her running shoes.

"Hi Mum. You been for a run?"

"Yes David, would you like to come with me next time?"

"Nah! We do it all the time at school."

"David, do you think you would be able to make a sceptre at woodwork at school. You're so good at making things out of wood. You know what a sceptre is don't you? A special stick that kings hold. Then we can all take it round to Dad and give it to him, and tell him that from now on, he's our leader, our king."

"Oh yeah. I could do that," said David cheerfully. "You draw a picture of a sceptre and I'll make it for him."

CHAPTER NINE

Secret Number Six
Enjoy your homemaking

TUESDAY night, Angela sat at the dining room table to make up her Goal List. After about an hour of thinking, writing, crossing out and rewriting, she completed it.

She felt pleased with herself. Reading the goals and the inspiring messages made her smile and feel good, even excited.

She read them through again, and then did as the Fascinating Womanhood teacher instructed and imagined herself as having already achieved them.

My Goal List

1. Ted is back home with me and loves me, and shares his thoughts with me. He is a wonderful husband.

2. I run 3 km, four times a week and look slim and healthy. I weigh only 53 kg.

3. Every day, in every way, things get better and better and better.

4. I feel peaceful and serene and always speak softly to Ted and the children. I love to smile and sing.

5. I praise and admire Ted and David at every opportunity.

Angela smiled again. She folded her list, took it to her bedroom and put it in her cosmetics case.

Angela was late for the Fascinating Womanhood class the following Wednesday evening. She had forgotten that her mother didn't have her car available this night. She only remembered at the last minute, that she had to go and pick her mother up to come and stay with the children.

Angela was tense from the stress of rushing as she entered the classroom. She slipped into a chair in the back row.

Kathy was beginning to share an experience.

Kathy. True Experience.

"My husband and I have always been happily married, but something was missing. I picked at my husband, was the boss, yelled at the children, had a violent temper, managed the finances and was down right miserable."

"If this course didn't help, I was going to a psychiatrist. That's now all in the past. I can see no need for a psychiatrist now. My problems with myself are not all solved but I am on my way."

"Thank you Kathy," said the teacher, smiling.

"Yes class, as we learned last week, generally we can heal all our emotional problems by doing just three things. Firstly, forgiving those who have hurt us. Secondly, repenting of hurts we have caused others. And finally, changing old bad habits with our Goal List."

"Now Helena, you also have an experience to share with us."

Helena. True Experience.

"Before this course I thought my husband and myself had a normal marriage. These past weeks I've been practising accepting him at face value, and making him Number One."

"Two weeks ago, I was served breakfast in bed for the first time in about two years. Last weekend my husband and I were dancing alone in our living room, when half way through the dance he looked at me and said, 'If everyone in the world were just like you, it would be a perfect world.' I was left speechless. My husband had never said anything like that to me before."

"As a matter of fact, before the course, everything I did was wrong according to my husband."

"When the course started, to tell you the truth, I kept thinking, 'Why don't they have something for men. They are the ones that need it, not us girls.' Now I know that I needed to change, not my husband."

"I think we are the happiest married couple in the world now, and we owe it all to Fascinating Womanhood."

"Thank you Helena. That was beautiful. Have you started your Love Book yet? What a lovely compliment from your husband to write in it."

Helena smiled radiantly, her olive skin glowing. "Yes, I started my Love Book this week."

Angela made a mental note to also start her Love Book. She had been meaning to, but kept forgetting.

"Now," said the teacher, "before we learn Secret Number Six, I want you to think carefully about this question. What is the most noble and important work in the world?"

The class was silent. Beth raised her hand. "Yes Beth?"

"I suppose, being the leader of a country, a prime minister, or a president."

"Yes, that is an important job Beth, but there is a more important one than that. Without this calling being done well, no one can effectively rule any country."

Marina raised her hand. "Yes Marina?"

"Are you meaning the rich businessmen and bankers?"

"Supreme court judges?" said Beth.

The teacher smiled. "The results of the work I am talking about, last forever, not just a few decades."

Elsie spoke. "I think I know what the teacher is getting at, the work of motherhood is the most important work in the world."

Motherhood – the most noble and important work on earth

The teacher beamed, as she often did when she heard the right answer.

"Thank you Elsie. Yes, Elsie is right. The calling of motherhood is the most noble and important work in the world, and the most rewarding."

"We are linking hands with God. We are creating eternal beings, children who will live forever. Yes, we mothers join hands with God as we bring his children into the world. He has given us the great responsibility of training their trusting little minds. Isn't it wonderful? Oh what other work can even begin to compare?"

The crucial early years of a child's life

"The hand that rocks the cradle rules the world," said Elsie.

"Yes indeed," said the teacher. "During their young years, and especially during the first three years of our childrens' lives, their little characters are developing. They look to us, their mothers, for example and guidance. I believe we mothers largely determine what their innocent little spirits will become as adults."

"Really, we shouldn't complain about men. We women play such a huge part in making them what they are. If we always criticise our sons, they can grow up to be recluses, or brutes, even monsters sometimes. But if we praise them, admire them, and be tender with them, they nearly always grow up to be fine, noble men, caring and gentle."

The satisfaction of raising happy secure children

"Is it easy to be a good mother? No, it's not easy. It takes lots and lots of sacrifice. It means loss of sleep, and fatigue at times. And teenagers can be very, very difficult."

"But it soon passes. They grow up and leave home, all too quickly. Don't they Elsie?

Elsie nodded. "Yes, but sometimes they come back for a time. Not always a good thing. They appear to revert back to dependent children again. Once they leave home I feel we should encourage them to remain independent, much as we

Being a grandmother brings back the fulfilment of raising children all over again, and without the sacrifices.

would love to have them home with us again."

"Yes, Elsie is right. We must release our children to fly."

"Sometimes we even need to push them out of the nest, like a mother bird does."

When they've gone, we look back and think of the sad times, and the happy times, and our mistakes, and our successes."

"It's a poignant feeling. Who's heard the song from 'Fiddler on the Roof' called *Sunrise Sunset*? The Jewish milkman sings it as his daughter is about to marry and leave home."

The teacher sang a verse in a pure, sweet soprano voice.

> *"Is this – the little girl – I carried?"*
> *"Is this – the little girl – at play?"*
> *"I don't remember growing older."*
> *"When – did – they?"*

"Oh it brings tears to my eyes. It's a beautiful sweet, sad song. I love that musical."

"But even though it's sad when our children leave home, there's so much satisfaction when we see our precious children as happy secure adults, working, marrying, raising their own children. It really is so satisfying. Nothing else in life begins to compare."

"Yes, being a good mother is a challenge, but it's our greatest source of fulfilment as a woman. Do you not agree Elsie?"

"I certainly do," said Elsie. "And being a grandmother brings it back all over again, and without the sacrifices. My grandchildren bring me so much happiness."

"Oh yes," said the teacher. "Our precious grandchildren. How many grandmothers do we have among us?"

Elsie, Diane and Marina raised their hands.

"How wonderful." said the teacher. "Elsie, tell us about your grandchildren."

The extra joy and satisfaction of a large family

Elsie's face lit up. "I have eighteen marvellous grandchildren, and I just love them all so much. Every bit as much as my own nine children. They keep me busy when they come to stay I might add, but young at heart."

"I feel sorry for women who limit their families to only one or two children. If only they could see ahead and know the joy and the satisfaction that a large loving family can bring in later life."

"I know they blame the cost of living, but my husband always earned a low wage, but we managed. I didn't go out to work until my youngest was a teenager, and then only for a few hours a day. And yes, you are right Harmony. It was only to buy a few luxuries. And you were right too, about my husband not really wanting me to."

"Thank you for sharing that with us Elsie," said the teacher. "I'm sure you were a good mother to your large family."

"I hope I still am." said Elsie. "It never really stops you know. There are always problems coming up that I am able to help them with. Life is never boring with nine children, I can assure you."

"I know EXACTLY what you mean Elsie," said the teacher.

Never express regret for becoming pregnant

"Now, while we're talking about larger families, we should understand than men respect women who desire to bear children."

"Even though they themselves may not want more children, they still expect us to desire more children."

We should never express regret for becoming pregnant. It can repel and depress a man's love for us. We become degraded as a woman in his eyes."

"I've raised a large family also. Eight children, not quite as many as Elsie. And yes, I have suffered and sacrificed, and made mistakes, like we all do, but they seem to have turned out all right. They're not all perfect, but I love them."

Then she smiled brightly. "And now every year Milton and I are becoming more and more spoilt by all of them. They are all married except our youngest daughter. We've got twenty-one grandchildren, even more than you Elsie. Soon it will be twenty-three. And like Elsie, I too love them dearly."

"You know, I've got so carried away by all this I've forgotten to give you the secret. You might have already guessed what it is."

She turned to the board and wrote . . .

If you don't enjoy your homemaking you be too rushed for time. Often it's man's work taking up your time.

SECRET NUMBER SIX
Your God-given role is that of mother and homemaker. Enjoy it.

Bev raised her hand. "Yes Bev?"

"Hang on a bit there teacher. I love being a mother. I always have. Especially peeping at my boys when they were little and curled up in bed at night. They looked so innocent. But housework?" Bev screwed up her nose. "Are you telling me I should enjoy housework?"

"Housework is like any other job Bev, part pleasant, part not so pleasant, but mostly pleasant if we're not rushed. And there's always that feeling of satisfaction when a job has been finished and done well."

Motherhood and homemaking is our lifelong career

"To enjoy our role as women we need to accept that motherhood and homemaking is our God-given career. Our families really depend on us to fill this role well. We should take a pride in this career, and do it well, and do it femininely."

"Most women who don't enjoy motherhood or homemaking

are either too rushed for time, or are being influenced by media into thinking that managing a home is unfulfilling."

"Our natural feminine instincts are to enjoy motherhood and homemaking. Nearly all young girls enjoy playing with dolls and doll's houses. They love pretending to be Mums."

"But if we're crowded for time, by going out to work, or by poor organisation, we are robbed of that enjoyment."

"We should ask ourselves, 'What am I doing with my time that is more important than my joy in homemaking?' Often it's man's work that is taking up our time."

"Helena, you had your hand up."

"Yes, my mother always taught me that we women are happiest being homemakers. I get a lot of happiness from running my household, but only when I do it well."

Miss Taylor Caldwell.
"Fulfilment comes from
the feminine role."

No lasting happiness in a career outside the home

"I strongly disagree with all this," said Beth. "You are all beginning to sound like my mother. Homemaking is not for every woman. As you know I study and work full-time. I work in a law office part time and when I graduate and qualify as a lawyer early next year, I've been offered a full time job with them. I'm having a baby soon, but I'm still going to continue my career after my baby's born. My husband supports my decision. I've put too many years into my career to give up now."

The teacher smiled graciously. "Thank you for being so honest in sharing your feelings Beth. I appreciate it. I really I do. You feel that all your education will be wasted if you don't carry on with your career."

"But is our education and experience ever wasted? I trained and worked as a medical nurse before I married. And that experience has helped me and my family, and allowed me to help others, hundreds and hundreds of times during my life. It still does."

"And higher education helps to develop our minds, so we can continue to educate ourselves in the future. It's never wasted. I even believe we take our mental and spiritual development with us into eternity. I believe our minds live forever."

"Could I suggest that you be courageous and ask your husband to tell you honestly what he would really prefer you to do. Your child and any future children you bring into the world are going to need a full time mother more than this world needs another lawyer. Children last forever Beth. I'm sure the love between you and your husband will also last forever."

"Can I read to you all, the words of a famous lady author that touched me very much. Throughout her long career, this woman Miss Taylor Caldwell received all kinds of awards, including the Legion of Honour. But later in life, after three failed marriages she wrote these words."

"There is no solid satisfaction in any career for a woman

like myself. There is no home, no true freedom, no joy, no expectation for tomorrow, no contentment."

"I would rather cook a meal for a man and bring him his slippers, and feel myself in the protection of his arms, than have all the citations and awards I have received world-wide."

"My property and my bank accounts, they mean nothing to me, and I am only one among the millions of career women like myself."

"There is nothing there of real value. Not from a woman's standpoint, because fulfilment comes from the feminine role."

Miss Taylor Caldwell

"Miss Caldwell is right when she says that fulfilment comes from the feminine role. If a woman is to be truly fulfilled, she must succeed in her home. She won't find lasting fulfilment or happiness in the world of men."

"Our children need to feel that they're more important than their mother's career. They just need us to 'be there' like the sun in the sky. To our children, a home is just not a home without mother there."

Another story that has touched my heart is an account given by a travelling church evangelist Spencer Kimball who flew in early to a city for a missionary meeting that evening. He went to a local minister's family home. The busy minister had to go out, but told the evangelist to make himself at home so the evangelist settled down in the minister's home and worked for several hours preparing for the evening meeting. Then mid-afternoon this experience happened. I'll read the evangelist's actual words.

"It must have been about 3 pm. The father was out at work, the mother was upstairs ironing. The front door opened a crack and a child's voice said, "Mother!"

"I heard the warm loving voice from upstairs say, "I'm up hear, dear. Do you want something?"

"Nothing mother," said the little boy, and he slammed the door and went out to play."

"In a few minutes the door opened again. Another boy stepped in, and a little older voice called, "Mother!" Again I heard the voice from upstairs say, "Here I am darling. Do you want something?"

"No!" was the reply, and the door closed again and another child went out to play."

"In a little while, there was still another voice, that of a fifteen year old girl. She came rushing in, surprised to find a stranger in the home. She too called out, "Mother!" And to this, the response was again, "I'm up here darling. I'm ironing." That seemed to satisfy this young girl completely and she went about her piano practice."

"A little later there was a fourth voice. A seventeen year old girl's voice. The call upstairs was repeated and the same mother's voice responded. But she just sat down at the living

room table, spread out her books and began studying.”

“Mother was home. That was the important thing. Here was security. Here was everything the child seemed to need.”

Do you feel guilty working, and guilty staying home?

Angela spoke. “Yes, all this makes a lot of sense to me. I work as a school teacher so at least I can be home about the same time my children come home. But about two years ago I worked full time for a short while in an office helping one of my brothers, from nine o’clock in the morning until five at night. I felt very guilty that I wasn’t there when my children got home from school.”

“And it seemed to affect them too. My daughter started wetting the bed at night. So I gave up the job and stayed home full time for a while. But do you know what. I still felt guilty. I felt I was stagnating. Most of my friends were working.”

Cherry laughed. “I know just how Angela feels,” she said, “Guilty if we stay home, and guilty if we go out to work.”

The class laughed. The teacher smiled and said, “Remember what Elsie said two lessons back? *When you are in step with the world, you are out of step with God.”*

Involve yourselves with other women with similar interests to yourself.

“Fascinating Womanhood brings us back into step with God. Back into step with truth and goodness. I sometimes think, on the Day of Judgement, what is God going to be more concerned with? How many words we typed a minute in our office job, or how well we raised our precious children?”

“Remember God’s plan. The man provides and the woman nurtures. We are both happiest in our distinct roles.”

“Fascinating Womanhood encourages mothers to stop working outside the home when at all possible. Yes, we might buy fewer luxuries than our neighbours, but that’s more than made up for by the joy of tender and loving relationships with our husband and children. And there is the added bonus of much more free time to develop our minds and our interests, and to enjoy our homemaking and spending time with our friends.”

How to avoid being bored at home

Beth spoke again. “You do make some valid points, and I can see that you believe in what you are teaching, but I would be bored stupid staying home all day.”

Elsie spoke, “You’ll be too busy to be bored once your baby is born Beth.”

“What Elsie says may well be true,” said the teacher, “but the reason many women go out to work is not because they are bored from having nothing to do, but because they are bored from lack of adult company.”

“You’re so right,” said Cherry. “I couldn’t agree more. My husband reckons we should pull down all the fences in our neighbourhood, so we women will mingle more with each other and stop each other going bonkers."

"There's a lot of truth in what your husband says Cherry," said the teacher. "We women today do live in an unnatural way. We shut ourselves away alone in our homes with our labour saving machines, far away from our parents and grandparents, and our brothers and sisters."

"Yet men still mingle with other men in their work, which is probably why men suffer less emotional disorders than women."

"Some women are outgoing and make friends easily, but most of us do not. When we combine this seclusion from other women, and career women's attitudes towards mothers who stay home, we can understand why so many women today get depressed, and sometimes 'go bonkers' as Cherry puts it."

"So what's the answer?" asked the teacher. "How do we overcome this isolation from other women?"

Sonia raised her hand. "Yes Sonia?"

"I used to feel a bit like what you said, but now that I take my little girl along to Play Centre, I enjoy talking with the other mothers, and I've made a new friend. We visit each other all the time. It's made all the difference in the world."

Marina spoke. "My church helped me when I was a young mother. We had 'Young Mums' day every Wednesday. We had get-togethers at each others homes. Those who had cars would pick up those of us without transport. They were happy days. I don't know what I would have done without my church friends."

"Yes," said the teacher looking pleased, "Sonia and Marina have found the answer to our question. So to enjoy our role as mothers and homemakers we should . . ."

She turned and wrote on the board:

> Involve ourselves with other women
> who have similar interests to ourselves.

"We can mingle together, sew together, exercise together, learn together, just as we are tonight. Or even just chat together. That's how friendships are built. We are all becoming friends through this course? When we finish we will have a friendship link between us that will last a life time."

"Life is so rich and so enjoyable with friends, especially close friends. Even if we have only one close friend."

"And don't feel guilt because you're home enjoying yourself with your friends, while your husband is out working to support the family. It's not your role to do that. That's your husband's role. Leave it up to him."

"Generally if you're happy, your husband will be happy."

Staying home gives you time to read in the sunshine, listen to music, create or play your own music, enjoy your hobbies develop your skills, educate yourself and mingle with your friends.

Why women need the friendship of other women

"We women all need at least one close friend to confide in. Someone we can talk to heart to heart. Our husband is our friend, but he can't meet all our special needs."

"Most men don't like to talk much anyway. Research has shown that our female brains are more highly developed in verbal areas. We women can speak about 50,000 words a day before we become tired of talking. But most men can only manage about 25,000.

That's one of the reasons most men don't feel like talking much when they come home after work. They've used up their quota during the day."

"Also women and men have different interests. How many of us are really interested in the mechanical details of cars, or the play skills of rugby players?

Use a desk-top calendar planner diary to become better organised.

The need for challenge in a woman's life

"Marina, you had your hand up?"

"Yes darling. You know, sometimes I think I would like to live like those women in native villages who are always mingling together, washing clothes in the river, and collecting water from the well. They always look so happy on TV, just following the traditions of their mothers. No stress."

Some of the class laughed. Some agreed with her.

The teacher smiled. "Yes, I must say that most do appear to be very content. But I would imagine they have their own peculiar challenges, just as we do Marina."

"I believe that life is designed by God to challenge us. We need challenge to grow. Life is a learning experience. God is preparing us for a greater life to come."

"So let's sum up what we've covered so far:

Firstly. Fascinating Womanhood teaches us that we achieve far more by staying home and building up our husband and children than by going out into the work force and joining the hunt with men. No success in a career can ever compensate for failure in our home."

"Secondly. We are generally more pleasant wives for our husbands to come home to if we have at least one friend to talk to during the day, even if it's only by phone. Close friends are vital."

"Thirdly. Staying home gives us free time to be with our friends, to enjoy our children, to read in the sunshine, to listen to music, to create or play our own music, to enjoy our hobbies and to develop our skills and educate ourselves."

"Overall we feel far less pressured and store up lovely memories of treasured moments with our children. We become more feminine and therefore more delightful to our husbands."

Men's most common complaint about their wives

"Now let's move on to something else very important, organisation. How well organised are we?"

"Many women have difficulty organising themselves. I know it is hard at time, with all the demands made upon us, especially by our children. But most men with their orderly minds are very intolerant of disorganised women. It's the most common complaint they make against us."

Angela thought of the muddle she had got herself into earlier that evening about picking her Mum up. Also how she still hadn't got round to starting her Love Book.

How to become organised

"However, there is a simple way to become organised. That is to write down the things we need to do, the moment we decide to do them."

"There are several ways we can do this. I use one of those small desk-top calendar planner diaries that some businessmen use. You know the ones with a little ring binder that sit on a wooden or plastic base and you turn over a new page each day."

"I keep mine next to my bed and I have a pen tied to it with string. It doesn't look very elegant, but it works a treat. Or you can keep it in the kitchen if you like. As long as you see it every day."

"Or you can use book type diary. I did that for a while. The kind that opens to a full week at a time is good. You can also take it with you when you go out. But it's too easy to forget where you put it. I never lose my wooden one. It's always in the same place next to my bed."

"Whenever I get ideas, or have things to do, or something to buy at a future time, I go and write it down on my calendar, on the exact day I need to do it. Then I don't have to worry any more about remembering it."

"And every night, I sit up in bed and cross off the things I've done that day. That's so satisfying, and I transfer the things I didn't get done to another day on the calendar. Then I can relax and go to sleep with a peaceful mind."

"My husband uses one of those little computer thingys in his cell phone to do the same thing. But I prefer pen and paper."

"And every morning, just before I get up, I read my list of things to do that day. If I have some things to do away from home, I'll write a separate list to take with me in my purse."

"I also keep a little notebook and pen in my purse to take notes if I'm away from home. I transfer them to my desk-top diary in bed at night."

"A system like this works very well when you get into the habit of using it daily."

"You can also use it to list your weekly, two weekly and monthly regular household tasks, like watering the pot plants, cleaning the windows, vacuuming, polishing the woodwork, regular outings, meetings and birthdays."

"Some women also like to have a writing board in the kitchen. They re-write each days things to do, from their diary, in the order they plan to do them. A woman in one of our classes used the side of her fridge. She wrote on it with one of those white board pens that wipe off with a cloth."

Elsie raised her hand. "Yes Elsie?"

"There's an old saying, *"The weakest ink is better than the finest memory."*

"Thank you Elsie. Yes, that's so very true. I like that saying." The teacher reached for her purse. "I'll write it in my little purse notebook right now, to share with future classes."

Angela liked the saying also. She found a pen in her purse and wrote the saying in small print on the front of her cheque book. She also wrote underneath:

> Buy Love Book.
> Buy desk-top diary.
> Buy writing board for kitchen.

When Angela had written down her list of things to do, she unexpectedly felt more relaxed. She wondered why this should be. Then realised that she was now free of the anxiety of trying to remember to do these things.

She smiled contentedly. Fascinating Womanhood was providing answers to all her problems.

What men want from their wives as homemakers

"Now," said the teacher, "let's quickly look at some of the feminine skills we need to master to be successful as mothers and homemakers, and to keep our husbands and families content."

"First, meal preparation. How organised are we here? Men look forward to coming home to a tasty meal that is ready on time. But even the most placid husband will get very annoyed with his wife when she is so disorganised that she's always running late with the meals."

"And what about our ironing? Is it always up-to-date? Enough towels? Socks? Men get very upset when we lose one of their favourite socks."

Bev laughed loudly. "Hey, I think there's a sock-eating monster living in my washing machine. And he only eats one of each pair. You wouldn't believe how many single socks my family end up with."

All the class laughed.

"Yes, I must admit to that problem also," said the teacher, "especially when my children were at home."

"How many of us hoard those odd socks for years, hoping their mates will turn up?"

"Don't you think class, that we hoard too much stuff in our homes? Toys, clothes, gadgets, cosmetics, pills, magazines. The more we have, the more there is to make clutter. As a general rule, I suggest that anything non-essential that we haven't used for two years, we should consider disposing of. We can either give it away, sell it, recycle it, or dump it."

"Another very important thing Fascinating Womanhood teaches about homemaking is to have a fragrant, clean smelling home, with little feminine touches here and there.

As your husband's love and tenderness for you increases, the more inclined he will be to offer to help you.

House plants, china and wall pictures are nice. And craft and art objects, especially those we have made ourselves."

"Your husband may not comment about these things, but these feminine touches will gladden his heart."

"And outside our home we can plant flowers and fragrant plants, in pots if we don't have a garden."

"A fragrant, clean smelling home is so important. Men identify us with our homes. If our home is smelly and untidy, guess who gets thought of the same way? So let's keep our kitchens, toilets, laundry and bedding clean and fragrant. Remember that our home is our husband's castle, and he is Number One. Let's make sure it's clean and tidy and comfortable for him."

Diane spoke, "Should we ask our husbands to help us with the housework?"

"No, we shouldn't ask him to help us with the normal housework Diane. We are talking about things like the dishes and vacuuming the floors. Unless it is a masculine job, or requires a lot of strength. Wait for him to offer. If he doesn't offer, we should just accept it. We must remember that the housework is our area of responsibility, not his. He has his own responsibilities to take care of."

"However we will find that as our husband's love and tenderness for us increases, the more inclined he will be to offer to help us."

"We learn more about asking for our needs in Secret Number Nine.

There are so many feminine skills you can develop at home, and many of them can save you money.

How to be more interesting to your husband

"Now the other common complaint that husbands make about their wives is that they are dull and boring. That they are only interested in children, make-up, gossip and TV programs. I wish this wasn't true, but with too many women, it is a valid complaint."

"Don't misunderstand me however. Men don't want us to compete with them verbally, or debate with them, or have 'man to man' discussions. They just expect us to know something about current affairs and other things they often talk about. Or at least to show an interest in what they are saying."

"They also like us to develop our minds and our feminine skills. We should always be learning something useful or creative. We can do this by reading widely. Do we all belong to the library? If we don't enjoy reading, there are instructional videos and DVD's available at most libraries. And there are night classes like this Fascinating Womanhood course."

Diane raised her hand. "Yes Diane?"

"I've just finished a night course in artificial flower arranging. I loved it. I'm going to make all my gifts this Christmas. I think the money I'll save will probably more than pay for my course."

"Very good Diane. And I'm sure your personally made gifts

will be treasured by those who receive them. And that's the kind of hobby we can do with a friend."

"There are so many feminine skills we can learn at home, and many of them save us money. Embroidery, toy making, cake decorating, flower arranging, all kinds of handwork."

"I love to bake my own whole grain bread. I'm a bit of a health fanatic. Most men like their wives to bake for them."

"What are some more ideas?"

"I used to write stories for a children's magazine," said Angela.

"Why that's great Angela."

"I grow roses" said Helena.

"I like to draw and paint," said Diane.

"I teach a Sunday School class for children" said Marina.

"Excellent. Very good", said the teacher looking pleased. "You're such an interesting class. I love you all. Keep it up. All your lives. Let's all develop our minds to the fullest. Let's leave our TV off more often. Let's be interesting to our husbands. Remember life's great rule, *Use it or lose it!*"

"We can really enjoy our homemaking. We are never bored when we have friends to mingle with. And there is no greater joy in the world, and no more important work than be involved with our children."

"But it's important that you have a break from young children every so often. You should try and go somewhere without them at least once or twice a week. You'll love and appreciate them more that way."

"This is where we grandmothers are useful. Give them to Granny for a day, or overnight. Let her spoil them a little. Or take turns with your friends. Look after each others children. Give each other a break. Enjoy your whole home to yourself sometimes, or go out on a date with your husband."

Men respect motherhood

"Are we starting to catch a vision of our woman's role as God intended it to be? Isn't being a mother and homemaker challenging and rewarding?"

"But it does require skill. It also requires wisdom, and most of all love. Lots and lots of love."

"Let's not be influenced by a few discontented women who degrade our beautiful role. The media will always magnify conflict and make it seem more widespread than it really is."

"Men never degrade motherhood. They never degrade the woman's role. Men love and respect their mothers too much. They realise how noble and beautiful motherhood is."

It's a glorious role. A role that shines brighter and brighter as our families mature. I believe our honour as a mother, and a wife, continues to increase as our descendants increase, even throughout all eternity."

Remember your spiritual growth

"I firmly believe we are eternal beings. We need to remember our spiritual growth. It's so easy to get caught up in short term worldly views. The powers of darkness and deception have great hold on the world today, especially through the media. So let's spread some light and reach out and be kind to those outside our family circle."

"Let's develop the unconditional love that Jesus spoke about. You remember the story of the Good Samaritan that Marina shared with us last week. We should help any person in need and always be charitable."

"I read two pages from my Bible every morning. It reminds me of eternal things. I don't watch TV much now. I believe we should try and leave this world, and all our friends better for having known us. I'm sure you all believe that too. I believe God is preparing us in this life for a higher and more joyful life in the next world."

Teach your children to pray and love God, by example.

How to be treated with respect by professionals

"Sonia, you have a question."

"Yes. I would like to think that we mothers are respected like you say, but when I take my little girl to the doctor, he treats me as if I'm just a kid."

The teacher nodded in sympathy. "I know exactly how you feel Sonia. Even my own husband used to be guilty of this. It is a harsh truth, that many people, especially busy professionals who are dealing with the public every day, quickly sense our self-esteem and treat us accordingly. "

"But as our self-esteem improves, so does the courtesy with which others treat us."

"Keep working on Secret Number Five Sonia, Inner Serenity. That's the key. Do your Goal List. Watch your posture. Stand erect, head up, chin pointed slightly out and up. Learn to smile readily. Put a cheerful feminine lilt in your voice. Then watch the change in the way professionals treat you."

How to raise your children successfully

"Now class, to close off tonight's lesson I want to hand out this list of 10 proven rules for raising well-balanced children. Let's read them through together."

10 RULES FOR RAISING WELL-BALANCED CHILDREN

RULE 1 Allow your children to be themselves. Teach them right from wrong and discipline them, but don't try to mould their personalities into what you would like them to become.

RULE 2 Praise your children's accomplishments, no matter how small. Praise far more often than you criticise, and never tease them.

RULE 3 Never compare one child with another.

RULE 4 Always build up the image of your children's natural father.

RULE 5 Be fair and always keep your word, so that your children will respect you.

RULE 6 Allow your children to win against you sometimes.

RULE 7 Present a united front with your husband.

RULE 8 Never shield your children from life's difficulties. Overcoming difficulties is how character is developed.

RULE 9 Have your children earn all their pocket money. Teach them the satisfaction of work.

RULE 10 Teach your children to pray and love God, by example.

"Any comments class?" asked the teacher when they had read them through.

"Very sound rules," said Elsie. "I would add, 'Give them lots of warm loving hugs, and read them stories at bedtime when they are little."

"Be a good listener," said Marina.

"Thank you Elsie and Marina. Yes, hugging and listening to our children is very, very important, and reading interesting stories to them when young develops in them a love of reading and of books."

"Now here are this week's assignments."

ASSIGNMENTS. SECRET NUMBER SIX

ASSIGNMENT ONE. Obtain a desk-top calendar planning diary with a page for each day (or a similar planning aid) and plan out your next two weeks.

You might include:

Homemaking duties
Hobbies
Skills development
Spiritual development
Exercise
Children's development
School activities and holidays
Music
Ideas
Shopping
Get-togethers with your friends
Family outings
Holidays
Husband-wife dates
Meetings
Time or outings without the children
Books to obtain and read
Library visits
Birthdays and anniversaries

ASSIGNMENT TWO. If you go out to work, list all the advantages of giving up. Ask your husband to read the list and tell you honestly how he feels.

"Our two guests tonight are Charlene and Tessa. It's so nice to have you both with us tonight. Charlene would you speak first, and then we'll hear from Tessa."

Charlene. True Experience.

"Oh, the heartache I need not have gone through with our oldest son. He is just twenty years old and has had his Mama telling him what to do and when to do it for too long. Now I can see what caused his rebellion in the first place. Me!"

"He returned home this summer to work on the farm for his father, and with the help of Fascinating Womanhood things went smoother than they have for years."

"I now know what I'm doing on this earth, and what happiness can come to a woman. Before, I never felt that a woman was anything but a 'yes dear' dummy. But I couldn't be happy that way, and it resulted in my being in competition with men, and especially with my husband."

"I made the decisions for us, and tried to help my husband. I made every effort to convince him that I had a brain on my shoulders. All of this sent me further from what I really wanted – his love."

"How much easier it is now. How much more fun it is to have my whole day to do for him the things I should."

"The romantic days of our engagement and early marriage are coming back. I now enjoy being a woman. It's really fun."

Tessa. True Experience.

"During the first Fascinating Womanhood class, lots of things the teacher said grated on me. But I was having trouble with my marriage and thought that my thinking would change. I was frustrated with working full time at a job I enjoyed, and yet having to do all the household duties myself. I was hoping to find ways to get my husband to help with domestic duties."

"Well, needless to say, I've undergone a complete about turn. Our marriage has improved and I have been gathered up into the enthusiasm of our teacher and class members who really believe in two sexes."

"The most important change was when I began accepting my husband's small faults as part of him, and realised that he probably never would change. It has relieved me from the feeling that I must teach him until he realised the 'right way' to do things."

"All our married life, my husband has talked endlessly about buying an airplane. I've always argued about the

SECRETS OF FASCINATING WOMANHOOD

safety factor, cost, frivolousness, etc."

"Finally I said, and meant, 'Wayne, you've wanted an airplane all your life, I really think you owe it to yourself to buy an airplane."

"Well, he was so happy. But the next day he told me that he really didn't think he should buy one at this time, and gave me all the reasons I'd been harping on for years. It all happened because I supported him rather than fought him. I'm also happier with housework. Thank you so much."

"Thank you Charlene and Tessa. It's wonderful to have you come along and share with us your experiences."

"In closing class, I would just like to testify to you all how much I enjoy being a mother and a homemaker. I love it. I treasure my role. At this stage of my life I feel brimful of satisfaction. I wouldn't change it for anything."

"Good night everybody."

The next morning, on the way to school, Angela stopped at the gas station to get petrol for her car. As she took her card out of her cheque book folder to pay, she noticed the reminders she had written on her cheque book the night before.

So during her lunch break, she drove downtown to a stationers and bought herself a desk-top calendar for the following year, and also a medium size, glossy white writing board, with little flowers around the edges to put on the wall of her kitchen and a blue felt pen that wiped off with a cloth.

She couldn't find a note book with a pink or red cover for her Love Book, so she bought an ordinary note book and some pink paper to cover it with.

Feeling pleased with herself Angela drove back to school.

That evening she asked her son David to attach the writing board on the kitchen wall with the adhesive strips supplied.

"OK Mum," he said cheerfully.

Angela was surprised how willingly David agreed to this task. Then she realised that he saw it as a masculine task.

Over the next few days David and Tiphony wrote all sorts of things on the board until the novelty wore off. After that, Angela found it highly useful to keep note of things to be done, and household items and food that needed replenishing.

She looked forward to the new year coming up in about six weeks time, when she would begin using her daily planning diary.

CHAPTER TEN

Secret Number Seven
Make the most of yourself

SATURDAY afternoon, Ted came by and picked up the children and took them back to his flat to watch a video.

It was raining, so Angela stayed inside the house and caught up with many of the tasks she had been forgetting to do over recent months.

As they had occurred to her during the week, she had written them down in her purse notebook, or on the new writing board in the kitchen.

Later that afternoon, Angela covered the Love Book that she had bought, with pink paper. She also pasted on a favourite photo of Ted and glued some little colourful flower pictures around the edges.

Then she went outdoors and sat on the covered patio, out of the rain and wrote her first entry in her Love Book, Ted's words to her on the phone, *"Your notes were nice Angie. They even brought tears to my eyes."*

After writing Ted's words, Angela felt relaxed and peaceful. She sat and watched the late spring rain falling, enjoying the warm moistness of the air and the lush green of the lawn and trees.

Angela pondered her future. "How wonderful it will be when Ted comes back," she thought. "It will be so nice to snuggle up to him at night in bed. And how good it will be not to have to go out to work. I enjoy teaching my students, but it's such a strain having to come home to another full time job. It will be so much nicer to stay home and enjoy doing my homemaking well, and to visit my friend Ami. And I want to start learning the piano again, and catch up on my reading, especially about health."

Her father's sudden heart attack and death had aroused in Angela a deep desire to know more about health.

She remembered again her Dad's words. "Everything will

turn out all right Angela. You'll see." She smiled softly and felt her eyes fill with tears of love for her Dad.

On Tuesday after school, Angela took her two children to the shopping centre to buy groceries.

She parked the car outside the supermarket and asked Tiphony to go to the chemist and pick up the photos that were being printed, while she went into the supermarket to buy groceries. David remained in the car.

When Angela returned to the car, she saw Tiphony and David looking through the photos laughing. She put the groceries in the boot of the car then sat inside and looked through the photos also. She was appalled when she saw one photo that David had taken of her from behind, two weeks ago.

"Oh no!" she said staring at the photo. "I'm not that fat am I?"

"Let me see," said Tiphony, plucking the photo from her mother's hand. "Yep. You've got a fat bum."

"Bottom! Not bum," snapped Angela. "Don't use that word. Its crude."

"Well you've got a fat bottom then," said Tiphony handing back the photo.

"Mum's got a fat bum. Mum's got a fat bum," sang David from the back seat.

Angela swung round to whack him, but David ducked and she missed.

"No TV for that tonight David," she said. "I won't have your cheek."

"I was only kidding Mum," said David.

"Well I'm not," said Angela, feeling upset. She had known for some time from the tightness of her clothes that she had been putting on weight, but had not realised just how large her hips had become. The bathroom scales had stopped working last year.

They drove home in silence.

The next night Angela decided to walk the 3 km into town to attend her Fascinating Womanhood class. It was a sunny mild evening and Angela enjoyed her walk.

The fragrance of newly mowed lawns and blossoms wafted onto the footpath from time to time. The low evening sun was warm on her face and it was peaceful during lulls in the traffic.

Occasionally she saw a person out running. Twice she saw women around her own age. Both of them had figures that looked slim and lithe. Angela thought of the goal she had written on her Goal List last week to run 3 km, four times a week. She had only managed to get out for one short run since then. She would have to organise herself better.

"Good evening everybody," said the teacher cheerfully, when everyone was seated. Tonight the teacher wore an attractive, white, calf-length dress and had a yellow flower pinned above her ear in her shoulder length, silver hair.

The teacher looked slender and lively as always, however Angela felt comforted by the fact that most of the other women in the class were plump like herself. Bev was grossly obese. Even Diane, who had formerly been thin, had gained considerable weight during the six weeks of the course. Cherry was solid and robust, but energetic and athletic in her movements and build. Only Kathy and Beth were slim.

"Now, who's going to share a Fascinating Womanhood experience they've had during the week?"

Many hands went up. The teacher looked pleased.

"Bev. You've had an experience you'd like to share. That's excellent. Come on up."

Bev blushed as she spoke, but looked radiant.

Bev. True Experience.

"My husband came home late Friday and expected me to be mad at him. But I met him with a smile, and he responded with a loving pat. Later in the evening, he said he was sorry he was late and he felt guilty."

"He said he likes the new me, and if I'm really going to go the extra mile to please him, he was going to try to please me too, and Saturday night he took me and the boys out to dinner, and to a show."

"Thank you Bev. That's wonderful. Remember class, the most important time of your day is the moment your husband comes home. It is a highly sensitive time for him. It's the time when he will most appreciate a little tenderness and sympathy from you. It can make a world of difference to your marriage."

"Also remember to say nothing about yourself or any household problems until you have comforted him and he has eaten."

"Now Diane, you too had your hand up. Come and share your experience with us."

Angela marvelled at the change in Diane. She was now nothing like the thin, depressed women of the first class. Not only had she gained weight, but each week she seemed to have grown in confidence. The thinness had gone from her voice and she now held herself well and was becoming a handsome woman.

Diane. True Experience.

"In the past I felt that motherhood was about the only real joy of womanhood for me. I used to envy men and their role in life and society. I felt trapped at home, and resentful that women were placed in obedience to men."

"This new concept and respect for my sex is one of the most wonderful things that has happened to me."

"Already my marriage is happier than I could have believed possible. My husband has a new spring in his

step, and a new note of authority in his voice which thrills me. I am finally really satisfied and happy with being a woman."

"Thank you so much, Diane. Isn't life wonderful when we live correct principles? Isn't it thrilling when our husband steps out and leads us with confidence and authority?"

"Now, on to Secret Number Seven. This secret is one of the most neglected secrets among married women."

The teacher turned and wrote on the board.

SECRET NUMBER SEVEN.

Make the most of your hair, your figure and your health.

Bev groaned. The teacher glanced around and smiled. "What's wrong Bev?"

"You're picking on me teacher."

The teacher laughed. "Sorry Bev, but a woman's figure is important to a man."

"My husband doesn't complain," said Bev.

"Men know better than to criticise their wife's figure," said the teacher. "But that doesn't mean they're happy with it. A woman's figure means a great deal to a man."

"Yes, just watch their eyes when a curvy girl is around," said Cherry, rolling her own eyes. "Especially when they think we're not watching them."

Plumpness can be attractive to a man

"It's not only Bev's problem, it's mine too," said Angela. "I am too embarrassed to tell you what my children said about me yesterday."

"Children can be painfully truthful," said the teacher, "But let's not be too hard on ourselves. Many men prefer their wives on the plump side. But what puts them off are rolls of fat around the waist, blubbery thighs and loose flabby skin on our upper arms."

"But if our contours, or curves as Cherry puts it, are smooth and firm, and in proportion, men will still find us very attractive, even if we are plump, or large boned."

"It's the hour-glass shape that men find attractive, not slimness. In fact you'll find that most men regard modern skinny, models as most unattractive."

"My husband says they look hideous," said Cherry.

Why your appearance is important to your husband

Beth raised her hand. "Yes Beth?"

"Aren't you making us out to be sex objects. I expect my husband to love me for my personality, not my appearance."

"Well Beth, to men, our bodies and our hair ARE part of our personalities. They can have very powerful influences on their love for us."

You can't separate a man from his sexuality. It's inter-

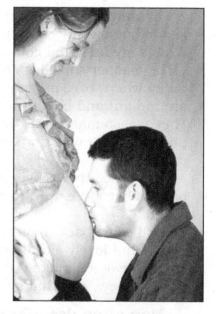

To your husband you are radiant and beautiful when pregnant, but his rosy viewpoint only lasts until your baby is born.

woven into his nature. It's a constant part of him."

"When a woman combines cheerful enthusiasm, child-like humility, femininity, the sex appeal of an hour-glass figure, and appealing hair, she becomes a highly delightful creature to a man, almost irresistible, especially when she smiles."

Why your body is still attractive to your husband when you're pregnant

"You may be right," said Beth. "But now that my stomach is swelling up, my contours aren't exactly hour-glass. What's my husband going to think when I get bigger still?"

The teacher smiled. "Most of us feel unattractive and bulky when we're pregnant Beth. But to our husbands we are radiant and beautiful. They are so proud of themselves. They feel so masculine. To a husband who loves his wife, pregnancy is mysterious and fulfilling, even holy and sacred."

"Of course, his rosy viewpoint doesn't continue after our baby is born. We need to regain our figures as quickly as possible."

"We'll come back to our figures a little later. Lets first talk about that lovely aid to our attractiveness, something few married women make the most of, at least from a man's point of view, and that's our hair.

Most men prefer longer flowing hair on a woman.

Men often describe women by their hair colour

"Do we fully realise how important our hair is to a man? Have you noticed that it's usually the first thing men notice about us?"

"Men often describe us by our hair. They talk about blondes, brunettes, redheads, raven haired beauties."

"A woman's hair is very important to a man. Your hair is important to your husband. Men wish we understood this a little more, but they don't like to hurt our feelings by criticising our appearance."

Most men prefer longer hair on a woman

"And our length of hair is important. Most men, not all men, but most, prefer longer hair on a woman. Remember that opposites attract. To be attractive to men, we need to look at what men do, and do the opposite. Most men naturally prefer have their hair short. Therefore they can perceive a woman with very short hair as masculine, especially if her figure is on the fuller side."

Angela could not resist glancing at Bev with her frizzy, orange red hair. Bev appeared embarrassed and was smoothing her hair with her hand. Angela felt compassion for her.

"I had long hair before I got married", said Kathy, "But it took such a lot of looking after."

"Yes it does Kathy, but it can be most worthwhile. It is highly appealing to a man to see his wife preening herself, and brushing her long hair in front of a mirror. It's ultra feminine. Your hair doesn't have to very long, but long enough to get away from the manly, short back and sides look."

Angela remembered back to when she and Ted were courting. He often said to her, "I just love your hair Angie," and he would run his fingers through it, then lift it up and kiss her neck. Mmmm, what a lovely, warm, sweet feeling it was when he did that.

Angela had already decided to let her hair grow long again, after what Ted said to her on the phone two weeks ago, "I love it long and shiny."

Beth raised her hand. "Yes Beth?" said the teacher.

"My hair is long, but it's stringy and dull. And it's got worse since I've become pregnant. It seems to be falling out, especially in the shower."

"A hundred brushes each night helps keep long hair glossy and silky Beth. But it sounds as if you have a nutrition problem. Your baby gets first call on your available nutrients. We talk about nutrition later in this lesson."

Hairstyles men find highly appealing

"Now, Fascinating Womanhood teachers often get strong reactions from women in their classes to this next statement I'm going to make."

"So here we go. Do you know which hairstyles men find most delightful in women? They are the cute hairstyles we do naturally for our little girls. Men find them highly appealing in women of all ages. They are cute and feminine."

"I have some pictures here of hairstyles that men find particularly appealing. I'll hand them out to you before you leave and you can study them at them at home."

"Judging from reactions of previous classes I have taught, you might think some of them are terribly old fashioned. But if you could look through the eyes of a typical man you would find them very appealing. Fashion is irrelevant when it comes to what a man finds attractive in a women."

"Flowing, lustrous hair on a woman is highly appealing to a man. He finds it delightful. Especially when she smiles."

"Even when a man has been married to a woman for years and years, he never tires of it. She looks so feminine, he cannot help feeling more masculine by comparison. Remember how we learnt in Secret Number One, that men love to feel masculine.

Why most men don't find permed hair attractive

"How many of you had your hair permed during the last year?"

Most of the class raised their hands.

"Whose idea was it, yours or your husbands?"

There was silence.

"It was your idea wasn't it?" said the teacher.

"Now here's a little known secret, class, but an important

It is highly appealing and ultra feminine to a man to see his wife preening herself, and brushing her long hair in front of a mirror.

one. Men feel obliged to compliment a woman when she has had her hair permed or set. But it's usually done without genuine enthusiasm. Why? Because most men prefer longer, soft, flowing hair on a woman. Hair with a natural shine."

"Short boyish hair, teased hair, or frizzy tight curls are unappealing to most men. Too masculine."

"I'm not saying we older women should pretend we are still young, or be 'mutton dressed up as lamb' as the old saying goes, but there is nothing wrong with mature women retaining longer hairstyles, and feminine mannerisms. Men find them delightful in women of any age."

"Even at my age, and I'm approaching 60, I still receive the occasional genuine compliment from a man since I've worn my hair long. One man told my husband he wished women would do more with their hair as they grow older. Most men are just not attracted to matronly hairstyles."

Hair styling that appeals to men

"But shiny, natural looking hair, styled femininely as we naturally do for our young daughters, is highly attractive to men, especially with a feminine ribbon, or a hair band, or flower, or other ornament added."

Some of the class laughed. Beth spoke, "A ribbon? I gave those up years ago, when I was a little kid. I wouldn't be seen dead wearing a ribbon at my age."

The teacher smiled, "I often get this sort of reaction when teaching this secret of Fascinating Womanhood. But remember, we have to start looking through a man's eyes. We women find boyish good looks highly attractive in a man don't we? Well the opposite is also true."

"If you don't believe this is a true principle, ask any man what kind of hairstyle he prefers on a woman, and insist that he tell you the real truth. Remember, men do not like to criticise a woman's appearance."

"But I get a real lift from having my hair permed," said Diane.

"Yes Diane, I know. The attention we receive in a hair salon does give us an emotional lift. But it does little to please most men. It's probably better for us to spend the money on having our hands and nails done, or buying feminine clothes. Men appreciate lovely hands and nails and feminine clothing."

Hair colouring must look natural

"Well what about colouring our hair? I like to have a rinse put through my hair sometimes," said Diane.

"Yes, when our hair begins to grey, colouring our hair is fine. As long as it still looks shiny and natural. But we should steer clear of unnatural colours. It should not look dyed."

"When my naturally brunette hair started to go grey, I began putting brunette rinses through it. That was OK with my husband. In fact I think he much preferred it to the grey. But one day I went out and had it all dyed honey blonde.

I thought it looked gorgeous, but my husband did seem pleased at all. He did not compliment me on it at all, in fact he said nothing. I got the silent treatment. When I asked him outright what he preferred, he told me that he married a brunette, not a blonde. So I went back to brunette for a few more years."

"I colour my hair silver grey now, as I'm nearly totally grey. Perhaps I'm not entirely practising what I'm preaching here, as silver grey is not really natural, but my husband has told me that he likes it, and that's the important thing."

"But colouring our hair when we are young, hardly ever improves our appearance in the eyes of a man. A 'bottle blonde' can be striking to a man at a physical level, but he typically regards such a woman as 'artificial' and 'cheap,' or a 'girl about town.' He is not attracted at the level that will develop into true love and marriage."

"Natural hair has numerous highlight colours, but dyed hair is usually all one shade and can therefore look unnatural and unattractive to a man's eyes."

"Some unnatural shades are even regarded as cheap and degrading. My husband once confided in me, that back in his single days, young men used to refer to the unnatural dark red shade that was popular with many girls back then as 'slut red'."

"So natural is best, but partly greying hair in a woman is generally not very attractive to our husbands or any man."

The first five secrets of Fascinating Womanhood the most important

"Now, before we go any further with this secret class, I want to stress the need to keep a correct sense of proportion with these Fascinating Womanhood secrets."

"This Secret Number Seven, which is about making the most of our appearance, is important, and WILL enhance our attractiveness and the relationship with our husband, but this secret and the ones that follow, are not as important as the first Five Secrets of Fascinating Womanhood."

"Most harlots probably keep Secret Number Seven to perfection, and they can attract men strongly on a lustful or physical level, but they can never win a man's love."

"Why? Because for a woman to win the genuine love of a man, her physical attractiveness must be combined with goodness and inner serenity, as we learned in Secret Number Five."

"And equally important, she needs to meet his innermost needs. The needs we learned in Secrets Number One, Two, Three and Four."

"A plain woman, who makes the most of herself and lives the first Five Secrets of Fascinating Womanhood, will win the love of a man every time, while the ravishing beauty, who lacks inner goodness and understanding of a man's deeper needs, will miss out every time."

The secret of permanent shapeliness

"Right, now, let's get back to our figures. How do we keep ourselves reasonably shapely and alluring to our husbands? How do we get rid of fat rolls, blubbery thighs and flabby upper arms?"

Marina raised her hand. "Yes Marina?"

"I once fasted for a week darlings. I lost six kilograms, but you know, straight away I put back on three kilograms."

"Yes, fasting can work well Marina, but most of our initial weight loss is water. Who's tried dieting?"

"Don't talk to me about dieting," said Bev. Look at me! I get bigger after every diet."

"So do I," said Helena.

"Yes dieting drops our weight temporarily," said the teacher. "But we usually pack on it back on even more efficiently once we stop our diet."

"That's for sure," said Helena.

"Here's something to think about," said the teacher. "How often do we see a normal active child with rolls of fat? Almost never, right? When we go to a school playground what do we see? Children running all around the field, except for the overweight ones. And what are they doing? They're usually sitting around talking."

"Yet all active children seem to eat like horses don't they? Especially when they come home from school. And what do they like best? Cakes, biscuits, ice cream, hot dogs, hamburgers, soft drinks, lollies. All the fattening foods. But they still stay slim, even skinny most of them. Why?"

"Because they're always on the move, burning up calories," said Cherry.

"That's right Cherry. That's exactly the right answer. In other words they are exercising."

The teacher turned to the board and wrote in big letters.

EXERCISE.

Some of the class groaned. "I knew it wasn't my night," said Bev.

The teacher smiled. "Believe me class, if we want to be physically attractive to our husbands, all our lives, exercise is a must. I'm 58 and I love to exercise. I feel as young and as fit as I did in my teens."

Then to Angela's surprise the teacher ran on the spot about thirty times and then bent and touched her toes five times.

"Bev, I was close to your size about twelve years ago, after my last child. Diets only made me bigger still when I went off them."

Angela saw Bev suddenly perk up.

Bev said, "Well come on teacher. Hurry up. Tell me how you did it. I'll try anything that works."

"Well Bev, all I did was to start riding a bicycle again, and staying on my feet more, and sitting less. And also going for

Once you get up to a certain level of exercise, your body will normally maintain its ideal weight.

148

long bush walks with my husband and the older children."

"Gradually, over a few months, my weight just melted off. I still ate about the same amount of food, but only a light meal at night. And I was never hungry all the time like when I was dieting. My husband, daughter and I still have only a light meal at nights. None of us have a weight problem at present, and we seem to sleep better than when we had a large meal at night."

"Nowadays for exercise, my husband and I mostly run and walk. He's a doctor and has made a of study of weight loss. It appears that once we get up to a certain level of exercise, our body will normally maintain its ideal weight. That's as long as we don't over eat at night, and we stay away from sweet drinks. Sweet drinks are one of the worst foods of all for putting on weight. That includes diet drinks too. The artificial sweeteners in some of them can damage our appetite control."

Too much sitting the main cause of weight gain

"So class, exercise is really the only answer. Too much sitting is the main cause of our weight gain. Even just moving around doing light housework on our feet uses three times as many calories of sitting down, 180 calories an hour, compared to 60 calories while we're sitting down, or lying in bed."

"Think about that for a moment class. It is very, very significant fact. WE BURN THREE TIMES THE CALORIES JUST MOVING AROUND ON OUR FEET, COMPARED TO SITTING. It's the key to slimness. That's why active children stay slim."

"Brisk walking, hiking, or cycling uses even more calories, 250 per hour. Steady running uses 700 calories, and fast running uses an enormous 1100 calories an hour. These figures are all for women. Men burn more with their bigger muscles.

One kilogram of fat, which is 2.2 pounds for us oldies, contains about 9000 calories. So you can see, its just plain arithmetic. Burn off 9000 calories and we have lost 1 kg of fat, that's 1300 calories a day over a week. That's why long distance runners are so skinny."

"And another big benefit from exercise is that we work off our stresses. Things don't seem to worry us so much, and we sleep better."

"She's right," said Cherry enthusiastically. "I started doing aerobics nine months ago at the women's gym. I was about Helena's size then. Sorry Helena," said Cherry grinning at her. "And look at me now, though I'm big boned." She stood up and wiggled her shapely hips.

"And teacher is right about stress. I used to get wound up and resentful towards my husband. Not any more. Now I just float round like a butterfly."

"Yes, Cherry is a good example to us," said the teacher. "Aerobics, running, or for the larger breasted woman, brisk walking, hiking and cycling, are all excellent exercises for staying slim, and working off tensions and worry."

"You can also use equipment at home like exercycles, steppers, rowing machines and walkers while you read or watch TV. And music always seems to make the time pass more quickly. And there are woman's gyms, as Cherry mentioned. They're popular nowadays."

"My husband Milton and I try and go for a run in the park three mornings a week. We walk there, or drive there, and I still ride my bike on quiet streets. I enjoy it, but not in heavy traffic. Sometimes I go for bike rides to parks with my grandchildren.

We mustn't let exercise become boring. So it's good to do it with others where possible."

"If you decide to take up running, which is the fastest way to burn off fat, use proper running shoes, and run on smooth, flat surfaces where possible."

"Oh it's a lovely feeling to run and feel the wind streaming past your face. I feel like a young girl again, and it seems to tighten up my tummy. But running is not for every woman."

The amount of exercise necessary to stay permanently slim

"Angela, you had your hand up?"

"Yes, I've just started running too. Now you told us earlier that your husband had discovered there's a certain level of exercise that will maintain our ideal weight. Just how much is that?"

"I'm pleased that you've started to exercise Angela, and it's a good question you've asked. Yes evidently research has shown, that if we exercise enough to double our resting pulse rate, for three hours each week, say for example, half an hour a day, six days a week. And we eat within our normal appetite, with hardly any sweet drinks and don't binge on sweet foods, our body weight should steadily drop until it maintains its ideal weight, and then stay there. And it seems to work; don't you think so Cherry?"

"It sure does," said Cherry. "I gave up soft drinks too, even fruit drinks. I eat whole fruit now instead."

"Very good Cherry. Now if doubling our pulse rate is too vigorous for us, we need only increase our pulse rate by half, but for double the length of time, say six hours a week, or any combination in between.

"Your pulse rate is the measure. First know your resting pulse rate. Its usually about 70 beats a minute for women. Men tend to be lower. Then try different speeds of exercise and check your increase in pulse. You can buy little electronic gadgets to do it for you, or just use your finger on an artery like I do, and time it with a watch."

"For example, if you choose brisk walking as your exercise, and your resting pulse is 70, you should walk fast enough to raise it to 105, that's a 50% increase, and be able to keep it around there for at least half an hour at a time. It

Running half an hour a day will normally maintain your ideal weight, and also help you to feel relaxed and sleep well.

takes about twenty minutes for exercise to start being really effective. Short bursts are not as effective for weight control."

"Is that clear?"

"Clear as mud," said Bev. "I'm hopeless at maths. Can you write it on the board?"

"Well I'll try Bev, although maths is not one of my strong points either."

"I can do it said Cherry. I've got it sussed out in my head." She walked up to the board and picked up the marker and said. "OK, lets say our resting pulse is 70 beats a minute. Now, any of these three combinations I'll write will give us the amount of exercise the teacher is talking about." Then she wrote on the board.

Resting Pulse 70		Exercise needed
Increase by 50% to 105	=	6 hours per week.
Increase by 75% to 122	=	4½ hours per week.
Increase by 100% to 140	=	3 hours per week.

"Does that make sense now?" she asked when she had finished. Most of the women nodded their heads and Cherry sat down.

Bev spoke. "So I need to exercise one hour a day, six days a week, at about 105 beats a minute. Then I'll be back to where I used to be? Correct?"

"Well, yes Bev." said the teacher. "That's what the research shows. Or you can do it in two half hour periods a day. It's worked for Cherry and I. And my weight loss seems to be permanent. As long as I continue to exercise and eat within my appetite. And just a light meal at night and no eating before bed. I've kept the same weight for years now."

"OK teacher. You win. Look out for the new Bev. If you can do it, I can do it. You just watch me!"

There was a determination and excitement in Bev's voice that surprised Angela. Angela felt excited also. This all made perfect sense. She had always been trim and active before marriage.

The teacher beamed at Bev. "I believe you really mean it Bev. But don't overdo it at first."

"I'll be starting tonight," said Bev.

"What sort of exercise is best of all?" asked Sonia.

"That all depends on what we enjoy Sonia.," said the teacher. "To increase our pulse rate 100% we need to do something very vigorous, like aerobics, or running, or swimming, or a stepper, or a rowing machine, or riding a bike or an exercycle very fast, or climbing steps, or hills, or playing netball."

"To increase our pulse only 50% or 75%, we can do the same things, but at a more comfortable pace. Or play tennis, or do exercises like trampolining or brisk walking."

"Brisk walking is popular. It's a good exercise, especially when you include some hills, and a friend for company. Or you can take a little radio with head phones, or an Ipod like my husband does when he runs or walks alone at night sometimes."

"As we can see with what Cherry's written on the board, an average 50% increase in pulse rate for an hour a day, six days a week, or an hour and a half a day, four days a week should keep us slim. I love to go bush walking with my husband. There are lots of beautiful walks in the hills around here."

"But long periods of exercise can be tiring at first when you're building up your fitness and carrying a lot of weight, so ease into your exercise and enjoy it. Fitness increases rapidly when we do it every day."

"Boredom is our biggest enemy to exercise. WE NEED TO GET OUR MIND OFF WHAT WE'RE DOING. A friend, or music, or listening to talk back radio, or tapes. Anything to distract our mind from the effort."

"And we should keep picturing in our mind the firm, shapely body we are regaining. It should be a goal on our Goal List."

"But don't overdo it. Overdoing exercise can stress our body and make us unwell. If any day you feel below par, give it a miss, but never, never give it up. Make it a life-long thing. And enjoy it. I do."

"You'll be amazed how more energetic you feel, and how much warmer you feel during winter. And how much more relaxed and free of worry. Also, vigorous exercise helps protect us from osteoporosis which is so common among older women."

"Now, two last points, before we move onto nutrition. If you choose an exercise where only your leg muscles are used, include another exercise to firm up your upper body muscles, especially your upper arms. Swimming and weights are especially good for the upper body, or a rowing machine, or the old traditional exercises like push ups and chin ups."

"And the last point, when you get down to your ideal weight, and for a period of time you find it impossible to exercise regularly, weigh yourself every day, and as soon as your weight increases by just 1 kg, get it off quickly by skipping a few meals, or halving your meals, or by exercise."

Beth raised her hand. "Yes Beth?"

"I believe in exercise. But I'm so busy I never get time to exercise."

"Beth, leg exercise during pregnancy is very important. It helps us prevent ugly, varicose veins."

"There's also the old saying that applies to all of us, *'Those who have no time to exercise, will sooner or later have to find time for sickness.'*

Obtain some good nutrition books and check your diet carefully to see if you're getting all the necessary nutrients. Minerals are especially important.

"We have to plan time for our exercising. We should use our desk top planners, or whatever we decide to use. If we just wait for time to come available, it hardly ever will."

How to eat for maximum health

"Now let's look more closely at nutrition and our health.

We need to be healthy to be fascinating to our husbands. Good health brings out qualities in a woman that are highly attractive to a man. I'll list some on the board."

Fresh complexion
Shiny hair
Vivaciousness
Sparkling eyes
Liveliness
Cheerful voice
Optimism

"Do we have these qualities?" asked the teacher.

"Maybe before marriage," said Kathy, "But after four children, what do you expect?"

"Nonsense," said Cherry "That's just an excuse we women make. I was a mess nine months ago, but now I feel great. I don't mean to show off, but everybody's telling me how good I look. All I did was to get my diet sorted out and to exercise regularly."

"Cherry's right," said the teacher. "Improving our diet can benefit us greatly. Most of us are probably eating too much sugar, and too much white flour, and drinking too much caffeine, and not eating enough whole grains and fruit and veges and nuts."

"We are what we eat," said Elsie.

"Yes, so true Elsie. And we are also what we don't eat too. If you haven't yet done so, obtain a few good nutrition books and check your diet carefully to see if you're getting all the necessary nutrients. Minerals are especially important."

"If you can't afford to buy books, you can go to the library."

"You could be amazed at how unbalanced your diet really is. I know mine was, and my whole family. Now we hardly ever seem to get sick any more, not even colds and have no arthritis pain. And we always seem to have enough energy."

"As a quick guideline, most of our food should be whole grains, legumes, nuts, and white, yellow, and dark green vegetables. We should try and avoid white flour products as most of the minerals and fibre are missing, and also soft drinks, and white sugar, and over-heated fats, and processed meats."

"Beth, the stringy and falling hair problem you mentioned earlier does sound very much like a nutrition problem. You might need more zinc and protein. And folate is very important during pregnancy. And too much worry, or constant perming can also dull our hair. Good nutrition generally puts the shine back in our hair."

A lovely, innocent smile is a priceless asset to a woman. If you feel self-conscious about your teeth, get them fixed up by a dentist.

Tips for life-long health

"Now we've got time for a few more health tips before we close. Creating beautiful things always seems to help a woman's health. So we might like to include a creative hobby as part of our personal growth."

"Also, going to bed early and getting up early is important

for life-long health.”

"She's picking on me again," said Bev.

The class laughed. The teacher smiled. "I haven't finished yet Bev. And plenty of fresh air, even during winter. We shouldn't close all our windows so the air gets stale. Our body needs fully oxygenated air to stay healthy. Oxygen is very important for health. We die in four minutes without oxygen."

"And of course I don't have to mention smoking do I? It's so unhealthy, and so unpleasant to non-smokers, and it's unfeminine. And what a terrible example it sets for our children."

"Nearly all men loath the smoking habit in a woman, Especially non-smoking men. And most men are non-smokers."

"I wasn't as big as I am now when I smoked," said Bev.

"Bev, exercise will soon have you looking and feeling like a teenager again," said the teacher.

"And if we want to enjoy continual health, we need to avoid emotional upsets, like getting angry, or even too much excitement. We shouldn't worry about the future, or dwell on the past. Just live one day at a time."

"Another thing, we should never take tranquillisers or sleeping pills. Or at least, never for longer than a week at a time. They are highly, highly addictive. I know. I speak from experience. Exercising is a much better way to relax and to sleep well."

"Singing and laughing also relax us, or going to church, or listening to our favourite music. We should try and enjoy some nice music every day."

"And most important, we should smile. Smiling cheers us up like nothing else does, and makes any woman look more beautiful to a man."

Do your teeth hinder your smile?

"A lovely, innocent smile is a priceless asset to a woman. It should come easily and spontaneously. If you feel self-conscious about your teeth, get them fixed up by a dentist. Yes it might cost your husband a lot of money, but when he sees you smile confidently, he will know it was worthwhile. We should have our teeth looking their nicest. It makes us more kissable also."

"Well that's all for tonight class. Here are this week's assignments."

ASSIGNMENTS. SECRET NUMBER SEVEN

ASSIGNMENT ONE. Ask your husband to tell you truthfully, what hair length and hairstyles he thinks you look nicest in, and wear your hair that way for him.

ASSIGNMENT TWO. Start an enjoyable exercise program that you can continue throughout your life.

ASSIGNMENT THREE. Obtain some good books on nutrition. Study them carefully, and work out a balanced diet for yourself, and also your family if they will accept it.

"Our visitors tonight are Lillian and Kate. Both these fine women have found happiness after broken marriages by living the Fascinating Womanhood principles. Thank you for coming along to be with us tonight. Can we hear from you first Lillian and then from you Kate."

Lillian. True Experience.
"I first heard of Fascinating Womanhood when our marriage was avalanching to a sad ending. This after thirty-two years of marriage and six children. But I was resentful, what about the feelings I have, don't they count, I thought."

"The situation went from bad to worse, we separated, and I lived alone in a rented flat. When I came home from work at night I had time to think, and relive my life."

"I went through a tremendous soul-searching period. I was ready to accept myself as the blame for our problems. I began to read over again, slowly, the Fascinating Womanhood teachings, with an entirely new outlook. Sure, there it was! Why couldn't I have seen it before? I silently thanked God for his guidance."

"I didn't have to act the part. I felt it. My life has changed. I am back home with my husband and we have found our old love renewed. We both look forward to a bright future."

"Don't wait until it's too late to apply these teachings. There's no age limit for these secrets. What have you got to lose? Believe me, they work."

Kate. True Experience.
"I've had three previous marriages, and the man I was engaged to had two. We were about to break our engagement due to my critical attitude. During this time I had been praying daily that I might discover what my mistakes were, so that I might correct them before it was too late."

"Then I heard about Fascinating Womanhood and I had a strange compulsion to know more. I knew somehow this would be the answer to my prayers, and it certainly was!"

"Within one day of applying Fascinating Womanhood he began putting his arm around me again while we watched TV."

"Within two weeks, he told me as he held me tenderly,

that he'd begun to love me lately like he used to. I was so happy that I burst into tears."

"We were married two months later and have been happy ever since. He brings me flowers. Today he came home with a beautiful pot of Azaleas and for no apparent reason. That's twice he's done that. No one ever brought me flowers before. That's what Fascinating Womanhood has done for me."

"Aren't they lovely experiences?" The teacher gazed at Angela and then smiled and said. "Angela, perhaps you too will soon be able to share a lovely experience of being reunited with your husband."

Angela blushed but felt her hopes rise higher.

"Good night everybody, see you next week. But before you go, here are the drawings of feminine hairstyles that most men find highly appealing."

"Next week we learn the secret of getting men to pay more attention to us."

That night Angela went to bed earlier than normal, at 10 pm. The next morning she arose at 6-30 to go for a run.

She ran and walked alternatively for a full thirty minutes.

As she was enjoying a shower after arriving back home, she resolved to run every Monday, Wednesday, Thursday and Saturday mornings. She would build up her fitness until she could run thirty minutes non-stop.

Angela felt a glow of health and satisfaction as she awoke David and Tiphony at 7-30 am.

Hairstyles men find appealing.

CHAPTER ELEVEN

Secret Number Eight
Femininity delights a man

David came home from school on Friday, waving the wooden sceptre he had made for his father and looking pleased with himself.

"Mum, I've finished it," he shouted.

The sceptre was about a metre long. David had shaped it using the school woodworking lathe. It had varying curves, like an expensive curtain rod. He had also flattened off a part in the middle and burned in the words "DAD THE KING."

Angela was thrilled with how it had turned out. She praised David as she admired it.

"You've done a lovely job David. I'm very proud of you. We can stain and varnish it tomorrow before we give it to Dad."

David grinned and flushed with pride.

On Saturday afternoon, Angela showed David how to stain the wood a rich shade of mahogany, using stain and a small cloth. Then she let him brush on a coat of clear varnish.

It was dry by evening. David wanted to take it around to his father's flat that night.

"No David, we'll take it round to him during the week," said Angela.

Sunday evening, Angela baked two chocolate cakes. One for Ted, and one for David and Tiphony.

On the following day, Monday, while at school, Angela asked a fellow teacher to phone Ted's workshop and ask to speak to the apprentice. Then Angela took over the phone.

"Is that you Alex?" she asked.

"Yes. Who's speaking?"

"It's me Angela. Ted's wife."

"Oh yeah."

"Alex, my children and I are planning a surprise for Ted tonight, around at his flat. I just want to be sure that he'll be there. What time does he normally leave to go home? He's not listening is he?"

"No, no, he's out talking with a customer. Oh I don't know. He normally leaves here about 5:30. Sometimes he goes for a beer. But he'll probably go straight home tonight, being a Monday."

"OK Alex. That sounds good. Don't say a word to him. But if it looks as though he's going to work late, can you phone me at home after 3:30? I'm still in the phone book under Ted's name."

"Yeah OK."

"Bye Alex."

"That evening, Angela put on her new pink dress. She also clipped onto her hair a white ribbon that she had folded into the shape of a flower. She felt highly anxious.

Ten minutes before 6 pm, Angela and her two children David and Tiphony drove around to Ted's flat. Angela saw his van parked up the driveway.

"So far so good," she thought. "Oh I hope he's alone."

Ever since Ted had left, Angela had dreaded the day she would find him with another woman.

They left their car out on the street and walked up the gravel driveway to Ted's flat. Angela carried the chocolate cake. David held the sceptre.

Angela felt her heart pounding as she knocked on the door.

The door opened immediately. Ted was still in his overalls and looked highly surprised to see them. He smiled when he saw the chocolate cake.

"What's all this about?" he said, still smiling.

"Look what I've made Dad," said David, excitedly waving the sceptre and nearly hitting Tiphony in the face.

"It's from all of us," said Angela. "Where shall I put your chocolate cake Ted?"

"Come in. Come in," said Ted, opening the door wide. Angela was enormously relieved to see that Ted was alone.

As she walked inside she sensed an atmosphere of loneliness within the two roomed, cheaply furnished flat.

Ted had been reading the paper at the table. There was no sign of a meal being prepared. Angela suddenly felt an overwhelming sorrow for Ted. A lump came to her throat.

She put the cake on the kitchen bench. The children were chatting with Ted while he admired the sceptre. Angela wondered what she should do next, and whispered a prayer for guidance. As she did so, a strange confidence seemed to come over her. She walked over to Ted.

"David, Tiphony, that's enough now. Your father's had

a busy day. Ted, that sceptre is a symbol from all of us. It shows that we accept you as the leader and king of our family. If you decide to come home and look after us, we all promise to follow your leadership one hundred percent."

Angela saw Ted's eyes fill with tears at these words and quickly looked away so as not to embarrass him. The children didn't appear to notice.

"David, you and Tiphony sit over there and watch Dad's TV. Let him change and rest, while I cook him a nice meal."

Ted seemed pleasantly surprised, and somewhat dazed.

Without saying a word he went into his bedroom to change while Angela looked in the cupboards and fridge for some food.

When Ted came back out, Angela went up to him and squeezed his hand and said, "You sit and finish reading the paper. Would a nice omelette with onion be OK? And some yoghurt and fruit for dessert?"

"Yes, that would be lovely Angie," said Ted, still looking dazed. He picked up the newspaper and sat down on the couch. Tiphony and David immediately went and sat either side of him. He put the paper down and put his arms around them both. Then he said "Pass me over that sceptre David. Let's have a closer look."

A little while later, Angela put the plate with Ted's omelette on the table, along with a yoghurt and fruit salad dessert. She also cut him a slice of the chocolate cake.

"Your omelette's ready Ted," she said. Ted was now reading the newspaper and the children were watching TV.

Ted folded the newspaper, picked up his sceptre and sat down at the table. He laid the sceptre on top of the table, looked at his food and smiled.

"This looks really good Angie," he said. "Smells good too."

Angela's feminine instinct told her it was now time to leave.

"Come on David. Come on Tiphony. Turn the TV off and let's go and leave Dad to eat in peace."

"Can we have a piece of cake before we go Mum?" asked David.

"We've got our own cake at home David. That's Dad's cake. Then she handed David the car keys and said quietly, "Please go and wait out in the car."

When they had gone, Angela took a deep breath and then went over to Ted at the table. She put her arm around his shoulders and kissed his prickly cheek.

"Goodbye Ted. I love you so much," she said.

As she closed the door behind her, she heard Ted break into enormous sobs. She didn't turn around, but hurried down the gravel driveway to the car.

Tuesday evening, Angela was thrilled when her brother Robert phoned. He thanked her for the letter she sent him. and apologised for the way he had treated her in the past.

Angela was amazed at the warmth and personality in his voice. Totally different from the cold monotone he normally used toward her. It was uncanny how much like her father he sounded.

Wednesday evening, Angela ate her usual light meal. She had done this now every evening since last week's class.

David and Tiphony did not think this was a good idea and ate their normal large meal, especially David.

Angela however was convinced it was wise to cut down her food. She had been sleeping more soundly and waking up more alert each morning.

Already she was feeling much lighter and more lively. And her clothes were looser on her body.

To attend the Fascinating Womanhood class tonight she chose to wear her pink dress and white ribbon flower, instead of the slacks she normally wore.

Although a gusty wind was blowing and the sky overcast, she again decided to walk to her class.

"It's good for my figure," she said to her mother who expressed concern. "Cherry will give me a ride home afterwards."

"Despite the wind, Angela enjoyed her walk. Her mind was serene. She was pleased that she had not lost her temper once during the past week.

When Angela walked into the classroom and sat down, she saw that most of the women were wearing more feminine clothing and hairstyles than previously.

Bev had recoloured her orange hair a natural brunette shade. And instead of it being frizzy and sticking out, she wore it styled closer to her head in gentle waves. She also wore two long gold ear rings. Angela thought she looked quite regal. Even Bev's normal florid complexion seemed a healthier hue.

Sonia had plaited her long brown hair into two plaits and wore a pale yellow ribbon in each.

Beth wore a conservative, amber coloured, hair band.

Diane had completely lost her tense look and was conversing animatedly with Helena.

"How radiant they all look tonight," thought Angela. She felt elated inside and smiled at the other women and relaxed.

"Good evening class," said Harmony the teacher. Angela was surprised to see that tonight she had her silver hair in a pony tail, and wore a striking, ankle length, white skirt, with lace frills circling it at intervals.

"I must say you all seem to be aglow tonight," she continued. "And I see some very feminine hairstyles. Was I right about men's tastes in women's hairstyles?"

Elsie spoke. "Well, I must admit I had my doubts. I've always worn my hair short. But I finally plucked up enough courage to ask my husband to tell me the truth about what hairstyle he prefers. You'll never guess what he

said? He said he would like to see me in a pony tail. Me?
A grandmother, in a pony tail. I just laughed. I thought he
was kidding me. But he wasn't. Then I come along tonight
and what do I see? My teacher, who's also a grandmother,
wearing a pony tail."

"Anyway, I've decided to let my hair grow a little longer for
a start. But I don't know that I could possibly wear it in a
pony tail. What would other women think?"

The teacher laughed and flipped her pony tail. "Come on
now Elsie. Be daring. Fascinating Womanhood teaches us
to please our husbands. Not please other women."

"Well, that's enough about hair. Have we all started our
exercise programs? And have we got our nutrition sorted
out?"

Bev said, "Well I don't know about the others teacher, but
you've fired me up to beat this weight problem once and for
all. So guess what? I've taken up jogging."

Some of the class laughed.

The teacher didn't laugh. "Good on you Bev," she beamed.
"Tell us more."

"Well, I've been out three nights now. I don't dare run in
the daylight. I wait until it's nice and dark. The first two
times I went out, I could only jog slowly for about a minute
at a time. Then I'd be puffing like a steam engine. So I
would walk and then run again for about a minute. But
on the third night, guess what? I ran for three minutes.
Without stopping. How's that for progress. Gee I felt good as
I showered afterward."

"Now I'm going to save up and buy myself some proper
running shoes. Then I'll keep it up until I can run for a half
hour without stopping, just like when I was at school. I
used to love athletics. So if any of you ladies happen to see
a hippopotamus jogging past your house late at night, you'll
know who it is."

"Bev, you keep that up for a few months, and none of
us will recognise you," said the teacher. "How does your
husband feel about this?"

"Hah! He laughed at first. But now that he can see I'm
serious, he's encouraging me. He says he'll buy me a new
dress and take me on a holiday if I can get as slim as I was
when he married me."

"He's really changed. We're all going to AA now. And you
know, he rang them himself. I didn't ask him. He hasn't had
a drink now for two weeks, and he's saving his money. He's
even sold our motor mower and bought a push mower so he
can get some exercise too."

"Oh Bev, I'm so pleased to hear that," said the teacher.
Angela could see the tears shining in the teacher's eyes.

"Now don't you give up your jogging, whatever you do.
You're a real inspiration. I'm going to call on you to visit
some of our future classes to share your experience. "

"Can I share one now," asked Bev. "Things are really

starting to happen in our home."

"Certainly, come on up."

Bev. True Experience.

"Before taking this Fascinating Womanhood course, I had just about given up on my marriage. In fact, two days before my first class I had been to see a lawyer about getting a divorce from my husband. He was unbearable. He drank too much, had no interest in us, and each weekend would take off and spend most of his wages."

"When I told him I had seen a lawyer, he begged me with tears in his eyes not to leave him."

"Then I had my first Fascinating Womanhood lesson on acceptance. It was a blow to self-sacrificing me. I had to admit I made mistakes too. Could it have been my fault all along for not accepting him?"

"So finally I told him I accepted him the way he was. I said I had made a lot of mistakes in our marriage, and would sincerely try to do better."

"A wonderful, shocked expression appeared on his face, and he said, 'You mean I can go out and spend all the money and you won't care?"

"He hasn't gone out one time since I've been applying the secrets. I still have a lot of work to do, but our marriage has become better each week."

"Oh that's excellent Bev. I'm so proud of you. I commend you for what you're doing."

Anybody else? Diane, come on up.

Diane. True Experience.

"When I came to Secret Number Seven and I started to pay more attention to my appearance, my husband started to compliment me all the time, which made my self esteem and confidence improve immensely."

"Recently my husband left early one morning to visit his mother. When I got out of bed I found love notes stuck all over the house for me."

"I then realised just how happy our marriage had become since living Fascinating Womanhood."

"Isn't that lovely class? Diane, remember to write what each of those love notes say in your Love Book. Or even stick the notes themselves in your book. I just love reading my own Love Book."

"Now, let's put tonight's secret on the board. This secret builds on last week's Secret Number Seven, on making the most of ourselves. It teaches us how to be noticed and admired and liked by nearly all men. Especially our husbands."

Most women had femininity in abundance as young girls, but somewhere along the way, as they grow up, they lay it aside, or have it educated out of them.

SECRET NUMBER EIGHT
Femininity delights a man.
Depending on him arouses his love.

Femininity and childlike purity are the heart and soul of Fascinating Womanhood.

"First what is femininity? What is this quality in a woman that is so delightful to a man?"

Helena raised her hand. "Yes Helena?"

"I suppose it's the opposite of masculinity."

"Yes. What an excellent answer Helena." said the teacher looking pleased. "That's probably the best way of all to describe it. Femininity is doing the exact opposite of what men do."

"It is the opposites of femininity and masculinity that attract men and women to each other? This seems obvious really. But so many women still make the big mistake of acting like men, to try and win a man's love and respect."

"It just doesn't work. In fact it has the opposite effect. Masculine behaviour in a woman repels most men."

"But a truly feminine woman, a woman who looks and acts femininely, is highly attractive and delightful to a man."

Are you a feminine woman?

"Let's look again through the eyes of a man. What is a feminine woman? What is it that delights him?"

The teacher picked up a picture of a young girl and held it up. The girl was wearing a pretty, frilly dress and wore her hair in two little pig tails with ribbons. She was smiling shyly.

"A little girl like this comes closest to a man's ideal of femininity. Most of us have femininity in abundance when we are young girls, but somewhere along the way, as we grow up, we lay it aside, or have it educated out of us."

Beth spoke. "Are you teaching that we should act childishly? Surely no man is attracted to that?"

A smile multiplies your attractiveness to men many times over.

"No. That is definitely not what I am teaching Beth. Now class, please don't get this principle of Fascinating Womanhood wrong. We are not talking here about scatty, giggly, girlishness. Nor are we talking about self-centredness, or the whining voice of some children. Beth is right. No man is attracted to that kind of immature behaviour."

"But to be childlike is different. It is to have the noble virtues of a child. These virtues are openness, innocence, humility, trust, dependence and a carefree charm. Qualities that are found in most young girls up to about twelve years of age."

"Many women in these Fascinating Womanhood classes resist the idea of allowing these childlike qualities they once had as young girls, to reawaken within them. They think it's an insult to their intelligence and maturity. They believe that sensible men will be repelled by such behaviour. But on the contrary, even the highest calibre men are greatly attracted to these childlike qualities in a woman."

"A woman who retains, or re-awakens her childlike humility and innocence, is regarded as charming and highly attractive by men. Try it. You will see that this is so.

Marina raised her hand. "Yes Marina?"

"Childlikeness is also a beautiful quality in God's eyes. Jesus once called a little child to him and said to the adults around him, *"Truly I say, unless you repent and become like little children, you will never enter the kingdom of heaven."*

"Thank you Marina. That is so appropriate. The femininity and the purity of a child is the heart and soul of Fascinating Womanhood. A delightful blend of childlike charm, vivaciousness and serenity. And a dependence on men for care and protection."

"Femininity wins a man's heart. Nearly all women have it, but it usually needs to be reawakened."

"But remember class, these feminine qualities will only enhance our husband's love for us when he is completely free of resentment toward us. That's why it is so vital that we live the first Four Secrets of Fascinating Womanhood. In order to make the most of these last secrets."

"Now we look more closely at feminine qualities that appeal most to men.

Men can be repelled by a serious faced or frowning woman.

Why your smile delights a man

"Firstly our smile. Why is our smile so delightful to a man? Because it signals friendliness, serenity and contentment. These feminine qualities are highly appealing to a man."

"On the other hand, men can be repelled by a serious faced or frowning woman. A tense, clamped mouth puts them right off."

"But men are highly attracted to a smiling woman. We all look more attractive when we smile. In fact a smile multiplies our attractiveness to men many times over. It is a major feature of our appearance. Even more than our hair and clothing."

"And remember how we talked about the importance of our teeth last week? How we should get them fixed up if they hinder our smile."

Let your tender emotions show

"Now let's move on to feminine tenderness. Feminine tenderness is very appealing to men, especially when we display it towards children or animals, and even flowers and plants. Or when we shed tears over a sad or moving story."

"Our husband might tease us a little at times, but we shouldn't hide our tender emotions. Or hold back our tears."

"Our tenderness and our tears, and even his teasing of us make him feel manly and strong. His own tenderness and love is aroused and awakened."

"Any questions so far? Yes Kathy?"

"What are some things that we women do that men find unfeminine?"

More than anything else, a woman's choice of words and the tone in which she speaks them, will make or break her marriage.

Things men find unfeminine in a woman

"Well Kathy, there are so many nowadays. We cover the more common ones a little later in this lesson."

"But in short, they are the things that men do themselves. Like drinking alcohol, using swear words, loud laughing, telling jokes. Just about any loud, boisterous behaviour, even whistling, are unfeminine in the eyes of men."

"But there are lots of other things we should also avoid too, like shaking hands too firmly, driving a truck, or even a van, or too large a car, or a high powered sports car, or riding a motorbike. If we don't feel feminine doing it, we should try and avoid it."

"There is a Golden Rule of Fascinating Womanhood, WATCH WHAT MEN DO, AND DO THE OPPOSITE."

Beth spoke. "I can see what you're driving at. But it's very difficult when you're working all day with men, and doing the same sort of work as them."

"You are so right Beth. It is difficult. That's why Fascinating Womanhood teaches that we should not try to succeed in man's pushy, aggressive world."

"Our femininity diminishes by degrees without us noticing it. We sacrifice our gentleness and our grace."

"On the other hand, a feminine environment enhances our femininity. It allows our charm to blossom. Just as the moon, when it moves out of harsh daylight into it's own world of the night sky, is enhanced in beauty and splendour."

The enormous influence of our tongues

"Now we look at something that has a very, very big influence on our femininity. And therefore our appeal to men. In fact, above all else. That's our tongue. The way we speak."

"Whether our marriage is a heaven on earth, or a hell on earth depends more on how we use our tongue than anything else we do."

The teacher's voice became serious. "What I am now about to say is extremely important. And this applies to all ten secrets of Fascinating Womanhood."

"More than anything else, our choice of words and the tone in which we speak them, will make or break our marriage."

"Let me repeat that, MORE THAN ANYTHING ELSE, OUR CHOICE OF WORDS, AND THE TONE IN WHICH WE SPEAK THEM, WILL MAKE OR BREAK OUR MARRIAGE."

"OUR TONGUE WILL BRING US HAPPINESS ON EARTH, OR HELL ON EARTH. WE HOLD THE KEY."

Angela was astonished at the emphasis in the teacher's voice. Yet the words had a profound effect upon her. Deep down she knew they were true.

"So, let's look at some guidelines we can use."

"First and foremost, we must think before we speak. We

should ask ourselves."

    "Is it kind?"

    "Is it true?"

    "Is it necessary?"

    "How will it make my husband feel?"

"Then, when we do speak, we should phrase what we say in a positive and loving way. This can be hard to do when we are irritated, or angry, but it is so vitally important. It makes all the difference in the world."

"Every sentence we speak to our husbands should be phrased and spoken positively and lovingly. Otherwise it is better to remain silent."

"Now let's see how this works. Give me some everyday examples of things we say to our husbands negatively. They usually call it nagging. Let's see if we can rephrase them positively to show what I mean. I'll write them on the board. Who's going to start us off? OK Sonia."

Negative	Positive
"When are you going to mow the lawns? They look awful?"	"In this case we say nothing. He can see they need doing. That's his area."
"Don't be late home tonight will you. I've got to go out at 6:30."	"I'll have dinner ready for you by 5:30 tonight darling. I need to go out soon after." (Say it as you kiss him goodbye in the morning.)
"The car's nearly out of gas again. Why don't you keep an eye on it."	"Is it OK for me to use the card to fill the car darling? It's nearly out of gas. I know you're busy."
"Why do you sit there in front of the TV and watch those stupid sports all weekend? There's loads of jobs need doing. The clothesline's falling to bits."	"Darling, please fix my clothesline when you get time today." (Say it with a smile and maybe a kiss on his forehead and as you do something nice for him, like bringing him a cool drink.)
"Don't touch me, I'm not in the mood for sex."	"Darling would it be all right if we waited until another night when I'll feel more in the mood? You turn over and I'll snuggle into your back."

Men like to devote all their concentration to a difficult task. And even though they love you, they can become irritated when you try and converse with them.

"You can see the difference, can't you?" said the teacher.

"And when we phrase our words positively, and speak them lovingly, our voice takes on a pleasing tone. Sweet and melodious to a man's ears. Highly feminine."

"But when we speak negatively, or critically, or crudely, or even too loudly or forcefully, our voice takes on an unpleasant, irritating tone to a man. It can immediately arouse resentment."

"We come across as nasal, or harsh, or masculine. It causes his tenderness and love to wither. Just like spraying a lovely flower with weed killer."

"When our husband hears us yelling at the children, it has almost the same effect on him. He loses respect for us. We fall off our pedestal so to speak."

Speak cheerfully, with a melodious lilt in your voice

"So unless it is a very serious subject, our voice should have a cheerful, gentle, smiley tone to it. It should radiate confidence and serenity."

"When we speak like this, our voice takes on the melodious quality and musical lilt that is highly appealing to men."

Beth raised her hand. "I'm not sure what you mean by a musical lilt," she said.

"Well, it's not that easy to describe in words Beth. The opposite would be a depressed monotone. I can probably best describe it as similar to the voice we women use to talk to babies. Sort of melodious and musical. Full of love and delight. And smiling as we speak. Men find it delightful and highly feminine."

Some of the class laughed.

"It's true" smiled the teacher. "Our laughter should also have this same musical lilt. And be spontaneous, yet gentle."

Know when to stop talking

"Now finally, we should not talk too much to our husband when he's busy or preoccupied. Of course when he's bored, he'll probably love us to chatter on. But we need to be sensitive."

"Watch for his little signs of restlessness. Remember he doesn't like to hurt our feelings by telling us to be quiet. He will enjoy our company much more if we instinctively know when to remain silent."

"Sometimes men need to be left entirely alone, such as when they're concentrating on a difficult task. Men do not like distractions when they are concentrating."

"We women can multi-task, but men like to apply all their concentration to a difficult task. They often become irritated when we try and converse with them when they are concentrating. Even though they love us. Sometimes they apologise afterward."

The enchanting effect your singing can have on your husband

"Any questions?"

Angela raised her hand. "Yes Angela?"

"I like to sing when I'm happy. How do men feel about us singing?"

"Oh, I'm glad you brought that one up Angela. How do they feel about our singing? They love it. When a husband hears his wife singing sweetly and happily, it uplifts his spirits. It inspires a feeling of pure love."

"There is probably no greater joy for a man than to hear his wife singing with a happy heart. Why? Because it's like pure admiration to him. It signals to him that you are happy with the life he is providing you."

Again Angela felt an awakening of truth. She had always loved to sing. But she had been so depressed the last two years she had seldom felt like singing, and especially not when Ted was around.

A vivid memory suddenly came to Angela's mind. It was soon after she and Ted were married. She had arisen early one weekend morning to catch up with her housework. She was in the lounge and her spirits were high. She was singing one of her favourite songs *'The Loveliest Night of the Year.'*

Ted came out of the bedroom into the lounge, still in his pyjamas and embraced her. He told her how much he loved her, and then he danced with her around the lounge, telling her to keep on singing.

Angela thrilled at the memory. She couldn't resist singing quietly to herself.

> *"When you are in love,"*
> *"It's the loveliest night of the year . . ."*
> *"Stars twinkle above . . ."*

"Elsie, you have a question," said the teacher.

"Yes. I know my husband loves to hear a woman sing. But what if you're like me and can't sing?"

"Oh that's nonsense Elsie. You can sing. I'll bet you sing beautifully in the shower."

"Well yes. Perhaps so. But that's different. Nobody's listening."

"The only difference is your self confidence Elsie," said the teacher. "Why not write yourself this message on your Goal List, *'I now enjoy singing in the presence of my husband.'* How does that sound?"

"Oh, I don't think I could do that," said Elsie, looking worried.

"Please try and do so Elsie. Once you've broken the ice it will be easier. It's truly delightful for a man to hear his wife sing. But we should try and stay in tune, and get the words right. Men like things to be technically correct, even in romantic matters."

"Now let's sum up the Fascinating Womanhood rules for femininity when speaking to men."

1. "We should always phrase our words positively and lovingly."

2. "Our voice should be cheerful, clear, confident and gentle."

3. "Our voice should have a melodious lilt to it, like we women use when talking to babies."

4. "We should be able to laugh freely and often, but not loudly."

"These qualities are feminine and highly appealing to men. But even more appealing is feminine singing and gentle, spontaneous, feminine laughter."

Feminine mannerisms that fascinate men

"Now we move on to feminine mannerisms. These are the natural female actions and gestures that so allure and fascinate men."

"Here again remember the Golden Rule 'WATCH WHAT MEN DO, AND DO THE OPPOSITE.'"

"Are our hand and wrist movements feminine and delicate? Do we make full use of our eyes. Men just adore feminine eye expressions, like widening our eyes, or rolling them, or fluttering our eyelashes. I am serious about this."

"And there's also the little girl pout, or tossing our hair. Charming to men. Even stamping our feet when we are angry, and folding our arms and turning away with our chin in the air. Fascinating to men. Don't ask me why. They just are."

"And what's our walk like? Men like to see us walk erect and smiling, with light, short steps. And they love women to be graceful, and supple, and relaxed, like a Tahitian Hula dancer. No striding, or swinging our arms. Why not Cherry?"

"Too masculine," said Cherry with a laugh.

"Exactly," smiled the teacher. "And the same with the way we sit, we shouldn't swing a leg up across our knee like men do. Or sit with our legs apart. Or stand with our hands in our pockets."

Avoid telling jokes

"Now we come to humour. We must be so very careful here. Humour can be a real minefield in our relationships with men."

"We should try and have a sunny, smiling sense of humour. And although it might be all right to gently tease a man now and then about his masculine traits when he's alone, we must never, never tease him or make a joke about him in the presence of other men or women."

"But whether done in private or public, unless our teasing or our joke makes a man feel more masculine, and that is rare, he will never appreciate it."

"In fact, if it mocks his masculinity in ANY way, he will be

When a woman dresses femininely, she tends to act femininely.

deeply hurt. HE MAY NEVER FORGET.”

“This is so serious to a man, that in a courting situation it can easily kill his developing love for a woman, stone dead.”

“His relationship with her will effectively end there and then. The woman is often mystified as to why, and the man will not reveal the real reason.”

“So please remember, teasing or joking with your husband, or any man, or your son, about his masculine shortcomings can seriously wound his pride.”

“Besides all this, a woman cracking jokes and making smart remarks in mixed company is seen as behaving in a masculine manner by most men. She is degraded as a woman in their eyes.”

Feminine clothing is highly appealing to men

“Next we move into the very, very important topic of our clothes. Never, ever under estimate the long term effect that your clothing can have on your husband’s feelings for you. It can have a profound, sub-concious effect on his relationship with you.”

“This is also another area, like our hair last week, where many women, especially married women, fail to make the most of their femininity. In fact, most women’s clothing nowadays repels men, rather than attracts them.”

“And men suffer away in silence. They just don’t like to criticise a woman’s appearance. Maybe our behaviour sometimes, but not our appearance. It’s not in their nature to do so.”

“Two wonderful exceptions are the way we dress our young daughters. And the way women from India dress with their colourful, feminine Sari’s. And we’ve all seen pictures of native African women in colourful, feminine clothing.”

“So here again is our standard.” And the teacher held up the picture of the young girl again. Dresses, frills and softness. Light or bright colours and patterns. Delicate, silky fabrics. Nice and feminine. When we dress femininely, we tend to act femininely.”

“Yes, I know it’s not fashionable. But women’s fashions don’t interest a man much, If at all. In fact some women’s fashion clothing is quite masculine. But most of it is feminine, but still not all that appealing to most men.”

“We should avoid all tailored styles. And any suggestion of masculinity such as cuffs, pockets and lapels. The more unlike men we are in our dress, the more attractive we are to them.”

“Men tend to wear dark, rather drab, coarse clothing. So they like us to wear light, colourful, soft clothing that enhances our feminine shape. Or clothes that flow over our bodies, like filmy gowns. Full length silky dresses can really appeal on social occasions.”

“We should avoid loose trousers, shorts, coats and jackets made from coarse material. Or any fabric similar to what men wear. or baggy clothes. They have no appeal to a man.

They repel men. Overalls would have to be the worst of all."

"We should also avoid heavy shoes and socks."

"What about jeans?" asked Angela, knowing in her heart what the answer would be.

"Very masculine Angela," said the teacher smiling. "Jeans, especially loose fitting ones, are drab and ugly, and manly in the eyes of most men. They won't say anything, but the depressing effect upon them is very real. And long term this can be very damaging to our relationship, especially if we dressed femininely while courting."

"Of course, there are times when we do need to wear trousers. On these occasions, lightweight cotton trousers, with bright, bold colours or patterns, and a leg hugging fit can look very attractive to men. Provided our figure is OK. But jeans and especially loose fitting slacks or trousers generally repel men."

"If you must wear them, wear something else, ultra-feminine to balance the masculine effect. A soft, colourful top maybe, or a hair ornament, or ribbon or earrings."

"Men also dislike seeing bra-straps, or other exposed underwear."

"And we should never be immodest in our dress. This is most important. Men will notice us all right, but they won't respect us. Men just do not respect women who expose their bodies in public. A man cannot love or respect a promiscuous women, no matter how much he may be sexually attracted to her body."

"We should also try and make some of our own clothing. A woman who makes her own clothes, especially dresses, is seen as ultra-feminine by men."

"Even more so when she adds little feminine touches of her own design. Her husband will love the fact that no other woman in the world has a dress quite like hers. It makes her extra special in his eyes.

Does your make-up look natural

Kathy raised her hand. "Yes Kathy?"

"Do you have any rules about make-up?"

"Yes Kathy. We should not overdo it. Make-up should enhance our fresh, natural look, which is so appealing to a man. Ideally a man should not even notice that we are wearing any make-up."

"Especially avoid excess blue around the eyes, and unnatural shades of lipstick. This sort of falsity deadens a man's ability to feel tenderness and love toward a woman."

"A man can still be attracted at a sexual level however by the message he believes a woman is conveying by her excess make-up."

"Perfume and excess jewellery also convey an image of falsity. They seriously detract from the fresh, naturalness that arouses a man's love."

"Some men hate perfume on a woman, especially when it's overdone. My husband is one of those men. He says that I

Don't do this when there is a man around to do it for you.

smell beautiful without perfume. So only a hint if you must wear perfume."

"Besides, cosmetics and jewellery can never compete with a warm smile and a feminine, melodious voice. More often they detract from them."

"Would perfume and jewellery enhance a father's love for his daughter? I think we all know the answer to that."

Why being dependent on your husband arouses his love

"Now the second part of Secret Number Eight is the powerful effect that our dependency has on a man. Being dependent on our husband can have an overpowering effect on him. It arouses his deepest love and protection. Few women realise how powerful an effect their dependency has on a man."

"Angela, you have a question?"

"Yes, what exactly do you mean by dependency?"

"Dependency is when we appear to a man to want his manly care and protection."

"Of course, this doesn't apply to our feminine role as homemakers and mothers. Men expect us to be, and need us to be, capable in these areas."

"But in all non-feminine areas of life, the more trusting in him we appear to be, the more lovable we become in his eyes."

"This is another one of those powerful, Fascinating Womanhood principles that can make all the difference in the world to our marriage. All the difference in the world as to whether our husband truly loves us. Let me state it this way:"

"THE MORE YOUR HUSBAND FEELS THAT YOU WANT HIS PROTECTION AND HIS MASCULINE ABILITIES, THE MORE LOVABLE AND APPEALING YOU BECOME TO HIM."

"When you depend on a man, his masculine feeling of strength and power is delightful to him, even overwhelming at times. He longs to gather you up in his arms and protect you forever."

"We women often feel like this toward little children when they're upset, or hurt, or lost. It's a powerful, emotional feeling. It creates and builds deep love."

"Young girls, with their natural air of helplessness in masculine things, arouse these powerful emotions in their fathers."

"And so it is also with our husband. When he feels that we trust him, and depend on him, it arouses within him powerful emotions and deep love."

"But even these powerful emotions can be blocked by resentment. So we must be sure to live the first four secrets of Fascinating Womanhood."

Ask him to help you in masculine matters

"Because of this principle, we are not imposing on a man

Asking a man to help you with heavy work allows him to feel masculine and thereby increases his love for you.

when we ask him to change a wheel on our car, or remove a spider. In fact it makes him feel manly."

"If he's still resentful towards you, or very busy, he might grumble a bit, but he'll feel a glow of masculine satisfaction and pride after he's helped you. And most important, his love for you will increase."

"And we shouldn't hide any fears from him that we have. Fear of the dark, or of spiders, or strange noises, or even heavy traffic. He might tease us a little when we tell him of these fears, but it will make him feel strong and masculine, especially when we cling to him fearfully."

Self-reliant women never win a man's heart

"Can you understand this important Fascinating Womanhood principle now? Deep love in a man develops when we ask a man to do masculine things for us. That's why we must stop doing men's work if at all possible. Especially when men are about. That includes heavy lifting and anything else that makes us feel less feminine."

"A woman who does not rely on men will never win a man's love. Have you ever noticed how most spinsters and feminists have an air of capability and self-reliance about them? No wonder they fail to win a man's heart. Men might respect the minds of such women, but they cannot love and cherish them."

"Yet the gentle, dependent woman attracts men like bees to a flower."

Appear helpless in masculine tasks

"Beth, you had you're hand up."

"Yes, but what if you ARE a capable woman? I mean I'm just not the dependent, incapable type."

"We don't have to be incapable Beth, just appear so to men, and only in masculine tasks. It comes naturally to most of us. Little girls are experts. It wasn't hard for us to get Daddy to pump up our bike tyres, or fix our punctures was it?"

"Let's be honest here, there is a degree of role playing in male-female relationships. Just as there is in good manners. Men know full well that in emergencies, most women can do masculine things reasonably well, but they still prefer us to act as we're helpless at masculine tasks. Things like working a spanner, or backing a car."

"Men role play too you know. They pretend to be helpless at feminine things, like changing a baby, or sewing on a button. They would rather not do these things because their make up is different. But they can do them alright if they have to, just as we can do masculine things if we have to."

"It's just like good manners, not essential, but life is easier and more pleasant."

"So always let your husbands, and your sons, feel that their masculine help and protection is needed and appreciated. Let them feel that you cannot get along without

A man's smile is his way of complimenting a woman. The more your husband smiles at you, the more he loves you, and the more fascinating you are becoming to him.

them. Men like to feel this way. Most of us women like to feel this way too, once we've become used to it again. I don't ever want to change a wheel. I even get my husband to fill up my car with petrol. I don't like working that heavy filler-up thing at the petrol station."

"You know, husbands who have self-reliant wives sometimes even go as far as to frighten them, by driving too fast, or taking them out in sail boats. Just to enjoy the feeling of protectiveness and masculinity that their wife's fear arouses in them."

Are men put off by intelligent women?

Beth raised her hand again. "Yes Beth?"

"If men are so brave, why are so many of them scared off by intelligent women?"

"Well Beth, I don't think it's so much a woman's intelligence that puts them off, it's more the masculine air of challenge that many intelligent women project."

"A woman will never make a man feel masculine by appearing to be more capable than he is in masculine matters, or by winning an argument against him."

"Also, many men have painful memories of their sensitive boyhood pride being crushed by woman school teachers."

"Is that why so many school teachers are spinsters?" asked Cherry with a cheeky grin.

The teacher smiled. "Intelligence is a priceless asset to a woman when she understands Fascinating Womanhood. An intelligent, educated woman can be highly fascinating to a man, as long as she does not belittle his masculinity."

"All we need to remember is, that men like to excel women in all masculine matters. You can safely excel your man in Music, or English, or Biology, but don't let him feel that you excel him in Maths or Engineering."

Child-like charm in a woman of any age is delightful to a man

"Well that's our lesson for tonight class. Femininity and Dependency. Two delightful qualities in a woman, in the eyes of most men."

"Too delightful for some men. Often a shy man will think himself unworthy of such a delightful creature. Beauty contest winners often report this fact. However that's more of a problem our unmarried daughters than ourselves."

"For us who already have a husband, let's remember what we were like as young girls. How excited we could become. Our sense of wonder. Our cuteness. Our pretty dresses and hairstyles. Our childlike innocence. Our delightful femininity."

"Men are highly attracted to childlike charm in women of any age. Just as we women are attracted to boyish enthusiasm in grown men."

"Re-awaken your childhood femininity if necessary. Try it out and see. You'll delight your husband and make him feel more masculine. And the more masculine you make him feel, the more he will love and cherish you."

Watch for his smile – a man's smile is his compliment to you

"Your husband may be too shy to compliment you. So watch instead for his smile. A man's smile is his way of complimenting a woman. The more your husband smiles at you, the more fascinating you are becoming to him."

Angela felt a warm reassurance inside. The last three times she had seen Ted, he had smiled at her.

"Now we have a lot of challenging feminine assignments for this week. The first one can be difficult. but is most important. Men generally don't like to say hurtful things about their wives. But be persistent, and give him plenty of time to think before answering. It can pay off richly."

"Assignment Number Five, the dress making one, is a long term thing. I don't expect it to be completed this week, but try and obtain the pattern book this week, and have your husband select a dress for you to make."

ASSIGNMENTS: SECRET NUMBER EIGHT

ASSIGNMENT ONE. Say to your husband in your own words, "Darling, I want to become more feminine for you. Please tell me the truth. What do you find the most unfeminine thing about me?"

When he has told you, phrase the solution positively, then add it to your Goal List. Repeat Assignment One as a New Year's resolution each year.

ASSIGNMENT TWO. For two whole days this week, think before speaking, and phrase every sentence that you say to your husband in a positive, loving way. And say it with a melodious voice and a smile. Observe the difference in his reaction.

ASSIGNMENT THREE. Sing in the hearing of your husband at least once this week.

ASSIGNMENT FOUR. Ask your husband to honestly analyse your entire wardrobe, including footwear, nightwear and swimwear and rate everything feminine, or unfeminine. Then discard, or plan to discard anything he finds unfeminine.

ASSIGNMENT FIVE. Have your husband choose what he considers to be an ultra-feminine dress from a pattern book, and make the dress yourself. Get assistance from another woman if necessary. Add some additional feminine touches to the dress, that your husband likes, to make it unique to you personally.

ASSIGNMENT SIX. Have your husband take back at least one masculine task that you have been doing. You might say. "I don't feel very feminine doing this."

"Any questions?" asked the teacher.

"Yes." said Helena. "What if my husband rates some of my wardrobe neutral?"

"Take it as a masculine rating Helena, but don't discard them. Remember, most men are reluctant to criticise."

"What I also recommend class, when you have been successful in having your husbands rate your wardrobe, ask them to go through all the things they have rated feminine again, and re-rate them for feminine appeal in their eyes. You might ask them to rate them as follows:

A He loves to see me wearing it.

B OK.

C He doesn't like to see me wearing it.

"Be prepared for some surprises. Any other questions?"

"I don't know about this singing assignment," said Elsie.

"Give it a try Elsie. Then watch for your husband's smile of approval. Remember everybody, your husband's smile is his way of complimenting you."

"I'm not very good at sewing," said Kathy. "I would love to make myself a dress, but I never learned how to dressmake."

"Invite a friend to help you Kathy. You'll enjoy it," said the teacher.

"I'll help you," said Bev. "I make most of my own clothes."

"Would you Bev?" said Kathy brightening up. "I'll take you up on that."

Beth spoke. "Yes, making a dress is something I've always wanted to do too. And would make a welcome change from all my studying. Most of my clothes aren't fitting me very well now. I could make myself a couple of maternity frocks over the Christmas break."

"The teacher smiled. "I made this dress I'm wearing tonight, with the help of a friend. My husband chose it from a pattern book. He also chose the material from samples I brought home to him. He loves me wearing it."

"Our visitors tonight are two delightfully feminine women, Mary and Sally. Mary can we hear from you first?"

Mary. True Experience.
"Let me tell you how discarding a brown dress changed my marriage."

"I have a particular brown dress which I find much pleasure in wearing. It's a house dress, and oh so comfortable. After I had worn it for some time, my husband let me know of his great dislike for it. I continued wearing it anyway, thinking, 'Oh well, it's only at home."

"Then I noticed my husband began to come home

with what seemed a negative attitude. Then the thought occurred to me, I had been wearing that awful brown dress a lot lately, due to much spring cleaning. My home sparkled, but I did not look "younger than springtime."

"Well, I got busy and bought a pattern for a very feminine house dress, with soft gathers at the scooped neckline and peasant sleeves. I made several of them so that I would have no excuses."

"That night when he came home, the look of approval on his face was something to see. He smiled and asked if this meant that I would throw the 'old brown bag' away? I didn't give him a definite answer. I'm going to cut the brown dress in half, wrap it up and give it to him on Mothers Day. Yes even a dress can change a marriage."

Sally. True Experience.

"My husband is charming, handsome and lovable. When we met, I felt 'Sir Galahad' had come to fetch me away."

"But not long after we were married, he started to become a little aloof, calculating and guarded. After a few years of his cooled manner I wondered if our marriage had a future."

"I puzzled over the problem for a year, picking up all the advice I could find."

"Then I came across Fascinating Womanhood. My first step was to 'turn his dull side away, and concentrate on his bright side'. That step warmed him slightly."

"My clothes seemed a weak point. Few things in my wardrobe were feminine, light, airy, childlike or charming. So I decided to wear only those few and to give the rest away."

"I have an outfit which can be worn with either skirt or pants. If I wear the skirt he compliments me, but with the pants he says nothing."

"Then I wore one of my few feminine dresses, went to him and said softly, 'May I stop doing the heavy work around here in order to become more of a woman for you?' He seemed flattered, approved of it, and has ever since taken care of it, hiring men where desirable. What a relief to say goodbye to it."

"I continued to follow the recipe for femininity, gentleness, tenderness, delicacy. After a few weeks my husband remarked. 'How feminine you've become, especially lately."

"Our marriage is much improved. He now confides in me easily. He is more generous with his heart and with his money. The mood is sunny. A million thanks Fascinating Womanhood."

"And a million thanks to you both Sally and Mary. It is just so true that opposites attract. To attract and delight men, we must be as unlike them as possible."

"See you all next week. Good night everybody."

"As Cherry drove Angela home, they enthusiastically discussed what they had learned the past few weeks in their class."

Angela felt a growing friendship bond with Cherry. Being a rather reserved woman herself, she enjoyed Cherry's lively, outgoing company. She sensed that Cherry also enjoyed her company.

They also lived near to one another and Angela felt that they were destined to become close friends.

CHAPTER TWELVE

Secret Number Nine
Just ask with a smile

SATURDAY morning dawned clear and sunny. Angela awoke early and went for her run.

Today she managed to run a full twenty minutes before getting puffed. She walked a few minutes to recover, then ran the five minutes back home.

After showering, she began sorting through all her clothing. She put to one side all her masculine, dark coloured slacks and heavy sweaters.

At the back of the wardrobe, she saw her bright red, flared dress with frilly white sleeves and neck. Ted had bought her that dress during their courtship.

Angela had not been able to fit it, since becoming pregnant with David. However she was now slimmer than she had been in years, so she decided to try it on. It was tight around her hips and breasts, but Angela was thrilled that she was even able to fit into the dress.

She also put on the wide, white vinyl belt that went with the dress. By holding her breath she could buckle it up to the belt hole she had used when she was still single.

Angela admired herself in the mirror. She looked good. The fat roll around her waist was almost gone, and her upper arms and hips were noticeably slimmer.

She decided there and then to set herself a goal to lose enough weight over the next few days to wear the dress, fitting comfortably, to the next Fascinating Womanhood class.

Angela was able to smile at her reflection in the mirror, something she usually found impossible to do. Her spirits soared. She felt like singing aloud. "Why not?" she thought. "It's one of my Assignments for this week anyway."

"Oh, what a beautiful morning,"
"Oh, what a beautiful day."
"I've got a wonderful feeling,"
"Everything's going my way."

Angela continued to sing as she prepared breakfast cereal for herself and the children.

Her high spirits were contagious. When David and Tiphony came into the dining room they were both smiling broadly.

"You're happy this morning Mum," said David.

"Yes. It's a beautiful morning David," Angela said in a melodious voice. "I feel happy, and I love you both very much." She put her arms around them both and kissed them on their cheeks, first one side, then the other.

David was a little embarrassed, but his smile was even wider as he sat down to eat his breakfast.

Angela walked to class again on Wednesday evening. She wore her red dress with the white belt.

Since Saturday morning she had halved all of her meals. And had gone for a run every morning and every evening. Every night she had slept like a baby.

The red dress now fitted her perfectly.

Also her hair was now long enough to gather up into a small pony tail. Just as her father had liked it when she was a young woman.

As she walked along a main street, a car full of noisy young men drove by. They sounded the horn and whistled at her. Angela felt both embarrassed and flattered. This was the first time that had happened since she had married.

As she walked through the downtown area, she met Brian, a friend of Ted's, coming out of a restaurant doorway.

"Hi Angela," he said with a broad smile and glancing her up and down with obvious approval.

"Hello Brian," said Angela with a melodious lilt in her voice and smiled back at him.

"Wow! You look nice tonight. Can I give you a ride somewhere?"

"Thank you Brian. But I'm just going up the road a little further."

"How's Ted?"

"He's fine."

"Oh well. See you round Angela."

"See you Brian."

Angela walked on, feeling pleased. Feminine instinct told her that Brian had found her attractive.

Angela was early for her class, one of the first in the classroom. As the other women arrived one by one, Angela noticed that all of them were dressed femininely this evening. Up until now, most had worn trousers.

Tonight, all wore dresses, or skirts, except Cherry, who wore snug fitting, cream slacks with a bold orange pattern.

A young girl instinctively knows how to obtain her needs from her father.

Cherry also wore a yellow blouse and a small matching yellow scarf around her hair, which was French plaited down her back. Even Beth wore a white frock.

The Fascinating Womanhood teacher was obviously delighted. "How lovely you all look tonight," she said. Her eyes were shining, "And very fascinating to men," she added.

"Now, who has a feminine experience to share with us?"

Nearly the entire class raised their hands, including Angela.

"Beth, let's hear from you, and then Angela. And let's also hear from you too Helena, and you too Marina. We only have a short lesson tonight."

Beth. True Experience.

"I decided to try getting dressed up instead of being in slacks. Not that my husband ever complained about my slacks. But when I put on a dress, he said, "Gee, its nice to see you look like a girl once in a while. You sure do look pretty."

"And he's right Beth." said the teacher. "You look do look pretty in that white frock."

Beth smiled demurely and sat down.

Angela then stood and told the class how her weight was now down to the level of when she was single. And how she was able to speed up her weight loss in just a few days, by halving her meals and running morning and night. And how she was achieve her goal of being able to fit the red dress she was wearing. She also told of the whistles she received while walking to class and the compliment from Brian.

Helena. True Experience.

"I remember some years ago now, my husband had been rough and tumbling with our boys and my daughter wanted to be in on the fun. As soon as he grabbed her he felt the difference, her frailty, and he was automatically gentle, and even afraid to play with her for fear of being too rough and hurting her."

"I remember asking him why he didn't treat me with the same gentleness he did her. He said, "You know, somehow you lost your femininity when you'd disagree with me, and shout so loudly when we'd quarrel."

"That hurt, but I now admit it was true. In those days I had to fight not to be a door mat. Now I know better. I have come to realise my mistakes. I am regaining my feminine status in my husband's eyes. I am building him up and being more feminine. I can see his eager response."

Marina. True Experience.

"I enjoy sewing and I make most of my own clothes. But the other day my husband commented on the feminine dress I had made for last weeks assignment."

"He told me how much he appreciated me looking nice for him. He also said he hoped I'd never stop doing this."

"Then he asked me if I would please have my picture taken by a professional studio, as he wanted a wallet size, and a big photograph of me. We've been married for years and he never before asked for a picture."

Marina's gentle, dark eyes glistened with tears as she sat down.

"Oh I could listen to your success stories all night," said the teacher. "Thank you all so much."

"Now tonight's secret teaches us how to get our husband to say yes, when we ask him for things we need. Or ask him to do something for us."

She turned to the board and wrote:

SECRET NUMBER NINE
To obtain your wants from your husband, just ask with a smile, as a young girl asks her father

Some of the class laughed.

"You mean I should sit on his knee?" said Cherry with a giggle.

"Why not Cherry?" said the teacher. "That's a delightful way to ask your husband for something you need."

"This secret is so simple. Getting your husband to say yes is easy when you know how. But most women don't know how. They ask the wrong way and get turned down most of the time. And they often irritate their husbands at the same time."

How to ask for what you want

"Now, when we were young girls, did we have any difficulty getting what we needed from our fathers? No?"

"How does a young girl get what she wants from her father? It's simple. She just asks him, with a smile."

"Just a simple request. No reasons. Just "Daddy will you please?" Or "Daddy can I please?""

"No hinting. No explaining. No justifying. No arguing the point. Just a simple ask, with a smile and a please. And maybe a touch."

"Or sit on his knee," said Cherry with a grin.

"Yes, a young girl will sometimes sit on her daddy's knee when she asks for something. Or hold his hand, or put her arm around his neck."

"But the most important thing is the simple request, with a smile and a please."

Angela again felt the peaceful, inner confirmation come over her, that what she was hearing was truth. She recalled that this was the way she used to ask her father for her needs. And he always seemed to delight in pleasing her. Yet would it work with Ted? A thrilling idea began to form in her mind.

Respect his position of leadership

"Why do you think this way of asking is so effective class?" asked the teacher.

Marina raised her hand. "Yes Marina?"

"Because a little girl is trusting, and depends on her father so much. She makes him feel strong and masculine, just like we've been learning about."

"A very good answer Marina. Yes class, Marina is right. The way a young girl asks, shows that she respects her father's authority. She allows her father to enjoy his manly role as leader and provider. He just can't help but want to please her."

"Exactly the same approach works for us with our husbands. Why? Because when we ask submissively, we place him in his proper role of leadership. We make him feel masculine and strong."

"Therefore our husband will want to do what we ask of him, if he's able to do so. And he will enjoy doing it for us, especially the satisfying feeling he gets from pleasing us. And what's more, his love for us will also increase."

"A man will go to great lengths to satisfy the desires of the woman he loves. The more submissive and dependent on him she is, the greater will be his desire to please her."

"But here again, this is only true when our husband is completely free of resentment toward us."

"Many women actually arouse resentment in the ways they ask their husband for things."

Do you make these common mistakes?

"How do most women ask for things from their husbands?"

Kathy raised her hand. "Yes Kathy?"

"I'm probably typical of most women," said Kathy, flashing her cheeky grin. "If I want something from my husband, I'll usually start off by hinting for what I want. Then I'll make suggestions. Then if that doesn't work, and I still don't get what I want, I'll start demanding and arguing. And nagging, until hopefully he gives in to what I want, just to get some peace."

"A good answer Kathy. And thank you for being so honest. Yes, so many women do follow that kind of procedure. First the hinting. Does that work? Not often, does it?"

"What about suggesting? Yes, that can work sometimes. If our husband is in a good mood and what we want will benefit him too."

"What about demanding? No. That really stirs up resentment in a man."

"And arguing? Highly ineffective. It even encourages his opposition. Most men can shoot down any number of logical reasons we put forward. Men are very good at that."

"But they only do it to protect their position as leader. For by arguing with a man, we are telling him that we do not respect his judgement. He can only salvage his sensitive male pride by bettering us in an argument."

"Nagging only makes matters much, much worse. Nagging causes deep resentment in a husband. And in us too, if we don't get our way."

"And when our husband does eventually give in and we get our own way, it's at the expense of his love for us. His pride is so badly wounded, that his heart will be full of resentment for days, or weeks. Even years for some men. It's so important we don't make those common mistakes."

Simply ask submissively with a smile and a please

"But what a huge contrast when we ask the Fascinating Womanhood way. Just a simple request. With a smile and a please, and a melodious voice."

"There's no need to explain why we need what we're asking for. It's enough for most men that it's our wish."

"When you ask this way, you'll usually obtain an immediate favourable response. And you'll also feel the warmth of his love for you."

"Why is this so? It's because of a noble quality that God has placed in the hearts of men. This principle is so important to understand I want to write it on the board." The teacher turned and wrote:

> "A man loves a woman more, when
> he can do things to please her, and
> when he can sacrifice for her."

"This is a wonderful truth of Fascinating Womanhood. The more your husband feels he is pleasing you, the more he will love and cherish you."

Why its better for your husband to spoil you

"Therefore, we shouldn't hesitate to ask for our needs. We shouldn't be too self-sacrificing. It's better for our husband to spoil us a little."

"We women are inclined to do without things. We take comfort in feeling self-righteous. But when we do this, we rob our husband of his joy of pleasing us."

"Oh this is so important to realise. THE MORE OUR HUSBAND FEELS HE IS PLEASING US, THE DEEPER HIS LOVE FOR US WILL GROW."

Things you shouldn't ask for

"Elsie, you had a question."

"Yes. There must be some things we shouldn't ask for?"

"Yes Elsie, there ARE a few things we shouldn't ask for. There are some things that should come freely from a man's heart. Things like love, and tenderness, and most gifts. Or to be taken out somewhere."

"These things are only of real value when given from our

Your husband will love you more if you let him spoil you a little.

husband's heart, without us asking. They will come when we live Fascinating Womanhood to its fullest."

Asking for gifts

"Now let's speak about gifts. For major anniversaries, like your birthday, or Christmas, where you know from tradition that your husband is going to buy you a gift, you can ask in advance for what you want. He'll probably be relieved. Most men dislike the uncertainty and difficult decisions of shopping for gifts."

"But all other gift occasions should be spontaneous. They will also mean so much more to you. Some men will ask what you want. Others will prefer to surprise you."

"If he does ask you what you want, just tell him with a smile. Don't try and justify it. Just say to him you would love that for a gift. It's just what you want right now."

"You can even offer to buy it on his behalf. He will probably again be relieved. Most men are not very good shoppers for women's gifts anyway. And many of them hate that kind of shopping."

"But we shouldn't ask him for things he really can't afford, except on exceptional occasions. Like getting our teeth fixed for example."

"Nor should we ask him to do anything, or buy anything that demeans his masculinity. Or goes against his principles."

Why many men are reluctant to buy gifts

"Now while we're talking about gifts, we should understand that many men dislike the commercial obligation of having to buy gifts on occasions like Mother's Day, Valentine's Day and even Anniversary Days. And as I said before, many men don't like gift shopping."

"If your husband has these feelings, accept them. but tell him you no longer require him to give you gifts on these occasions."

"I can see from some of your frowns that this might be hard to do. But he will be greatly relieved, and may buy gifts for you impulsively. Or more likely, he will show his love for you in many other ways, such as being especially kind and thoughtful, or taking you out, or taking you on holidays."

"Whatever he does for you, show your appreciation with feminine joy."

How to show feminine appreciation

"This is so important. Whenever your husband has done something for you, or given you a gift, you must show your appreciation to him in a feminine way."

"How do we do this? How do young girls show their appreciation to their fathers?"

Cherry raised her hand. "Yes Cherry?"

"Well when my little girl gets a present from her Daddy, she gets excited. She jumps up and down. Her eyes sparkle.

Sometimes she claps her hands. Then she gives him a big hug and a kiss."

The teacher beamed. "That's right Cherry. They become exuberant don't they? Sometimes they exaggerate and say that their gift is the best, or prettiest thing in the whole world. And what happens? Daddy gets a grin of pleasure from ear to ear."

"Men love grown women to be exuberant too. Just like young girls. They find it fascinating and delightful. They just love us to get excited over the things they do for us. It's very feminine in their eyes."

Childlike exuberance when showing your appreciation will gladden and thrill his masculine heart.

"When we behave this way, they enjoy pampering us and spoiling us. Our joy and our pleasure is their reward."

"A formal *"Thank you."* Or worse, *"That's too expensive"* won't encourage our husband to be generous."

"But your childlike joy, or even tears of joy, will gladden and thrill his heart. You will make him feel manly and protective."

"I know many women are serious, or reserved by nature, but we can still awaken the child deep within us. Even the most serious children can show exuberance, smiles and spontaneity."

"Singing in the presence of our husband can help us become more outgoing. That reminds me, how are you coming along with that assignment Elsie?"

"Oh Harmony, I'm still trying to gather up enough courage," said Elsie. "But I have started my Goal List, and I've put that at the top of the list."

"In that case I'm sure you'll soon be doing it Elsie. Goal lists are powerful things."

Why some men won't work around the home

Sonia raised her hand and spoke shyly. "I believe what you say about asking for things like young girls do. My father still does anything for me that I ask. But if I ask my partner to mow the lawns, he says he will, but most times he doesn't. If I didn't do them they'd be knee high. It's the same with most of the other man's work around our house. But he'll soon go and help someone else if they come and ask him."

The teacher smiled. "I've heard this problem so many times before Sonia."

"There are four main reasons why a man won't work around the home. Fascinating Womanhood can overcome them all."

"First reason. He does not have the energy. He may be overworking outside the home, or be in poor health, or he might be heavily overweight."

"Second reason. He is depressed, because of overwhelming problems. Depression saps a man's energy and is a very common cause of apparent laziness."

"Third reason. He does not have the skills, or the money to

do what is required, and is too proud to admit it."

"Fourth reason. He feels resentful toward his wife and does not feel like pleasing her in any way."

How to have your husband attend to work around the home

"Living Fascinating Womanhood should overcome all these reasons for a man not working around the home. "

"Unless your husband is elderly, his health and energy levels will usually greatly improve. And because of this, his income often improves also. So if he has not got the skills to do the work himself, he can afford to pay another man to do it."

There are four main reasons why a man won't work around the home. Fascinating Womanhood can overcome them all.

"We should appreciate however that not all men are natural home handymen. Some men are born organisers. Some are artistic. Some are highly intellectual. Some work hard in business and professions outside the home. These types of men often prefer to hire other men to do the work around the home. My own husband is one of these."

"However these husbands are exceptions. Most men are capable, and learn quickly and get much satisfaction from doing the masculine work around the home."

"As far as the fourth reason is concerned, when a man begins to love his wife deeply, and becomes totally free of resentment toward her, he will go to great lengths to please her."

"Now let's get back to Sonia's situation. We should not tell our husband to do regular jobs that he clearly knows are his responsibility, like mowing the lawns. He can see when they need mowing."

"Rather, we should live and apply the Fascinating Womanhood principles to overcome the four common reasons that hold a man back."

"If we nag him and then end up doing the work for him, he will have no incentive to change."

"Now having said that, we do of course need to ask our husband to take care of things that he's unaware of. Let's suppose the tap in the laundry starts leaking. How do we let him know about it and have him to take care of it?"

"Simple. We just ask him as a young girl would ask her father in a similar situation. A young girl might say, "Daddy, my bike's got a puncture. Will you fix it for me please.""

"So we could say, in a melodious voice, "Darling, the tap in the laundry is leaking. Will you fix it for me please.""

"Or, if you know he hasn't the skills to do it himself and will need to arrange a plumber, you could say, "Will you get it fixed for me please.""

"Now don't say these words to him as questions. But say them in a tone of cheerful expectancy and finality. So that you communicate to him that you trust him to take care of it for you."

"However, because men often forget to repair things that

are not directly bothering them, also put a note somewhere where he'll see it every day. Or put the thing to be fixed where he will constantly see it."

"Don't remind him again unless you're certain he's forgotten."

How to give up man's work

"Now if you've been doing a man's job for years, habits will have been formed. Your husband is likely to be reluctant to take the job back. Most men are lazy to a degree. So here's what to do."

"First, you must be fulfilling your women's role one hundred percent. Then say to your husband something like this, "Darling, I don't feel very feminine doing this job. It's man's work. You can do it much better than I can.""

"Then let it go. Say no more about it. Turn your back on the job forever. COME WHAT MAY."

"Don't try and reason with him. His logical male mind will shoot down your reasons one by one. Always say, 'I feel.' Men find that feminine, if somewhat illogical. And they can't argue with it."

How to have your husband complete jobs that get left and left

Kathy raised her hand. "Yes Kathy?"

"What if there's a really big job that you know your husband's been putting off and off. Something he's said he'll do, but it looks like it'll be years before he gets around to doing it, if ever? Like building the outdoor deck my husband promised us two years ago. The timber's been sitting there since last Christmas."

The teacher smiled. "Well yes, there is a Fascinating Womanhood technique for getting action in these kinds of situations. It's a bit cheeky, but we are within our rights as a wife. And our husbands will feel satisfaction when the difficult job is completed."

"It takes some nerve and a knack for timing. But there's an old and true story that illustrates this technique. It concerns Abraham Lincoln's stepmother."

"Abraham Lincoln's real mother lived with her husband Tom Lincoln in a little log cabin with a dirt floor. She was a meek lady and Tom Lincoln was somewhat lazy. He never got round to building her a wooden floor."

"She eventually died. In due course Tom Lincoln married again. His new wife's name was Sarah. She was a more assertive woman. When Tom Lincoln brought her home to the log cabin, along with a wagonload of her fine furniture, she took one look at the dirt floor and then said in a pleasant voice, 'Oh my goodness Tom. I couldn't think of bringing in all my nice things on this dirt floor. I will just leave them in the wagon and you can build me a wooden floor tomorrow.'"

"Did Tom build her a wooden floor the next day? Yes he did. Why?"

"Firstly. Because she was within her rights as a wife."

"Secondly. She was pleasant and feminine in making her request."

"Thirdly. It was a clear, simple request with a time limit."

"Fourthly and most important. The furniture sitting outside embarrassed Tom into applying urgency."

"We can use similar situations in our own homes to have our husbands complete those jobs that tend to get left and left. When visitors are coming to stay is a good time to apply this technique."

"But always be within your rights."

"Always be pleasant and feminine."

"Always respect your husband's authority."

Sarah Lincoln, step-mother of Abraham Lincoln. An assertive woman who obtained a wooden floor from her somewhat lazy husband.

When you're unhappy with your husbands' choice

"Any other questions?"

"Yes," said Helena. "Sometimes my husband and I will go shopping to look at something he wants to buy for the home, or for me. And he likes it, but I don't. How do I handle a situation like that?"

"Good question Helena. For the answer, let's return to our young girl and her father ideal."

"A young girl is honest and outspoken. What would she say to her father in such a situation? She would simply tell him the truth wouldn't she? She would say, "I don't want that one Daddy.""

"So all we need to say is something like, "Darling, I don't want that one.""

"It's not necessary to give our reasons. Our husband may start shooting them down again, and then feel offended if we don't agree with him."

"As long as we are honest and pleasant, our husband won't be offended. Remember, he wants to please us."

"When we're open and honest with him, he knows for sure that we're happy with what he does for us."

How to give feminine advice

"Now, you might remember during our Secret Number Four lesson, the one about allowing our husband to lead, I said we would learn in this Ninth Secret how to give feminine advice."

"We sometimes need to do this, perhaps when our husband asks us for our opinion on something, or when we can see that he's about to make a serious mistake."

"We should also speak up if we feel that our husband is not making full use of his ability to do good in the world."

"Remember, men expect we women to be more noble than them in such matters. God has given women the power to motivate men to rise to greater and more noble heights then

they would otherwise achieve."

"However, giving advice should only be done on rare occasions. Our words will then carry much more weight. Most of the time it's best to say nothing and to let our husband have free rein as leader."

"It can be better for us to put up with the consequences of a few bad decisions, than to risk wounding our husband's sensitive pride, and causing resentment."

"So here's how to give feminine advice to our husband. Or any other man for that matter, including our sons."

"First. Always use non-challenging words like *"I feel"* or *"I like."* Don't use words like *"I know"* or *"I think."*

"Second. Phrase what you have to say in non-challenging questions, such as, *"Have you ever considered?"* or *"Do you think (such and such) might work?"*

A woman sometimes need to give a man advice, but it should only be done on rare occasions.

"Third. Always allow him to remain dominant in the conversation. For example, don't draw conclusions from what has been discussed, or sum up. Let him feel that he's the leader and you are his counsellor."

"And lastly, three more don'ts:"

"Don't speak as if you know more than he does."

"Don't offer too many suggestions."

"Don't ask too many questions."

Gain your deepest, most heartfelt desires

"Well that's Secret Number Nine class. How to obtain your needs from your husband. And increase his love for you at the same time."

"Remember, your husband will love you more if you let him spoil you a little."

"His reward is your childlike, feminine and enthusiastic response, and his feeling of manliness as you show your pleasure for what he's done for you."

"Fascinating Womanhood doesn't ask us to become self-sacrificing doormats to our husbands. We give up nothing worthwhile in living these secrets. On the contrary, we gain our deepest, most heartfelt desires."

"Most of all, we enjoy a warm, loving relationship with our man that just grows richer and deeper as time goes by."

"Just one pleasant little assignment this week."

ASSIGNMENT: SECRET NUMBER NINE

Think of something you really want and deserve and ask your husband for it in a simple, direct, childlike manner. When he has agreed to it, show your appreciation in a lively, feminine manner.

"Our two charming visitors tonight are Valerie and Hinemoa. Let's hear from you first Valerie.

Valerie. True Experience.

"After 15 years and three beautiful children our

marriage was in serious trouble. My sister introduced me to Fascinating Womanhood. My first impression was, 'It may work for others, but it will never solve our problems."

"We had long forgotten the little courtesies extended to each other during courtship and early marriage. We had even talked of divorce."

"I was the domestic type. Not once in all those years had my husband introduced me or referred to me as his wife, it was always "the missus" or even worse, "the boss."

"Willing to try anything to save our marriage, I started to live Fascinating Womanhood."

"Surprising results started to happen. Imagine how thrilled I was when he proudly introduced me to an acquaintance saying, "I want you to meet my wife." It sounded like music to my ears. Now, no matter where we go, he can't say "my wife" often enough."

"Ours is a happy home now. The children are more thoughtful and happy. My husband has even started bringing me chocolates and flowers, and telling me that he truly loves me. Love reigns supreme. I bless the day I heard about Fascinating Womanhood."

Hinemoa. True Experience.

"I was destroying my husband and our marriage by trying to change him. I was trying so hard to change him that love was being replaced by emotional and physical abuse."

"Of course, before Fascinating Womanhood I was too self-righteous and proud to even consider that I was the one who was wrong. Because of my pride it was hard to take the first step. But, oh how rewarding each step has been. There is a sparkle in his eyes now that I haven't seen since the early days of our marriage."

"What an unspeakable joy it was the night he took me in his arms and told me how he loved me. It had been so long since I heard those beautiful words."

"For the first time in years, I'm beginning to feel like the woman I've dreamed of being."

Thank you so much Valerie and Hinemoa. It's wonderful to hear how well everything is going for you both."

"Now next week is our last lesson. Would anyone like to bring along a cake to celebrate?"

"I'll make us all a cream sponge," said Bev.

"Mmmm, that sounds nice," said the teacher.

"But we won't let you eat any of it Bev," said Cherry with a laugh. "We're all going to make sure you fit that new dress your husband's going to buy for you."

"Of course she can have some Cherry," said the teacher. "You can run an extra mile afterward, can't you Bev? How is your running going? You do look slimmer."

Bev looked pleased. "Would you believe I've lost three kilograms, and I'm still eating the same amount of food as before. But I eat it mostly for breakfast and lunch and just have a light meal at night."

"Excellent Bev," said the teacher. "If you really want to speed up your weight loss, just eat the same way you are now, but only half as much food. Just like Angela did this week to fit her dress. But especially cut down the white flour and sugar. They are highly fattening."

"Well, I might just try that," said Bev.

"We can go out running together sometime Bev," said Cherry.

"Let me get fitter first Cherry," said Bev. "I'm going to ask my husband for a pair of running shoes this week. I'll try out what I've learned tonight."

The teacher smiled approvingly at Bev.

Then the teacher said, "Now for those of you who haven't yet completed all your assignments, please make a special effort to catch up by next week."

Angela felt excited as Cherry drove her home.

She said to Cherry, "If only I had known this secret before. It's so simple. Just a smile and a please. That's the way I used to ask my father for things. He would do anything for me."

"Yes, my daughter even asks me for things that way too," said Cherry. "And I love doing the things she asks me to. As long as it's good for her of course."

When Angela awoke next morning, it was clear in her mind what she should do.

She had pondered for the past two weeks on the best way to persuade Ted to come back home to her. She had rehearsed the arguments and reasons she might use.

But Ted had always 'shot down' her arguments in the past, as the teacher had so aptly put it.

She was thinking of putting her best reasons into a letter and giving it to Ted, but after last nights lesson she could clearly see now that it was wrong.

All she needed to do was to simply ask him. Just like a child. It would also fulfil this week's Assignment.

Angela decided she would be bold and do it that very evening.

Most of that day at school she was nervous and felt sick with worry in her stomach. She had not had any breakfast and did not feel hungry.

Fears kept running through her mind. What would Ted say tonight? What if he laughed at her? What if he was in a bad mood? What if he got angry with her? What if he had just found another woman? She wondered if she still could go through with it.

Finally she remembered the comforting power of prayer. She sat on a seat under some trees in the school grounds during the morning play break and offered a silent prayer for courage. Immediately she felt a negative oppression lift from her. She became much calmer and was impressed to leave it all in the hands of God, come what may.

Angela also felt that she should continue fasting from food all day.

That evening, after preparing a meal for David and Tiphony, Angela put on her red dress, tied a white ribbon in her hair, and drove alone and anxious to Ted's flat.

She saw his van parked up the driveway. The driver's door was open.

She said another earnest prayer aloud in her car, that everything would work out for the best.

Then leaving her car out on the street, she walked up the gravel driveway. Her heart was beating fast and her hands were clammy.

Just as she reached Ted's flat, Ted came out the front door, wearing his overalls and carrying his laptop computer. He was obviously surprised to see Angela. But he smiled at her and put his computer in the van. Then he closed the van door and turned and looked expectantly at Angela.

Angela swallowed, tried to smile, then said in a quavery voice. "Ted, please come home and look after me." Then she burst into tears.

Ted was silent for a few seconds. Then Angela saw his lower lip quiver and his eyes fill with tears. Instinctively she flew into his arms and he held her tight. They both stood there hugging and weeping openly. Then Ted lifted Angela up in his arms and carried her inside the flat.

"Of course I'll come home Angie" he said. "Of course I'll come home." Tears were still running down his face. "My fridge has broken down anyway," he added with a silly grin.

He stood Angela down on the floor then recovered his composure quickly. "I'll move back tomorrow night Angie."

Then he smiled at her and said, "Isn't that the dress I bought you years ago?"

Angela nodded and wiped her eyes. "Oh Ted, I'll be the best wife in the whole world. I promise."

As Angela drove home, the lump in her throat disappeared and she began to feel elated. It all seemed so unreal. Like a dream.

When she told David and Tiphony that Dad was coming home, David became highly excited and did cartwheels in the lounge. Tiphony hugged her mother and cried with joy.

Later that evening, after David and Tiphony had gone to bed, Angela heard what sounded like Ted's van come up the driveway. Cautiously she went to the door and peeped out.

Suddenly Ted loomed up out of the darkness, lugging two suitcases and grinning all over his face.

"I couldn't wait till tomorrow," he said.

"Is that Dad?" called David's voice from his bedroom. Then

David came running out, followed by Tiphony.

"Hi David. Hi Tiphony," said Ted, "Dad the King's home."
He caught them both up together in his arms and hugged
them tightly.

CHAPTER THIRTEEN

Secret Number Ten
Handle anger femininely

ANGELA felt like a new bride for the next few days.

At first Ted was reserved. But Friday evening, when Angela comforted him after he came home from work, he began to speak more freely, and to confide in her.

Ted spent all day Saturday catching up with the repairs around the home. He also fixed the lawn mower and mowed the lawns. Angela found several opportunities to admire his masculine skills. Ted gave a shy grin each time she did so.

On Sunday morning, Angela wondered if she should ask Ted to take her and the children to church. But she thought it best to wait a little longer, or wait until he offered.

He did not offer, but he did take them all around to visit Angela's mother in the afternoon.

On Monday, after work, Ted brought his laptop computer and printer home. Later that evening, he sat at the dining room table and began using the computer to do his business accounts. To Angela's surprise he seemed very much at ease and confident in what he was doing.

When she praised his ability, Ted became highly enthusiastic and spent a long time showing her all that he could do with the business program he was using.

Angela knew more about computers than she let on, but was still impressed with the way Ted had mastered the program.

She however made up her mind not to have anything to do with the business, unless Ted asked her. She would keep herself free from masculine business concerns so that Ted could come home each day to a feminine, cheerful wife and be comforted.

Angela began to find the intimate side of marriage better than it had been for years. Being free of resentment, she was able to respond freely to Ted. Nor did she mind if she became pregnant again.

Ted had always wanted more children, but Angela had resisted this in the past. She feared what her friends might say. She had also wanted to be free to go out to work if necessary.

But now that she understood her feminine role fully, and had seen the joy and fulfilment of the Fascinating Womanhood teacher and Elsie, with their large families in their mature years, she realised how short sighted she had been.

Wednesday evening was Angela's final Fascinating Womanhood class. It was raining. After the evening meal, as she was clearing the table and the children were lying on the carpet doing their homework, Ted offered to drive her to the class.

Angela was about to say, "It's OK Ted, I can drive myself," when she remembered how a man enjoys helping a dependant and appreciative woman.

So instead, she smiled at him and said, "That would be lovely Ted," Then she walked over to where he was sitting in his chair, reading the paper. She put her arm softly around his neck and kissed him on the cheek. Ted smiled.

As Angela kissed him, she felt the prickles of his evening beard growth. She was about to say, "You need a shave." Then she remembered Secret Number One, 'Accept him as he is' and said nothing.

As she finished clearing the table, she congratulated herself on how she was gaining a good understanding of the Fascinating Woman principles.

Feeling pleased with how everything was going, she hummed as she worked. Then she began to sing aloud a song she loved, 'My Favourite Things.'

> *"Rain drops on roses, and whiskers on kittens."*
> *"Bright copper kettles, and warm woollen mittens."*
> *"Brown paper packages, tied up with strings."*
> *"These are a few of my favourite things."*

Angela went into the kitchen and was still singing as she stacked the dishwasher. Suddenly she felt Ted's long arms encircle her from behind and hug her strongly. Then she felt him lift up her hair and kiss the back of her neck.

"I really do love you Angie," he whispered.

Angela turned her head and saw Ted's eyes full of warmth and tenderness.

Ted returned to the lounge and Angela's heart almost burst with happiness. A lump came to her throat and tears of joy trickled down her cheeks.

Ted always liked to be early for appointments, so he drove Angela to her class ahead of time. The rain had now become a drizzle. They arrived just as the Fascinating Womanhood teacher was being dropped off by her husband.

Ted did not get out and open the door for his wife as the teacher's husband did, but Angela still felt proud and feminine, that Ted had brought her.

Angela entered the building and saw the teacher waiting for her inside the foyer. The teacher's eyes shone as she looked at Angela expectantly and asked, "Is it true? Is he home?"

Angela nodded her head, blinking back her tears. "Yes, he's come home."

The teacher squeezed Angela's hand, and together they went down the stairs. The teacher unlocked the door of the classroom and they went inside. There they hugged each other for a long time and wept freely.

"Oh Angela, I'm so proud of you. I'm so happy for you," the teacher said, and a beautiful smile shone through her tears.

Angela felt the now familiar lump in her throat return. She dabbed her tears away with a tissue and sat down.

Soon the other class members arrived.

Bev, who was looking noticeably slimmer, made a grand entrance, holding up the cream sponge she had promised to make. She looked much more confident than normal.

When the class were all seated the teacher said, "Well now, how did you get on with last week's Assignment, to ask your husband for something you need?"

Bev stood up and with an exaggerated air of nonchalance, walked out in front of the class and hitched up the ankle length dress she wore. She looked down at her feet and wriggled them. She was wearing a new pair of running shoes.

The class cheered and clapped.

"You got them," laughed the teacher. "Well, good on you Bev. Tell us how you did it."

"I just asked him sweetly, and with a smile. I said, "Aden, may I please have a pair of running shoes?"

"Yep. Of course you can," he said with a grin. So I acted delighted, which wasn't hard to do, because I was. I said, "Oh I'm so excited darling," and I kissed him."

"He gave me such a lovely smile. He looked years younger, and so handsome, even though he's nearly bald. The next morning he gave me a signed blank cheque and said, "Get yourself a good pair Mum." He always calls me Mum."

"Bev, you never fail to amaze me," said the teacher. "I am so very, very proud of you. And I really mean that."

Bev sat down. The teacher smiled directly at Angela and said, "Now I think someone else has an experience to share with us?"

Angela smiled and stood up.

A hush fell over the class as Angela shared her experience of asking Ted to come home, and the thrill of having him back.

Cherry, Helena and Elsie couldn't stop beaming. When Angela had finished speaking, she saw the eyes of every women in the room glistening with tears. She tried to hold back her own tears, but failed and stood there weeping freely.

Angela was aware that she had never cried so much in her whole life, since taking the Fascinating Womanhood course.

As she returned to her seat, both Cherry and Elsie stood up and hugged her tightly.

The teacher's voice was full of emotion as she said to the class, "Fascinating Womanhood teaches us to enjoy our woman's role. Both as a mother, and as a companion to our husband. But it also encourages us to develop our spirituality. This is best done by using our God-given talents and reaching out to others. Sharing truths that we have learned."

"I do this by teaching these Fascinating Womanhood classes. I want to share with you that the joy I receive is overwhelming at times."

"I also want to encourage every one of you to develop your spirituality by reaching out to others. It is so richly rewarding, far more so than working for money."

"We have time for another experience."

Elsie raised her hand. "Can I say a few words about how Fascinating Womanhood has improved my marriage?"

"Certainly Elsie. Come on up."

Elsie. True Experience.

"I have always had a good marriage. I took this course to gain more self confidence."

"I had always accepted and admired my husband, but never told him so. I thought he must know it. It was hard for me to start saying these things, so I started writing him notes."

"Then I progressed to saying complimentary things. His response was so great that I realised his need to hear these things."

"He started telling me the ways I pleased him, and this gave me the self-confidence I have always lacked."

"His tenderness towards me is fantastic. I feel like a bride again."

"The greatest thing was when he said with tears, "I have come to realise that you are the sweetest, the most feminine woman in the world, and I love you so deeply I can't tell you how much. You are my whole life."

"Oh Elsie," said the teacher, "What a lovely compliment to write in your Love Book."

"Now for our last secret. This secret teaches us how to handle an emotion that destroys many marriages. An emotion that usually bring out the worst in all of us. That emotion is anger, especially uncontrolled anger."

"When a person is angry, they can clearly know the right thing to do, but in the heat of their anger, that can do the exact opposite."

Kathy raised her hand. "Yes Kathy?"

"Whose anger are we talking about? Ours or our husbands?"

"Both Kathy. This secret teaches us how to handle both our anger, and our husband's anger."

She then turned and wrote on the board:

SECRET NUMBER TEN
Handle anger in a feminine and childlike manner

The teacher turned back to the class and smiled. "Most of you look a little puzzled."

She picked up her large black Bible off the table and opened it to a marked page and then said, "Marina, you shared with us some words of Jesus in our lesson on femininity. Can you read them for us again now?"

She handed the Bible to Marina who stood and read:

Jesus called to his side a little child and set him in the midst of them, and said, "Truly I say to you, unless you repent and become like little children, you shall never enter the kingdom of heaven."

The teacher took back the Bible and then said, "In this scripture, Jesus is teaching us to become like little children again. What are the qualities of little children that Jesus wants us to return to?"

Marina raised her hand. "Yes Marina?"

"Little children are teachable."

"Yes, a very important quality for us to have."

"Anybody else?"

"They are humble and completely honest," said Helena.

"Yes Helena, two very important qualities. Children are humble and honest, especially in the way they express their emotions."

"So tonight we are going to learn from little children how to handle this emotion of anger. Both in ourselves and in our husbands."

Men respect a spirited woman

"First we look at how to handle our own anger. We do need to stand up to men for our rights sometimes. Fascinating Womanhood does not teach women to be doormats."

"Men respect a spirited woman. One who'll get angry and stand up for her rights, as long as she does it in a non-challenging, feminine way. Men find a spirited woman quite fascinating."

When you have a right to be angry with your husband

"So when do we have a right to be angry with our husband?"

High spirited, ultra-feminine behaviour can distract a man when he's being too serious, or acting flirtatious toward other women.

Sonia raised her hand. "Yes Sonia?"

"I suppose when he has made a stupid mistake. Like if he loses a lot of money. Or when he's been lazy and hasn't mowed the lawn for weeks."

"Well Sonia, those are both areas of male responsibility. We have to allow him to choose for himself what he does in those masculine roles. We can influence him, but we don't have the right, and nor does it do any good to show anger toward him. It's all part of living Secret Number One, 'Accepting him as he is'. However there are limits, and we'll talk about those shortly."

Helena raised her hand. "Yes Helena?"

"What about when he mistreats us?"

"Yes Helena, that's when we can show anger toward our husband. When he mistreats us. Or when he insults us, or criticises us unfairly. Even if he overworks us, or ignores us."

"We cannot be happy in our marriage if we allow our husband to mistreat us or take us for granted. I'm not talking about little things. It's best to overlook those. Or to let them build up before speaking out."

Express your anger in a childlike manner

"So how do we express our anger in a way that doesn't arouse our husband's anger?"

"Let's look at how a child expresses anger. Cherry, tell us how your little girl expresses her anger."

Cherry laughed. "Well, sometimes she stamps her feet. And she has this cute way of folding her little arms, putting her chin in the air and going 'humph'. Then if nobody takes enough notice, she tosses her curls and stomps out of the room, glancing back to see what effect it's having. Tina's real cute when she's angry."

"Wow. A perfect answer Cherry. Just what we needed to hear. Yes, this childlike way of handling anger IS cute. We women find it cute. Men find it even cuter, whether in little girls or grown up women. It makes them want to hug us."

"Although some children, when they get angry, throw a tantrum and scream and yell and kick and say hurtful things. What happens then?"

"It arouses our own anger," said Angela.

"Yes. Exactly. Angela is right. It arouses our own anger. But when a child or woman expresses anger the cute, childlike way that Cherry's daughter does, it doesn't arouse the another person's anger. And more importantly, when a woman expresses her anger this way, it doesn't challenge her husband's masculinity."

"But when we start shouting, or arguing, or worse still, swearing, we arouse our husband's own anger. We instantly kill his affection for us. We just wither it up. Just like spraying a beautiful flower with weedkiller."

"Why is this? Because when we direct our anger toward

You have a right to show your anger when your husband mistreats you. But it must be done in a feminine way.

201

him in this way, we demean his authority and his masculinity."

"He becomes defensive, and tries and often succeeds in blaming us for the problem. We also fall from our pedestal in his eyes."

"So we must always express our anger in a feminine, non-challenging way. Without any harshness or ugliness. Without losing our feminine charm. Just as Cherry's daughter did."

"When you show your anger in this feminine way, you are far removed from arousing your husband's anger. In fact the opposite occurs. He sees you as cute and fascinating. You become adorable in his eyes. You actually enhance his love for you."

"What are some of the ways we can do this?" asked Diane.

"Well Diane, there are many feminine ways to let off steam without challenging our husband's masculinity. We can stamp our feet, or beat our fists on his chest, or put our hands on our hips and pout, or fold our arms and turn our back on him with our chin in the air."

"With a 'humph", said Cherry with a giggle.

"Yes, men find all these things fascinating. They feel manly and protective. We become more lovable in their eyes."

How to speak to your husband
when you're angry

"And when we speak, we can say things like, "I'll never speak to you again."

"We can even call them names if we like, but MAKE SURE THEY ARE MASCULINE NAMES, like "you hard-hearted brute" or "you stubborn, obstinate man" or "you beast."

"Men don't mind those kind of names because they enhance their masculinity. Men even smile when we call them names like these."

"But NEVER, NEVER USE NAMES THAT DEMEAN A MAN'S MASCULINITY, like "useless" or "little man" or "no hoper" or "dumb". Those kind of names arouse deep resentment in a man. They can permanently destroy his love for you, especially if he believes you mean what you say."

"This can be so serious that it's right up there with unfaithfulness in marriage. It's like your husband telling you to your face, "I have never loved you.""

Exaggerate your hurt

"Now when you tell your husband HOW he's mistreated you, it doesn't hurt to exaggerate a little, as a child does."

"You can say things like "How cruel" or "How mean" or "What a dreadful thing to do".

"We must come across to our husband like an adorable and helpless child who has been cruelly mistreated. Do you understand what I'm trying to say?"

The poor little me approach

"I can see Elsie looking horrified. Don't worry Elsie, there are more reserved methods of showing anger for a quieter woman. There's the 'poor little me' approach. This way of expressing our anger can be highly effective with any man. You know, the downcast eyes with our face in our hands. Or whatever comes naturally to your personality. Perhaps just a quiet "Oh dear".

"Genuine tears add greatly to all these ways of showing our anger. Genuine tears usually soften any man's heart."

"So these are all natural, feminine ways of handling anger. And they don't hurt our husband one little bit. Rather they increase his love for us. And they arouse in him a desire to make amends for our hurt."

Release your anger as soon as it arises

"Isn't it better just to be serene and keep our anger to our selves?" asked Elsie.

"In minor matters Elsie, yes. We can work off mere annoyances by vigorous exercise, or complaining out loud to ourselves when nobody can hear us. But even God gets angry over major things."

"Once strong anger has arisen, it's best to release it, or diffuse it as soon as possible. Otherwise it can settle into resentment and smoulder for years."

"Bottled up anger and the lack of forgiveness which usually goes along with it, can lead to depression and other illnesses."

"So we should release our anger quickly, as little children do. They flare up and then a few minutes later they are serene again. Its really healthy."

"But remember, we're not talking about mere annoyances. We have to learn to take these in our stride. Usually a good night's sleep is all we need to clear away these feelings."

"But when our husband clearly mistreats us, we should show our upset feelings immediately. We should not wait. We need to express it straight away, in a childlike manner."

"By letting him know as soon as we are hurt by his actions, a man can then immediately link his actions with the cause of our pain. He doesn't have to try and think back to what he might have said and done."

"Men like their us to be open and straight forward with them, as long as we do not challenge their masculinity or leadership."

Other ways of releasing anger

Kathy spoke, "I can see why we shouldn't show anger toward a man when he's failed in one of his masculine duties. But we're still going to get angry at times. How do we handle those angry feelings without criticising him?"

"First of all by forgiveness Kathy. Remember, we women have faults too. We can also use the techniques taught in

Genuine tears can soften almost any man's heart.

Secret Number Five, like writing out our angry thoughts."

"Or we can work off our angry feelings by vigorous exercise. Aerobics are good, even a long brisk walk."

"Some women just need to sit in a peaceful place for about an hour. That works for me. Would probably work for you too Elsie."

"But we are all so different. One woman told me that she drives off in her car and screams with all the windows up."

"I punch the bed," said Kathy with a giggle.

"That's OK Kathy. Just get it out. Don't bury it. When we release our anger, as a child does we are much healthier, and happier."

When your husband fails too often in an area of his responsibility

"Now it could happen that your husband has failed too many times in one of his areas of responsibility. We're talking of extreme cases here, where he has caused you so much distress, that it IS appropriate for you to express anger towards him."

"But it still must be done in a feminine way. Vivian, one of our visitors is going to share with us later how she used feminine anger to get her husband to fix a roof that had leaked for ages."

How to handle severe mistreatment

"Now one final thing, in cases of very severe mistreatment, such as unfaithfulness, it can be most difficult for a woman to be childlike in her anger. But it is still the best approach."

"Let me read you the experience of Belle, a woman who went through one of my other Fascinating Womanhood classes."

Belle. True Experience.
"One night my husband was out with another woman. As I waited in agony for him to come home in the early morning hours, I determined to act with childlikeness."

"When he came home, I ran to the door to meet him, threw my arms around him weeping, and said, 'Oh how could you do this to poor little me?'"

"My husband was aroused to compassion, and took me tenderly in his arms. This was the beginning of a new life for us."

How to handle your husband's anger

"Now class, we're going to move on to the second part of this lesson, on how to handle our husband's anger, when it's directed towards us?"

"Cherry, you did so well last time. Tell us how your daughter acts when her Daddy gets angry at her."

Again Cherry laughed. "It happened last Saturday. Tina had been playing with his chess set during the week and had lost one of his pieces."

"John really growled her, poor thing. Well, her little lips

quivered and she looked down and rubbed her feet together. Then tears started to trickle down her cheeks. John couldn't stay angry with her for long. He ended up cuddling her and telling her how sorry he was for growling her."

"Thank you Cherry," said the teacher looked delighted. "Another perfect illustration of Fascinating Womanhood in action. Of course he couldn't stay angry with her. She was a picture of helplessness."

"And that's exactly the way we need to react to our husband's anger. With helplessness and vulnerability. Again, allowing our tears to show is most effective."

"Have you all heard the proverb of wise King Solomon? 'A soft answer turns away wrath.' I'm sure you have. It really does work."

"These feminine reactions are charming to men. It makes them feel wonderfully masculine. Their anger just melts away and tenderness and love take its place."

Hear him out before speaking

"Now usually its best to let our husband pour out all his angry feelings before we say anything. But not always. Some men can say hurtful things when they're angry and the sooner we diffuse their anger the better. We need to decide for ourselves when it's best to speak. After all, we know our husbands best."

"But what if our husband is wrong?" said Beth.

"Well, even when we're innocent Beth, we should still hear him out. Before we say anything, we should allow all his angry feelings to come out."

"Then if we ARE INNOCENT, we just softly explain the truth without embarrassing him, or challenging him. Here again, let the tears come if you feel like doing so. But let him know that you understand how he made the mistake, and that you don't hold it against him."

"Now on the other hand, if we ARE GUILTY and he has a right to be angry, we must act helpless and vulnerable, as a little child would. Like Cherry's daughter did."

"Then we softly say something humble, like, "You're right. That was stupid of me. I'm sorry. Will you forgive me?"

"And what happens? His anger just melts away and his love for us increases. This increase in love might seem strange, but love seems to need emotional interaction to develop and grow. Even if it is anger."

"This feminine way of handling anger we learn in Secret Number Ten is just wonderful. It saves marriages. Really it does."

When your husband is niggly

Helena spoke. "Yes, what you're teaching us sounds good to me too. But what about when our husband is just plain niggly toward us? You know how men get sometimes."

"Well Helena, niggliness in a man always responds to kindness and sympathy. Unless it's caused by resentment. If that's the case then we are not living all the four secrets

of Fascinating Womanhood. Or we haven't done all the lesson Assignments. They are so important."

When your husband ignores you or flirts

"Now let's look at what to do if our husband ignores us, or flirts with another woman."

"The best way to handle that situation is by playfully teasing him. We should smile impudently and act ultra feminine, and also be a little saucy to distract him. Touch him in some way. Straighten his tie or smooth his hair, or sit on his knee. And we can also start talking about something frivolous."

"The same high spirited approach works when he's being too serious, or starts to lecture us."

"If he seems to be getting exasperated, we can pout adorably and give him cheeky glances that say, "You're not going to get angry with poor little me.""

"In other words, we do what came naturally to most of us as young girls to get our father's attention, or to distract him when we thought he was going to scold us."

"This may be too much for some dignified women, but still, it works, and it's delightful and fascinating behaviour to a man."

"Well, that's the end of tonight's lesson class, and also the end of our Fascinating Womanhood Course."

"There are no assignments, except to complete any assignments you might not have done yet. Please don't put them off. They have proven over and over again to have powerful effects for good."

"Our visitors tonight are Vivian and Joy. Vivian's now going to share with us her funny story about how she used childlike anger to get her husband to fix a leaking roof."

"Then Joy will share how she brought out the tender, romantic side of her husband by handling her anger using the natural feminine principles we have learned tonight."

Vivian. True Experience.
"Fascinating Womanhood lets us stamp our feet and shake our heads. Oh this is fun!"

"Getting my husband to do things had been next to impossible, or so I thought. By being impatient and nagging I had accomplished nothing. I became the fix-it man in our home, mowing lawns, painting, moving furniture."

"After many days of rain, our living room roof leaked along a ten foot section. So, trying to let go the man's role, I got pots, pans and trays and lined them up along the floor to catch the leaks. It was hard for me not to complain or nag, and even harder not to go up and repair the roof myself. I bit my lip and held my tongue."

"That night I was awakened by a noise. I leapt out of bed in the dark and rushed into the living room. I trod

on the edge of one of the pans of rain water, splashing cold water up my leg and all over my nightie."

"I remembered Fascinating Womanhood and bit my lip. I went outside and finding nothing wrong I returned through the living room, where I stepped into another pan, splashing cold water up my other leg and again on my nightie."

"That did it."

"I carefully walked back to the bedroom and switched on the light. There lay my husband, peacefully asleep. After awakening him, I stamped my foot, shook my head and punched him on one shoulder and said, "This is for one wet leg," then I punched him on the other shoulder and said, "This is for the other wet leg and a dripping nightie."

"Startled he asked what was going on. In a pathetic, appealing voice, almost crying I said, 'I'm dripping wet with rain water from a leaky roof." I said no more. He was too shocked to say anything."

"In the morning I was awakened by footsteps on the roof. I peeped out and there on the roof was my husband making the necessary repairs. When he came in, I praised his muscles and how strong he was and said that I didn't really know about repairs like he did. He had a delightful smile on his face."

"About a week later, as I was driving down the road I noticed my husband's truck overtaking me. He had been home and missed me. He presented me with a kiss and a gift, the most beautiful, gorgeous, white chrysanthemums with red satin hearts in the centre of each bloom."

"I was so thrilled I could hardly say a word. He had not been in the practice of giving gifts, or remembering special days. The card attached had a lovely message. "See dear, I don't forget. Love, Ron."

"We hold the keys to our happiness."

Joy. True Experience.

"My marriage was like so many, an armed truce. We had vowed 'for better or worse.' My husband never wore his ring and spent little time with me or our two children. He made it clear that he didn't need me at all. He seldom spoke and never touched me."

"One lonely day I poured out my heart to a friend who had been through the Fascinating Womanhood course. I can't count the times she said, "That isn't the way to handle it." I got mad at her, but she still persisted with Fascinating Womanhood."

"Shortly after, my husband and I visited with a bachelor friend of his who desired to get married. While I was doing the dishes, my husband began saying things like, "So you want to get married. Boy, you don't know when you're well off. Look at all the headaches a wife can bring."

"At first I took it as a joke, but soon it wasn't funny any more. I thought, "I know what Fascinating Womanhood says about anger. I'll give it a try."

"I turned around, stamped my foot, and said, "You big hairy beast. I'm never going to like you again, ever!" Then I walked out of the room, turning as I went to glance over my shoulder. He was grinning from ear to ear. "Did you hear what she called me?" he asked his friend, "Did you hear?"

"I found myself sitting in the bedroom thinking, "Great, but what now." My husband had never in eight years of marriage apologised. Yet, not two minutes later he entered the bedroom, sat down beside me and said, 'I'm sorry. I didn't mean to hurt your feelings. Will you forgive me?"

"I enrolled in a Fascinating Womanhood class."

"Two months later, I received my first birthday card from my husband. It was special, not only because he remembered it, but because he had selected a tiny card showing a cute little hairy beast. It said, 'Happy Birthday lovingly, from your Hairy Beast."

"He had actually looked for a special card."

"It's now five years later. They have been the best five years of my life. My third child was born by Caesarean section. My wonderful husband, who truly can't stand sickness or pain, was with me every minute he could be."

"The day I left hospital, the nurses told me that they, all of them, voted my husband the most tender, romantic husband they had ever met. And he is."

"My prayer is that every woman could know and accept Fascinating Womanhood."

"Thank you Joy, you certainly are doing your part to share the truths of Fascinating Womanhood with others."

"Thank you too Vivian for sharing the amusing feminine way you released your anger and motivated your husband to do his manly duty."

The teacher paused and smiled. "We have now come to the end of this course. I have really loved being your teacher. And I've loved hearing your successes. We have now become friends. Let us all stay in touch with one another, and encourage each other in living these wonderful principles."

"Now before we enjoy Bev's delicious looking sponge cake, can I share just one last word of encouragement."

"Some of you have had great success already with Fascinating Womanhood, but it's only the beginning. Most women take about a year to master these principles. Please don't give up if you fail from time to time. Fascinating

Womanhood is a one way road. We must go forward. Only happiness lies ahead. All your heartaches lie behind you. Allow two years for the magic to work fully."

"Some of you will have difficulty in accepting some parts of these teachings, especially acting childlike, and being dependent on your husbands, but these qualities are important to men, and they are a natural part of our feminine nature. We must be humble enough to accept all the teachings of Fascinating Womanhood. They have proved themselves over and over again, for years and years."

"Forgive, Accept, Admire, Comfort your husband. Make him Number One. Allow him to fully take over the reins of leadership. Then relax, free of worry and allow your femininity to blossom."

"Regain the carefree joy of your early childhood. When you do so, your husband will be fascinated with you. He will love you. He will cherish you. He will want to spoil you."

"Enjoy your role as a mother and homemaker. Take your time and do it well. Develop your talents and never stop learning. Surround yourself with pleasant friends and meet together often during the daytime. Share each others difficulties. Keep your standards high and encourage one another to grow spiritually."

"Comfort and pamper your husband when he comes home weary. Refresh him with your femininity. He will love you dearly and deeply. He will want to place you on a pedestal, so to speak. He will even worship you and treat you as his queen."

"Always, always, be feminine. Just as you were as a young child. Childlike femininity and charm in a woman of any age is always appealing to a man."

"Dresses, feminine hairstyles, hair ornaments, trim waistline, all these things delight men, and are important to them. But even these delights are no match for a woman's loving smile, with nice teeth.

"Be joyful and exuberant in showing your appreciation to your husband. It gladdens his heart. Men's tastes never change in these things."

"Remember that opposites attract. Do the opposite of what men do. You will be noticed and smiled at and fussed over. Men love to be around a truly feminine woman."

"And finally, remember God. Pray every morning and every night and nourish your spirit by reading good books, and the Bible. Set aside a certain time every day for this spiritual development. It will bring serenity into your life. Remember that your husband expects you to be a better person than him. So keep your standards high. Remain worthy of the pedestal that your man loves to place you on."

Then the teacher handed Angela a small, white book, opened to a marked page.

"Angela, you have a lovely reading voice. Would you close our Fascinating Womanhood course by reading the words of Ruth Stafford Peale."

"Ruth was the wife and woman behind the great writer and pastor Dr Norman Vincent Peale. It was she who inspired him to write his famous classic *"The Power of Positive Thinking."*

Angela stood and faced the class and read:

"No job, no hobby, no activity on earth can compare with the drama, and the exhilarating experience of living with a man, loving him, doing your best to understand his infinitely complex mechanism, and helping to make it hum, and sing, and soar, the way it was designed to do."

Ruth Stafford Peale and her husband Dr Norman Vincent Peale, on their 25th wedding anniversary.

Ted had earlier asked Angela to phone him from the foyer that night, when she was ready for him to come and pick her up.

Cherry offered to take her home, but Angela thought it best to depend on Ted and let him come and get her.

When Ted answered the phone, Angela was about to say in a matter-of-fact voice, "You can come and get me now Ted." Instead she quickly reconsidered and said in a cheerful, melodious voice "I'm ready darling."

"OK Angie, I'll be there in a few minutes." Angela noticed that Ted's voice was becoming deeper, more masculine, and more good natured. He also had a new confidence that thrilled her.

Angela waited outside. It had stopped raining and was a now a mild, clear night. The stars shone brightly.

Ted pulled up in his van, and for the first time since they were married, he leaned over and opened the door for Angela from the inside. She smiled her appreciation.

Angela chatted for a short time as they drove home, then, feeling content and loved, she softly started to sing *"The Loveliest Night of the Year."*

> *"When you are in love,"*
> *"It's the loveliest night of the year,"*
> *"Stars twinkle above,"*
> *"And you almost can touch them from here."*

Angela felt Ted's warm, strong hand take hold of her hand. As they drove homeward through the night, a street light briefly illuminated Ted's face. Angela saw that he was smiling.

The End

SECRET NUMBER ONE

Accept him as he is.
Look to his good side.

Don't try to change him.

Forgive him for past hurts.

Allow him his freedom.

Compile a list of his masculine virtues.

Humbly apologise to him for your past mistakes.

ASSIGNMENTS – SECRET NUMBER ONE

ASSIGNMENT ONE. Make a list of all your husband's masculine virtues. Read them every morning and night. Continue this until you have committed them to memory.

ASSIGNMENT TWO. Forgive him in your heart for all the times he has hurt you in the past. Ask God to help you if necessary.

ASSIGNMENT THREE. Then say the following to your husband, touching him as you do so:
"I'm glad you're the kind of man you are. I haven't always appreciated you in the past, and I've made some silly mistakes. I'm sorry, and I'm glad you haven't let me push you around. I'm glad you're the way you are. From now on I'm going to try to be a wonderful wife for you."

(You can rephrase this statement with words that are more natural to you if you prefer. But do not lessen its impact.)

SECRETS OF FASCINATING WOMANHOOD   SUMMARY – SECRET NUMBER FIVE

SECRET NUMBER TWO

Admire his masculine qualities. Never wound his sensitive pride.

A man's greatest need is to be admired for his masculine qualities.

His deepest misery is to be belittled by a woman.

ASSIGNMENTS – SECRET NUMBER TWO

ASSIGNMENT ONE. Praise one of your husband's masculine qualities before he goes to sleep tonight. Watch for his smile.

ASSIGNMENT TWO. By asking questions that require long, thoughtful answers, and giving admiration, try and have your husband talk to you about a past achievement, or a future dream, for at least five minutes. (Be openly attentive and strictly avoid interrupting him with your own thoughts as he speaks.)

ASSIGNMENT THREE. Every second day, sincerely tell your husband how much you admire him for one of his virtues that you listed as part of last week's assignment. Touch him and smile as you do so. Continue doing this until you have praised him sincerely for all the virtues you have listed.

SECRET NUMBER THREE

Make him Number One in your life. Comfort him tenderly when he is tired or discouraged.

Appreciate the heavy responsibility a man carries.

Use the great power of sympathy.

Comfort him lovingly when he comes home weary.

Do not raise problems until after he has eaten.

ASSIGNMENTS – SECRET NUMBER THREE

ASSIGNMENT ONE. At least twice during the week, greet your husband when he comes home, with a smile and looking your feminine best. Have your home quiet and organised. Make him comfortable. Listen to him if he wants to talk. Don't speak about your day or your concerns until after he has eaten.

ASSIGNMENT TWO. In your own words say to him. "I'm beginning to realise the great responsibility you have, to provide for me (and the children). I do appreciate it. It must be a big load to carry."

ASSIGNMENT THREE. Say to your husband, "I want you to know that you're the most important person in my life, and always will be."
(You must really mean this and never give him a reason to doubt it in the future.)

SECRET NUMBER FOUR

Your husband's God-given role is to lead you and provide for you. Allow him to do it.

Your role is to be his companion, a mother and a homemaker.

Let him know your views, but support his final decision 100%.

Let him worry about the finances.

ASSIGNMENT ONE. Draw up a 'Certificate of Leadership' made from cardboard, or make some other symbol of leadership that will last a life time, and present it (as an entire family if possible) to your husband. Tell him (and really mean it) that from now on, you will all follow his leadership 100%.

ASSIGNMENT TWO. If you are managing the finances, or any other masculine role, say to your husband, in your own words. "I don't want this responsibility any longer. It's a burden for me. You're a man. It's much easier for you."

SECRET NUMBER FIVE

Men deeply admire inner serenity and goodness in their wives.

Your husband wants you to be a better person than himself.

Goodness and inner serenity are required in a woman for a man to love her deeply.

Inner serenity develops in a woman when she becomes free of pride and self-righteousness, always does and says the right thing, is free of guilt, and has a forgiving heart.

ASSIGNMENTS. SECRET NUMBER FIVE

ASSIGNMENT ONE: (Stage One, Forgiveness, see page 105 for more details.)

Become totally relaxed. Divide a sheet of paper into two columns. At the top of the left column write your own name. At the top of the right column write the name of the first person listed below (ie, your father).

Then under your name, in the left column write, *"I now forgive* (father's name) *for all the hurt he/she has caused me."*

In the right-hand column opposite, write the first negative thought or memory that arises. Keep writing out the forgiveness message, and opposite any other negative thoughts or memories, until no more arise and you can smile and feel love inside you for the person concerned. Pray for help if forgiveness is difficult.

Start with your father, then your mother, then your immediate family members and then any of the other persons listed below who may have hurt you in any way.

Father	Husband
Mother	Other men
Brothers	Other women
Sisters	Yourself
School teachers	God

ASSIGNMENT TWO: (Stage Two, Repentance, see page 108 for more details.)

Become totally relaxed. Write across the top of a

215

sheet of paper, *"I (your name) have hurt the following people during my life."*

Divide the rest of the sheet into two columns and then list all the persons, living or dead, you have ever hurt, and briefly the nature of the hurt alongside each name. Keep adding names, using more sheets of paper in necessary until your conscience is totally clear.

Then, below your list of names, write, *"I, (write your name) am deeply sorry and repent of all the hurt I have caused these persons. From now on, I will be especially kind to these persons inasmuch as I am able, and I will follow my conscience in the way I act towards everybody."*

Finally, in the days ahead, do all in your power to make amends to these people for these hurts. For those whom you cannot make amends, ask God to bless them.

ASSIGNMENT THREE: (Stage Three, Re-programming your sub-conscious mind, see page 109 for more details.)

Start a Goal List of five positive emotional goals. Re-state your weaknesses as specific, positive goals you want to achieve. Read them every morning and evening. As you do so, picture yourself having achieved and enjoying the goal. Also include an inspiring message on your list.

Examples: *'I now enjoy jogging 2 km, four days a week.'*

'I feel fit and energetic, and weigh 60 kg."

'Every day in every way, I am getting better and better and better."

Review your goal list once a week, rewording, and replacing them as desired.

SECRET NUMBER SIX

Your God-given role is that of mother and homemaker. Enjoy it.

Motherhood is the most noble
and important work on earth. Enjoy the
wonderful satisfaction of raising happy,
secure children. Men respect motherhood.

Allow time to enjoy your home
making. Homemaking is a woman's
life-long career. Do it well.

Cultivate woman friends. Visit together.
Do things together. Confide in each other.
Develop your talents.

Plan your days in advance by using
a desk top calendar planning diary.

ASSIGNMENT ONE. Obtain a desk-top calendar planning diary with a page for each day (or a similar planning aid) and plan out your next two weeks.
You might include:

> Homemaking duties
> Hobbies
> Skills development
> Spiritual development
> Exercise
> Children's development
> School activities and holidays
> Music
> Ideas
> Shopping
> Get-togethers with your friends
> Family outings
> Holidays
> Husband-wife dates
> Meetings
> Time or outings without the children
> Books to obtain and read
> Library visits
> Birthdays and anniversaries

ASSIGNMENT TWO. If you go out to work, list all the advantages of giving up. Ask your husband to read the list and tell you honestly how he feels.

SECRET NUMBER SEVEN

Make the most of your hair, your figure and your health.

**Your appearance is important to a man.
Most men find longer, femininely styled
hair highly appealing.**

**Maintain your ideal weight by regular
exercise and sound nutrition.**

**A lovely smile is a priceless asset to a woman.
Have your teeth looking their nicest.**

ASSIGNMENT ONE. Ask your husband to tell you
truthfully, what hair length and hairstyles he thinks
you look nicest in, and wear your hair that way for him.

ASSIGNMENT TWO. Start an enjoyable exercise
program that you can continue throughout your life.

ASSIGNMENT THREE. Obtain some good books
on nutrition. Study them carefully, and work out a
balanced diet for yourself, and also your family if they
will accept it.

SECRET NUMBER EIGHT

Femininity delights a man, and depending on him arouses his love.

To be feminine and attractive to men, do and wear the opposite to what they do. Appear to be helpless in masculine matters.

Child-like charm in a woman of any age is delightful to a man.

Speak cheerfully, with a melodious lilt in your voice

ASSIGNMENT ONE. Say to your husband in your own words, "Darling I want to become more feminine for you. Please tell me the truth. What do you find the most unfeminine thing about me?"

When he has told you, phrase the solution positively then add it to your Goal List. Repeat this assignment as a New Years resolution each year.

ASSIGNMENT TWO. For two whole days this week, think before speaking, and phrase every sentence that you say to your husband in a positive, loving way. And say it with a melodious voice and a smile. Observe the difference in his reaction.

ASSIGNMENT THREE. Sing in the hearing of your husband at least once this week.

ASSIGNMENT FOUR. Ask your husband to honestly analyse your entire wardrobe, including footwear, nightwear and swimwear, and rate everything feminine, or unfeminine. Then discard, or plan to discard anything he finds unfeminine.

ASSIGNMENT FIVE. Have your husband choose what he considers to be an ultra-feminine dress from a pattern book, and make the dress yourself. Get assistance from another woman if necessary. Add some additional feminine touches that your husband likes, to the dress, to make it unique to you.

ASSIGNMENT SIX. Have your husband take back at least one masculine task that you have been doing. You might say. "I don't feel very feminine doing this."

SECRET NUMBER NINE

To obtain your wants from your husband, just ask with a smile, as a young girl asks her father.

**Just ask submissively, with
a smile and a please.**

**Your husband will love you more if you
allow him to spoil you a little.**

**Show feminine appreciation in
an exuberant, childlike way.**

ASSIGNMENT. Think of something you really want and deserve, and ask your husband for it in a simple, direct, childlike manner. When he has agreed to it, show your appreciation in a lively, feminine manner.

SECRET NUMBER TEN

Handle anger in a feminine and childlike manner

Men respect a spirited woman. Release your anger as soon a it arises, in a childlike manner.

Show anger against your husband only when you have been clearly mistreated. Express it in a feminine, childlike way that allows him to feel manly and protective.

FASCINATING WOMANHOOD PROGRESS CHART

Courageous women may wish to monitor their progress by asking their husbands to honestly evaluate them each year, using this chart or one of your own devising. However most men are reluctant to criticise women. Nevertheless a problem identified is half solved.

Just ask him mark alongside each quality an A, B, C or D according to his present feelings.

Rating grades
Excellent: A
Good: B
Average: C
Poor: D

Personality
Cheerfulness
Goodness
Truthfulness
Forgiveness
Patience
Charity
Tact
Trustworthiness
Friendliness
Charm
Serenity
Femininity
Self Discipline
Control of temper
Control of addictions
Personal cleanliness
Readiness to smile
Pleasantness of voice
Pleasantness of conversation
General knowledge
Overall personality

Appearance
Hair
Figure
Wardrobe
Overall

Homemaking
Motherhood
Thrift
Home organisation
Punctuality
Home cleanliness
Home tidiness
Cooking
Ironing
Overall

Relationship
Acceptance of husbands weaknesses
Appreciation of his strengths
Respect of his authority
Confidence in his abilities
Ability to comfort him
Willingness to praise him
Willingness to please him
Ability to discern his needs
Sex
Overall

Also mark with a tick one of the above qualities in each area you would most like your wife to work on improving.

Made in the USA
Monee, IL
16 September 2024

65874745R00122